Demystifying Career Paths after Graduate School

A Guide for Second Language Professionals in Higher Education

A volume in
Contemporary Language Studies Series
Terry Osborn, *Series Editor*

Demystifying Career Paths after Graduate School

A Guide for Second Language Professionals in Higher Education

edited by

Ryuko Kubota
University of British Columbia

Yilin Sun
South Seattle Community College

INFORMATION AGE PUBLISHING, INC.
Charlotte, NC • www.infoagepub.com

Library of Congress Cataloging-in-Publication Data

Demystifying career paths after graduate school : a guide for second language professionals in higher education / edited by Ryuko Kubota, Yilin Sun.

   p. cm. – (Contemporary language studies series)
 Includes bibliographical references.
 ISBN 978-1-62396-034-6 (pbk.) – ISBN 978-1-62396-035-3 (hardcover) –
ISBN 978-1-62396-036-0 (ebook) 1. English language–Study and
teaching–Foreign speakers–Vocational guidance. 2. English language–Study
and teaching–Vocational guidance. 3. English teachers–Employment. 4.
English teachers–Training of. I. Kubota, Ryuko. II. Sun, Yilin, 1953-
 PE1128.A2D434 2012
 428.0071'1–dc23

                                                          2012033286

CONTENTS

Acknowledgements...vii

Preface..ix

Foreword xi
Lía D. Kamhi-Stein

1 Introduction...1
  Ryuko Kubota and Yilin Sun

2 Seeking a Faculty Position 9
  Soonhyang Kim

3 The Research-Intensive University..23
  Yuko Goto Butler

4 Teaching-Focused University...35
  Ekaterina (Katya) Nemtchinova

5 Community College 49
  Yilin Sun and Ke Xu

6 Writing Center..63
  Lucie Moussu

7 Moving from North America to Overseas 77
  Noriko Ishihara

8 Working in Canada 89
  Ling Shi

9 Working in the United Kingdom 103
Constant Leung and Tracey Costley

10 Working in Hong Kong... 115
Xuesong (Andy) Gao

11 Getting Tenure 127
Manka M. Varghese

12 Getting Grants 141
Ulla Connor

13 Getting Published and Doing Research 151
Guofang Li

14 Involvement in Leadership Roles in Professional Organizations .. 163
Shelley Wong

15 Working as a Journal Editor 177
Suresh Canagarajah

16 Assuming Administrative Duties.. 191
María E. Torres-Guzmán

17 Balancing Professional and Personal Life 205
Suhanthie Motha

Author Biographies 219

ACKNOWLEDGEMENTS

We would like to acknowledge with gratitude Terry Osborn for his support of this project and graduate students at the University of British Columbia for their inspiration. We thank our authors for their expertise and valuable contribution to our project, as well as their support for the professional development of graduate students and beginning scholars. Special thanks go to Joel Heng Hartse for carefully negotiating authors' voices during copyediting.

PREFACE

As the internationalization of academe advances, the fields of second language education and applied linguistics have witnessed growing racial, linguistic, and gender diversity of their participants, including students and faculty members in higher education, members and leaders in professional organizations, and authors and gatekeepers in academic publishing. There has been a growing body of inquiry into the identities, experiences, and challenges of non-native English-speaking (NNES) and racial minority professionals in second language education and higher education in general in the English-dominant world, drawing increased attention to this group of professionals. Although these individuals do face various challenges, what is often overlooked in the existing literature is the fact that they *have* attained a great amount of success. Many of them are now tenured professors, publishing actively, serving as editors of academic journals, taking leadership positions in professional organizations, or assuming administrative duties in colleges and universities. But how did they manage to achieve such remarkable success? Reading academic research on linguistic and racial minority professionals usually provides very few answers to this pragmatic question, partly because they are often portrayed as sufferers of institutional oppression and partly because their victimized experiences are often described in research contexts. This book fills this gap by highlighting their *victories*—in other words, successes and achievements in their professional lives—and describing in concrete terms what hurdles exist and how they can be overcome.

This book is a career guidebook for graduate students and entry-level faculty members in second language education and applied linguistics, especially those from NNES and racial minority backgrounds, seeking em-

Demystifying Career Paths after Graduate School, pages ix–x

paternalistic (or maternalistic) attitudes, but because by doing so, we may help minority professionals to "successfully navigate their academic careers" (as Kubota and Sun put it in their introduction), ultimately contributing to a more diverse faculty body and a potentially broader research agenda.

Currently, minority professionals are highly visible in the form of scholars, leaders, and teachers. However, in spite of the many achievements of these professionals, and the many books and articles focusing on them, what had not yet been done was *deconstructing* the black box for them. After reading the chapters in this book, I can say that the box is no longer "twice as black" or even "black." *Demystifying Career Paths After Graduate School: A Guide for Second Language Professionals*, has, in fact, deconstructed the black box. I only wish this book had been published years ago! But, of course, this would not have been possible, given that it is only in recent years that minority professionals have become visible in our profession.

As I reflected on the contents of the book, I immediately noticed four things. First of all, I found the tone of the book to be celebratory, uplifting, though not naively so. Rather than describing the struggles and the challenges they face, the authors' goal in writing their chapters was to provide "tangible guidance grounded in successful professional and personal experiences with a vision of navigating toward victory narratives" (see Chapter 1, Introduction). The book certainly achieves this goal, since the authors of the chapters do not present themselves as victims or survivors of the educational system in which they function. In fact, after reading the chapters, I was left with the notion of "Yes, this *can* be done!" rather than "How will I *ever* achieve what this author has achieved?

The second point I noticed about the book is in relation to its positive, uplifting nature: I found the chapters to be enjoyable and highly readable— features that are not necessarily always present in academic books. All the chapters in the book open with a narrative and are written in the first person. These features contribute to making the authors, many of them at the highest levels of leadership in the field, more relatable than they would have been had they used the third person singular, thereby contributing to a sense of reader engagement.

Third, while the book was written with new faculty members and their mentors and advisors in mind, experienced professionals like me will also benefit from this book. For example, several of the authors describe a series of strategies that can be used to promote balance in one's life. As I read the chapters, I smiled to myself because finding professional-personal balance has been, with all probability, one of the biggest challenges in my own life. Therefore, as I read the suggestions, I took note of them (The Sunday Meeting, for example; see Chapter 17, Balancing Professional and Personal Life). Since I am writing this text on January 2, 2012, I have already added a couple of the strategies I learned from the book to my list of resolutions for this year.

Fourth, the book includes chapters written by authors with diverse experiences and backgrounds. For example, while some of the authors are well established in the field, others are relatively new to their fields. At the same time, some authors work for teaching universities, and others work for research universities or for community colleges. Some have teaching assignments, while others have administrative assignments. Some write from their position as authors of articles and books and others from their position as journal editors and manuscript reviewers. Some of the authors are male and many are female. And some authors write from their positions as academicians who are mothers and are juggling their academic and personal responsibilities (an issue that many minority professionals, both novices and more experienced ones—like me—struggle with). It is this diversity in voices that contributes to the strength of the book. There is something to be learned from every chapter and from every author. Kudos to the editors for that!

It's about time that a book like *Demistifying Career Paths After Graduate School: A Guide for Second Language Professionals* was published. When I graduated from my doctoral program in 1995, it was practically impossible to find minority professionals, and especially female minorities, who could serve as my models for success. Therefore, I had to learn how to deconstruct the black box by myself, though I was fortunate to have the strong support of my husband, an "old gringo" (because of his extensive experience) in U.S. academia. In contrast to me, the readers of this book will learn how to navigate the complexities of higher education systems from the diverse voices of professionals like us, language and racial minorities who have thrived and succeeded in the system. *Demystifying Career Paths After Graduate School: A Guide for Second Language Professionals* will be essential reading for my students and mentees, including those planning to get into doctoral programs and those about to get into the job market. I thank and congratulate Ryuko Kubota, Yilin Sun, and the authors of the chapters for producing such an outstanding much-needed book. *Tarea superada!*

REFERENCES

Kamhi-Stein, L. D. (2004, March/April). *Addressing nonnative English-speaking teachers and teacher educators needs.* Paper presented at the Academic Session, Teacher Education Interest Section, held at the annual convention of Teachers of English to Speakers of Other Languages, Long Beach, CA.

CHAPTER 1

INTRODUCTION

Ryuko Kubota
University of British Columbia

Yilin Sun
South Seattle Community College

In 1998, when the Non-native English Speakers in TESOL (NNEST) caucus was born in TESOL (Teachers of English to Speakers of Other Languages— now known as the TESOL International Association), perhaps very few people could imagine the remarkable achievements made by non-native English-speaking (NNES) professionals as well as professionals of color, who have since taken various leadership positions in less than ten years. The 2006 inauguration of Jun Liu as the president of TESOL—the first non-native English speaker and person of color elected to that position—epitomized this attainment. As in many other academic organizations, TESOL's leadership had been dominated by Caucasian native speakers of English, even though the field serves entirely non-native speakers of English, many of whom are people of color. This long-standing tradition was finally broken. In 2008, another landmark was made by the inauguration of Shelley Wong as the president of TESOL—this time, the first Asian woman in the position. This was followed by the 2008 election of Suresh Canagarajah as the second vice president of the American Association of Applied Linguis-

Demystifying Career Paths after Graduate School, pages 1–8
Copyright © 2012 by Information Age Publishing
All rights of reproduction in any form reserved.

tics (AAAL), a position that leads to the conference chair and then to the president. He is also the first NNES professional of color in this position.

Many other NNES professionals and people of color are increasingly filling academic and leadership positions in higher education as well as in professional organizations in the field of second language education and applied linguistics in North America and around the world. In the meantime, the globalization of higher education has expanded English-medium educational programs worldwide, both creating employment opportunities and intensifying competition among institutions (Mok, 2007). This highlights several issues: First, the professional door that once appeared closed to non-mainstream people is now open widely to them. Minority candidates applying for academic and other professional positions are successfully attaining their goals. Second, this, however, may not necessarily mean that NNES and racial minority professionals can sail through various obstacles to advance their careers. Growing diversity in higher education does not necessarily mean that racial, linguistic, and other kinds of discrimination have disappeared. Moreover, university faculty in some geographical areas still remains predominantly white. Third, as the job market is becoming tight, and competition among colleges and universities is intensifying, it is increasingly necessary for minority candidates to become familiar with how the system works in order to succeed in their academic careers. Familiarity from early on in their careers with issues such as job hunting, tenure, and promotion review, as well as participating in professional service activities, can tremendously help them to successfully navigate their academic careers.

VICTORY NARRATIVES

This book aims to provide graduate students and faculty members, especially students and faculty from NNES and racial minority backgrounds, with information essential for their career advancement in higher education in the fields of second language education and applied linguistics. It identifies critical turning points in career trajectories during employment in universities and colleges, describes institutional structures and practices, and provides NNES and racial minority professionals with practical suggestions that will enable them to successfully navigate their career paths. These successful professionals' personal accounts and recommendations allow graduate students to visualize a possible career path and institutional requirements. They also provide faculty members with strategies to successfully navigate new territory to advance their professional trajectories.

This book is inspired by the aforementioned pioneers in the field—Jun Liu, Shelley Wong, and Suresh Canagarajah—as well as many other colleagues, represented by the authors of the chapters in this book, who are

NNES and/or racial minorities who are making remarkable contributions to the advancement of the field.

This project is also motivated by everyday experiences in our professional lives. One of them occurred in a graduate class that addressed sociopolitical issues, including NNES teaching, accents, and race. One day, an Asian NNES female student expressed her frustration about having her manuscript for a book review rejected by a journal editor. The editor apparently judged the quality of the content solely based on some linguistic limitations contained in her email. As one of us sympathized with her by saying that some native speakers might not be sensitive about the challenges that nonnative writers face, another student spoke up in a rather annoyed way: "I hear a lot of victim narratives in this room, but look at you. You have made through thus far and accomplished so much. Can't we focus on victory narratives instead?" This statement was quite shocking; obviously, it failed to acknowledge the actual challenges that NNES professionals face in their careers. Nevertheless, it contained some legitimacy to ponder.

Another incident happened to a newly graduated NNES male student with whom one of us is acquainted. He was offered a tenure-track position but was unable to keep it due to his poor handling of various duties as a tenure-track faculty member, caused partly by his unfamiliarity with the institutional culture. Before he left, he emailed one of us and out of frustration, he wrote "Why can't any professors who look like me write something and share their experience and strategies to help us survive the tenure-track process!" We also remembered the times when we first landed tenure-track positions in new institutions and how we wished there could be a book like this one to offer insights and successful strategies to guide us in our journeys of navigating the higher education system in North America and elsewhere.

These incidents, among other exchanges with many NNES colleagues and colleagues of color, made us reflect on the trend of the scholarly and professional focus of our field in the last decade. There has been a proliferation of publications on NNES professionals in TESOL and minority faculty in higher education in general (e.g., Belcher & Conner, 2001; Braine, 1999; Casanave & Li, 2008; Curtis & Romney, 2006; Kamhi-Stein, 2004; Li & Beckett, 2006; Llurda, 2005; Mabokela & Green, 2001; Mahboob, 2010; Mayuzumi, 2008; Moussu & Llurda, 2008; Stanley, 2006; Vargas, 2002). While issues of NNES teachers are increasingly explored through an academic lens, professional issues of navigating the career path are often discussed with the vocabulary of struggle, challenge, discrimination, marginality, and survival, which does seem to confirm and reinforce victim narratives. As a greater number of us are moving into professional and leadership roles, it is necessary to steer more toward the exploration of concrete strategies for success. In the spirit of celebrating our accomplishments and advocating greater representation of minority leaders, this book provides tangible guidance grounded in successful professional and personal experiences, with a vision of navigating toward victory narratives.

In order to achieve professional success in higher education, it is essential for graduate students and novice scholars to understand institutional expectations for faculty members. In the following section, we provide a brief account of a career path for a regular academic faculty member in North America. Institutional differences obviously exist, and one should be careful not to draw crude generalizations. Also, there are different kinds of positions within higher education that involve slightly different types of tasks and responsibilities (see, for example, Chapter 6, Writing Center). However, we hope that the following descriptions provide readers with a general picture and background knowledge for the subsequent chapters.

PHASES OF PROFESSIONAL DEVELOPMENT

Job-Hunting as a Graduate Student

Toward the end of your graduate program of study, you make a decision on whether you want to pursue a teaching career in higher education or move in a different direction (e.g., working for a school district or a non-profit organization). Some might consider moving back to their home country (Chapter 7, Moving from North America to Overseas) or moving to a different country to pursue an academic career (Chapter 8, Working in Canada; Chapter 9, Working in the United Kingdom; and Chapter 10, Working in Hong Kong). No matter what career path you choose, in the current tight job market, academic achievements, including publications (e.g., peer reviewed articles, book reviews, book chapters, books, teaching materials), conference presentations, and grants enhance your marketability.

In North America, academic jobs are announced typically during the fall semester, and job interviews are conducted early in the spring semester. Employers are eager to attract the most qualified candidates, which influences when the job search is conducted. It is important to thoroughly organize your application materials and prepare for interviews (Chapter 2, Seeking a Faculty Position). Once you are offered a job, you have a chance to negotiate various conditions. Finally, you sign a contract and launch your new job.

Obtaining Tenure and Promotion

For a tenure-track position in North American universities and colleges, you are initially given the title of assistant professor. You are likely to be reviewed for reappointment during the third year and then for tenure and promotion during the sixth year. After you are tenured and promoted to associate professor, you have a chance to apply for a promotion to full professor usually after five or more years.

The components for tenure and promotion review usually include research, teaching, and service (see Chapter 11, Getting Tenure). The weight of these three components varies depending on the type of the institution. For teaching-focused universities (Chapter 4, Teaching-Focused University) and community colleges (Chapter 5, Community College), the weight on teaching is heavier than in research-intensive universities. In research-intensive institutions, research (i.e., publications) weighs significantly more (Chapter 3, Research-Intensive University). Knowing the expectations for tenure and promotion from *day one* is essential, because a careful allocation of your time and effort ensures success.

Teaching, Research, and Service

As mentioned above, the main responsibilities of faculty members are teaching, research, and service. The quality of your teaching is usually judged by the course evaluations that students fill out and class observations done by your colleagues and your unit administrator, typically before each tenure and promotion review. It is important to always improve your teaching by attending to the results of course evaluations (numerical and written comments) and other informal feedback from your students and colleagues.

Research involves publications, conference presentations, and research grants (see Chapter 12, Getting Grants; Chapter 13, Getting Published and Doing Research). Not all publications have the same weight. Education and applied linguistics are typically *article fields*, in which a sufficient number of refereed (peer reviewed) articles counts, whereas English and modern language teaching within the humanities, for instance, could be *book fields*, in which publishing at least one academic monograph along with other publications is required for tenure. Again, it is important to know the requirement in terms of the type and quantity of publications so that you can fulfill the expectation.

Service involves professional involvement in the departmental, university/college-wide, local, regional, and national committees, events, organizations, and professional associations (Chapter 14, Involvement in Leadership Roles in Professional Organizations; Chapter 16, Assuming Administrative Duties). Professionals of color might be frequently invited to serve on institution-wide committees and engage in other service work as minority representatives. It is important to prioritize your time and commitment, because teaching and research typically weigh much more than service for obtaining tenure.

While you, as an assistant professor, can engage in a leadership role in professional associations or professional journals outside of your institution, many of these activities are considered to be part of professional service. Thus, you would have greater freedom and opportunities to engage in such a role after you get tenure.

Leadership Roles

Leadership roles are found in research and service. As you establish your scholarship, you may decide to edit a book on the topic of your expertise, propose to guest-edit a special topic issue for a journal, or apply to serve as an editor of a journal (Chapter 15, Working as a Journal Editor). For professional service, you might take on an administrative role in your department or institution (Chapter 16, Assuming Administrative Duties). You can also get involved in the leadership roles in regional, national, or international professional organizations (Chapter 14, Involvement in Leadership Roles in Professional Organizations). You may volunteer to serve on a committee or you might be nominated for an officer's position and run in an election. Assuming a leadership role makes a significant contribution not only to the organization, but also to the NNES and racial minority groups at large in terms of visibility, support, and advocacy.

ENVISIONING VICTORIES

In paving our way to professional success, we need to recognize that each of us is endowed with not only unique talents but also diverse challenges. To succeed, one should capitalize on his/her strengths and at the same time overcome challenges that might not be shared by everyone due to racial, gender, linguistic, class, physical, and other personal differences. This implies that the strategies for success are not necessarily applicable across the board. For instance, many institutions of higher education are still male-dominated, and women tend to be marginalized as minority. A woman of color in public institutions is often called a *double minority*. Correspondingly, woman of color from a NNES background is a *triple minority*. Adding more minority categories increases potential disadvantages, making the institutional hurdle higher to clear. Furthermore, it is important to keep in mind that we are all human beings with personal life beyond work. Balancing work and private life is essential for not only professional success but also personal fulfillment and happiness (see Chapter 17, Balancing Professional and Personal Life). While not all of us are superheroes/heroines (and we do not have to be) who can juggle all the tasks well or make outstanding achievements all around, there are ways to make small successes and reach excellence in one's own way in the mainstream academic community and beyond. The key is to take small steps to clear institutional hurdles with a larger goal in mind. Sometimes, this involves wading into uncharted territories, like becoming the first representative of color on an important committee. But to do so successfully, as many of our predecessors have done, expands opportunities for more minority professionals to enter where they were previously excluded.

Career advancement in academia is challenging for anyone, and especially for non-mainstream graduate students and scholars because the ways a specific institutional system and culture work are often unfamiliar to them. Yet the greater presence of high-achieving NNES and racially minority professionals in our field attests to minority scholars' ability to succeed. The experiences of these professionals can provide readers with invaluable insights and suggestions for accomplishing professional goals and victories. By keeping the momentum going, we can further transform our field from within.

REFERENCES

Belcher D. & Conner, U. (Eds.). (2001). *Reflections on multiliterate lives.* Clevedon, UK: Multilingual Matters.

Braine. G. (Ed.). (1999). *Non-native educators in English language teaching.* Mahwah, NJ: Lawrence Erlbaum.

Casanave, C. P. & Li, X. (Eds.) (2008). *Learning the literacy practices of graduate school: Insiders' reflections on academic enculturation.* Ann Arbor, MI: University of Michigan Press.

Curtis, A. & Romney, M. (Eds.) (2006). *Color, race, and English language teaching: Shades of meaning.* Mahwah, NJ: Lawrence Erlbaum.

Kamhi-Stein, L. (Ed.). (2004). *Learning and teaching from experience: Perspectives on nonnative English-speaking professionals.* Ann Arbor, MI: University of Michigan Press.

Li, G. & Beckett, G. H. (Eds.). (2006). *"Strangers" of the academy: Asian women scholars in higher education.* Sterling, VA: Stylus.

Llurda, E. (Ed.). (2005). *Non-native language teachers: Perceptions, challenges and contributions to the profession.* New York, NY: Springer.

Mabokela, R. O. & Green, A. L. (Eds.). (2001). *Sisters of the academy: Emergent black women scholars in higher education.* Sterling, VA: Stylus.

Mahboob, A. (Ed.). (2010). *The NNEST lens: Non native English speakers in TESOL.* Newcastle upon Tyne, UK: Cambridge Scholars Publishing.

Mayuzumi, K. (2008). 'In-between' Asia and the West: Asian women faculty in the transnational context. *Race Ethnicity and Education, 11,* 167–182.

Mok, K. H. (2007). Questing for internationalization of universities in Asia: Critical reflections. *Journal of Studies in International Education, 11,* 433–454.

Moussu, L. & Llurda, E. (2008). Non-native English-speaking English language teachers: History and research. *Language Teaching, 41,* 315–348.

Stanley, C. A. (Ed.). (2006). *Faculty of color: Teaching in predominantly white colleges and universities.* Bolton, MA: Anker.

Vargas, L. (Ed.). (2002). *Women faculty of color in the white classroom.* New York, NY: Peter Lang.

CHAPTER 2

SEEKING A FACULTY POSITION

Soonhyang Kim
Pace University

About one year ago, the editors of this book invited me to write a chapter on seeking a faculty position, and initially, I didn't think I was the right person to do it; I was just a junior tenure-track Teaching English to Speakers of Other Languages (TESOL) faculty member. After some serious thought and reflection, I realized, however, that I am in a good position to write about the job search process and especially to give advice to second language doctoral students who are on the job market. I am a Korean-born, non-native-English-speaking (NNES) Asian woman who has gone through the process myself.

In the United States, I went through a number of academic trajectories from marginal or peripheral to legitimate peripheral to fuller participation, first as a master's student at a small, teaching-focused university in Kentucky and then as a doctoral student at a large, research-intensive university in Ohio.[1] Since graduation, I have been experiencing the same diverse career trajectories other NNES second language professionals experience, first as a tenure-track assistant professor of Korean, then as a tenure-track assistant professor and founding director of a master's level TESOL teacher educa-

Demystifying Career Paths after Graduate School, pages 9–21
Copyright © 2012 by Information Age Publishing
9

tion program, and now as a faculty member and coordinator of both English as a Second Language (ESL) and TESOL programs.

While acknowledging that there are many career options and job locations, this chapter focuses specifically on seeking a faculty position in the U.S. context (see Part 2 of this book for other countries). The chapter provides general job search tips and advice for all job seekers, as well as specific strategies that NNES professionals and professionals of color can employ for a successful faculty job search.

UNDERSTANDING THE FACULTY JOB SEARCH PROCESS

This section is organized by the chronological order of the stages of the job search—which consists of identifying jobs, applying for positions, interviewing, accepting a job offer, and negotiating—in a frequently-asked question format. These questions are the ones I often asked during my own job search and were also raised by graduate students in a mini-survey I conducted to write this chapter.

Identifying Jobs

What does the process of job hunting consist of?
   The entire job search process can take months and involve a job application, preliminary interview, campus visit, job offer, negotiation of conditions, and decision whether to accept the offer. Most second language education faculty positions for the next academic year are announced between late August and the following February for four-year universities and colleges, and until April for two-year community college positions. Applicants are asked to submit their job application materials by a certain deadline for initial screening. The search committee then selects several candidates for telephone or video interviews or a convention interview, which is an onsite interview at a conference or convention. From these interviews, two or three finalists are invited to visit the campus. A job offer is usually made two to four weeks after the campus visit, followed by negotiations regarding salary and other working conditions.

How do I prepare for job hunting?
   Your job search process and preparation start from day one of your graduate study. From the earliest stage of your graduate work, find out what specific skills, knowledge, dispositions, and experiences potential employers look for. After identifying your strengths and areas to improve upon, be prepared to accumulate the qualifications and experience you need in or-

der to be a competitive job candidate if you do not already have them. For example, if you discover that you do not have sufficient higher-education teaching experience, something that most universities and colleges prefer (if not require), but you find it difficult to obtain a teaching position at your own institution, feel free to search for a teaching opportunity at another university or community college to accumulate experience. Seeking an overseas teaching position during an academic break can be another way to add more diverse teaching experiences, especially in international contexts. This can be an especially good solution for some international doctoral students who have difficulty working in the United States during their study due to visa restrictions. Especially in the field of English language education, institutions are looking increasingly for candidates with teaching experience in both domestic and international contexts and in both ESL and English as a Foreign Language (EFL) contexts.

You should also look for other relevant teaching and work opportunities. A wide variety of work opportunities are available, though you need to actively search for them. You may be able to find work as a volunteer teacher, tutor, or coordinator at a community-based educational or outreach program developed specifically for minority groups. This may not be the direct higher-education teaching experience most faculty positions list as a requirement in a job announcement, but it can certainly be an advantage. Such experience indicates your strong commitment to promoting diversity and multiculturalism, improves your leadership skills, and adds to your experience of teaching and working with diverse people, all of which are essential characteristics second language educators are expected to have. Even with an unpaid, volunteer position, you should try to obtain some form of work verification and a written performance evaluation that you can add to your portfolio.

How can I build up work experience as an international student?

Even if you are an international student, it is not impossible to seek work experience. For example, current U.S. immigration law allows F-1 (student visa) holders to obtain authorization for temporary off-campus employment as long as the work is an integral part of their degree program. This is called Curricular Practical Training (CPT). You may also work in accordance with the requirements of Optional Practical Training (OPT) for one year after your degree is granted, provided the work is directly related to your degree area and consists of a minimum of 20 hours of work per week. If you fail to find regular paid employment, you may work as a volunteer (e.g., unpaid intern) to enhance your practical training experience while you continue to search for a faculty position.

Please keep in mind that immigration laws and regulations are complex and change over time. You need to regularly check the regulations and properly document your work history for future employment. You should always work with an international student advisor at your own institution who specializes in this matter whenever you make an employment decision. It is recommended you consult with an immigration lawyer should you have any complex immigration-related issues.

What kinds of positions are available for doctoral students after graduation?

Faculty positions in ESL, TESOL, second/foreign language education, bilingual/multilingual education, or combinations of these are some of the available career options in higher education. These positions are usually situated in departments of applied linguistics, education, English, foreign language, or linguistics.

You should consider the kinds of institutions (e.g., two-year community college, teaching-focused university, research-intensive university), types of jobs (e.g., ESL/foreign language faculty, TESOL faculty), types of appointments (e.g., tenure-track, non-tenure-track term lecturer, writing center director), and locations (e.g., U.S. or non-U.S. contexts) to which you intend to apply. The choice depends on your interests, strengths, and personal circumstances. Refer to Parts 2 and 3 of this book to understand different institutional environments.

Where should I look for a position?

Most positions for English, ESL, TESOL, and second/foreign language education are announced through online job search databases. Several examples are the career sections of the *Chronicle of Higher Education*, Modern Language Association (MLA), and TESOL International Association websites. (Refer to the resource list at the end of the chapter for the URLs and more details.) Most of them allow you free access, with daily or weekly e-mail alerts of available new positions once you register. Some include advice for academic job seekers, including tips on job applications and interviews. You may also utilize your personal network by letting your faculty advisors and other professional connections know that you are on the job market.

What skills and dispositions are necessary?

A strong academic background is required for all faculty positions. Research, teaching, and service are the three major elements all institutions will consider for hiring and granting tenure/promotion. Different institutions give more weight to certain areas than to others. For example, research-intensive universities may expect candidates to have experience with or the potential for publication, obtaining external funding, dissertation supervision, teaching research methods courses, and/or interest in developing a new course in the candidate's area of expertise. Teaching-

focused universities and community colleges are particularly interested in candidates with excellent records in teaching. Teacher education programs usually require experience in K-
12 teaching with a teaching certification. They look for candidates with experience in teaching practicum supervision and collaboration with local schools. Some institutions search for a candidate who can teach both undergraduate and graduate courses in the candidate's specialization area or his or her secondary areas of expertise. If an institution is creating a position in order to develop and implement a new program, it will look for someone with experience or potential in program administration, strong leadership and management skills, the ability to excel in research and teaching while also managing administrative tasks, and the ability to work both independently and in collaboration.

How do I decide which positions to apply to?

Whether to narrow your selections down to specific jobs you are highly interested in or apply to a large number of open positions depends on your professional and personal circumstances and preference. Some people cannot leave the area where they live because of their family situation or other circumstances. In this case, they have limited options. However, regardless of the situation, every applicant should narrow the application target to those jobs for which they are well qualified and want to pursue. The job market is fairly competitive, and the job search process can be extremely time-consuming. Therefore, reviewing each announcement carefully and systematically to select the best-fitting positions is crucial in order to save your time and energy.

If you do not have the required or minimum qualifications and experience listed in a job announcement, you may choose not to apply for the position. For example, it is not worthwhile to apply for a job that requires three years of public school teaching experience in the United States if you do not in fact have that experience. You may still consider applying for the position if the experience is listed as "desired" or "preferred" and if you have all the other required knowledge and skills.

Do not be intimidated or discouraged, even if you do not have extensive teaching or research experience. It is not uncommon for doctoral students to have little or no experience in research, grant writing, or teaching in a higher-education setting. Some institutions will still consider your potential as a scholar and researcher even if you lack direct experience. In fact, some job announcements state that they are looking for someone who has "experience, *ability* and/or *interest* in teaching." Even if you do not have direct experience in teaching university courses in second language education or other courses offered at a certain institution, you are likely to be considered capable of teaching such courses if you can demonstrate your content knowledge by showing a strong academic record during your graduate work. That is why some universities require academic transcripts as part of the application materials.

Is it OK to contact the search committee chair during the job application stage?

In general, it is OK to contact the search committee chair or any contact person with questions about the position and application process. Such communication can help you strengthen your job application by enabling you to understand the announced position better, especially when the posted job description is generic and without details. When you make an inquiry, do your homework first by researching background information on the institution, department, and program so you can ask well-prepared questions. However, do not contact the hiring university if the job announcement specifically prohibits phone or e-mail inquiries. Keep in mind that all contact is part of the impression you make and therefore part of the interview.

As a personal example, I once came across a generic job announcement that simply stated the department was looking for a tenure-track faculty member in TESOL. I first researched the websites of the institution and program and then contacted the search committee chair by e-mail. I provided a brief summary of what I had found about the institution and program and then asked several specific questions my research didn't answer. I was able to find out that they were looking for someone who had experience in TESOL program development and administration to run a new TESOL program. This information could not have been known without the contact I initiated. This contact helped me write a more targeted, customized cover letter for the position, and I was invited for a telephone interview. However, do not be disappointed if you do not receive a response. It may mean that the search committee is looking for a very specific candidate or is simply too busy to respond to most inquiries during the initial review process.

Applying for Positions

What does a complete job application package consist of?

All jobs require a letter of application, CV, and letters of recommendation or names of references. Some institutions may ask for academic transcripts, a teaching philosophy statement, a research statement, sample publications, or evidence of teaching excellence. Some examples of evidence of teaching effectiveness are student feedback and evaluations, colleague or supervisor evaluations of observations, and teaching awards.

How do I prepare my job application materials?

A cover letter is your first opportunity to present yourself to the search committee as a promising researcher and teacher. A good CV is a clear and concise description of your academic and professional background, skills, and experience that shows potential employers that you are the best candidate for the position. Writing a professional and descriptive letter is critical in order to grab the search committee's attention and to prompt it to do a thorough review of your application materials and invite you for an interview. Your cover letter should stand out among those of other applicants by highlighting the essential skills and abilities that you possess and that the institution is looking for. Each letter should be customized based on a thorough review of the institution and the position. If you have some personal, academic, or professional connection to the institution, such as having participated in a collaborative research with some faculty members at that institution, you should mention that information in the letter.

There are many ways to seek support in order to prepare a good job application package. Numerous online and offline resources and services are available to assist you. Several major professional organizations offer comprehensive tips and advice on job application materials (see the resource list at the end of this chapter). Your university career office may offer job search workshops, including cover letter and CV writing sessions, and usually will provide individual consultations. Your faculty advisor or professional mentors who know you well academically and professionally and are familiar with the job search process can also be good people you can consult.

Is it helpful or harmful to send more materials than asked?

In principle, you should follow the given instructions by submitting required materials only. You may contact the search committee chair first if you have any compelling reasons to send additional supporting materials. For instance, if you have more than three strong references who can talk about various aspects of your academic and professional life, even though the job announcement requests only three, you could contact the chair to determine the maximum number the committee would accept, with a brief explanation of how those additional references would comment on the qualifications and experience sought in the announcement. Some may say they are willing to accept additional letters of reference. If not, send only what they ask for. If you have additional supporting materials, such as a teaching portfolio, then you may include a statement at the end of your job application letter indicating that additional supporting materials are available upon request, and you can list them as an appendix in your CV.

Interviewing

What types of interviews are available?

Once you pass the initial application screening, you will be invited for a preliminary interview. Most universities and colleges conduct a telephone or video interview with approximately five to eight candidates. Some institutions will interview you between November and January at a professional conference, such as those for the American Council on the Teaching of Foreign Languages (ACTFL), Linguistic Society of America (LSA), or MLA, or sometimes at the end of March at TESOL. Two or three finalists from the initial interview are invited for a campus visit.

How do I prepare for job interviews?

Once you are invited for a telephone or convention interview, start another intensive research effort to find out as much as you can about the institution, the department, and the program. University websites provide good background information. After that, you may contact the search committee chair if you have any follow-up questions that would enable you to better understand the program and the position. Usually, you will be informed of who is on the search committee, but if not, ask and then do some research about their research interests and teaching specialization.

Anticipate questions that the search committee may ask and prepare responses in advance. You should be able to determine what the questions will be if you spend sufficient time understanding the institution, program, and advertised position. Write down every question that comes to your mind during the process, prepare an answer for each one, and practice them until you are confident. You may want to arrange for a mock interview with a faculty advisor or mentor who is an experienced job seeker or search committee member. Some university career offices or teaching centers offer mock interviews that can be recorded. You can review the recording later and make improvements to your responses, demeanor, and posture if needed.

What kinds of questions will be asked during the interview?

The questions you will be asked will be related to your fit and motivation for the institution, position, research, teaching, and service. You may be asked to explain your reasons for applying to the university and the specific position and any special contributions you can make to the university. At a teaching-focused university, many questions will be related to assessing your teaching effectiveness. The interviewers will ask about your teaching philosophy, preferred teaching methods, interest in designing a new course, strength as a teacher, teaching specialties, technology use in instruction, and so on. They may ask questions to evaluate your problem-solving abilities (e.g., "What challenges have you encountered in your teaching and how have you overcome them?" "Have you encountered issues with students, and how did you handle them?"). Research-intensive universities will be concerned with your ability to conduct original research and publish (10 to 15 peer reviewed articles within five years) to be tenurable. If the job involves some amount of administration, they will probably ask questions about your experience in administration and ability to handle program management and scholarly activities. Other possible topics the interviewers may ask about are your dissertation, professional goals, and ability to work collaboratively.

What kinds of questions are appropriate to ask the search committee during the interview?

You are expected to ask questions yourself, usually at the end of the interview, so prepare a list of questions to ask the search committee. Be ready to ask questions that demonstrate that you have done comprehensive research on the institution, department, program, and the advertised position. This demonstrates your enthusiasm for the position and your potential as a faculty member. It would be good to frame your questions to highlight your interest in the position and how you can contribute to the institution. For example, a question about the possibility for research collaboration and external grant writing would be a good indicator of your research ability, willingness to work with others, and potential for generating external funding. Another good question to ask in order to show your long-term commitment to the position would be about the tenure review process (e.g., expectation for research, publication, teaching, and service). Asking questions about faculty mentoring programs or the faculty learning community can demonstrate your interest in ongoing professional development in teaching. Avoid asking questions about salary and specific working conditions during the interview stage.

Receiving a Job Offer and Negotiating

How do I prepare for job negotiation after being offered a position?

Negotiations after a job offer include discussions about specific details regarding salary and the work environment. Be reasonable about salary negotiation. Figure out what they can offer by researching what the base starting salary is. You may find this information by accessing the faculty handbook and/or asking the search committee chair. Justify why you are asking for a higher salary than they offer, if you do. For example, I was able to negotiate a higher salary than what the college originally offered due to one year's previous work experience in a tenure-track position at another institution. This, coupled with the skills required in being a founding TE-

SOL director and the challenges associated with this role, justified a higher salary. Sometimes you may find it difficult to negotiate your salary but easier to negotiate for other working conditions or additional resources. As another personal example, I requested the support of a graduate assistant, staff, and technology in order to perform my work efficiently. All of these requests were accepted. You may ask for a spousal hiring, if needed. If you have another or better job offer, feel free to use it to negotiate for better conditions.

CHALLENGES, STRATEGIES, AND SUCCESSES

An international, non-native English speaking teacher (NNEST) doctoral student at a research-intensive university asked me via e-mail: "Where can I find jobs where there is no or less discrimination against NNESTs? I was told that I should avoid job locations where NNESTs are still underestimated and discriminated against." My response is that being a non-native English speaker in the field of second language education in the 21st century can be a positive feature you should highlight in your cover letter and during the interview. Your firsthand experience as a former learner of EFL and/ or ESL, as a native speaker of your own language, and now as a bilingual speaker makes a great contribution to language education.

Educational and cultural experiences in both U.S. and non-U.S. contexts, additional foreign language learning experience, and teaching experience in both the United States and your home country are several distinctive aspects, to name just a few, that NNES candidates can bring to the U.S. institution. As I said above, an increasing number of institutions are looking for such candidates in order to promote their international initiatives. Some institutions search for someone who can teach courses in second language education along with foreign languages and cultures.

Not many native English speaking candidates have the combination of such qualifications. Thus, you can be one of the most qualified candidates, someone who can add a great deal of diversity and internationalism to the institution and serve as a role model and mentor for students and faculty members once you are hired. How you highlight your unique strengths and contributions depends on your strategy.

Many institutions are committed to promoting diversity and internationalizing their campuses in order to meet the educational and economic needs they face. Therefore, hiring and retaining diverse faculty and staff are critical elements of this institutional effort. As long as you have the qualifications and experience they are seeking, do not be discouraged from applying to an institution, even if it has little or no minority faculty representation. This can be one of your very best opportunities, because some institutions with little minority representation might be eager to hire the best-qualified individual from an underrepresented group to showcase their efforts towards diversity.

SUMMARY AND FINAL ADVICE

What can doctoral students who are seeking a faculty position in second language education do to succeed? Here is a summary of the strategies and tips I shared in this chapter:

- Start your job search process and preparation from day one of your graduate study;
- Identify the best-fitting positions;
- Use personal networks;
- Find out as much as you can about the institution, the department, and the program prior to completing the application and interview;
- Follow the instructions in the job posting;
- Write an appealing cover letter and clear, concise CV;
- Seek professional support to prepare a good application package;
- Anticipate the questions that the search committee may ask, and practice your responses;
- Prepare a list of questions to ask the search committee;
- Be reasonable about salary negotiation;
- Negotiate for additional resources to work effectively;
- Highlight your strengths and unique contribution as an NNEST; and
- Do not be discouraged from applying simply due to your underrepresented status.

Earlier, I advised you to start being familiar with the faculty job search process as early as possible: the earlier, the better. You may feel discouraged if you are already at a later stage of your doctoral work but have not yet started your job search. Do not worry. There is also truth in the statement that it is never too late. When you invest time to identify the areas you are strong in and the job you want, you can be successful in job hunting. With luck, you will receive a job offer, after which you can begin negotiations and accept the offer. Then, celebrate your entrance into academia as a faculty member! Even if you find that you are unsuccessful in the first year of your job search, you will certainly find that the process has helped you succeed in your ongoing search.

NOTE

1. See Samimy, Kim, Lee, & Kasai (2011) to understand the growth and empowerment experienced by the three NNES graduate students, including myself.

RESOURCES

Online Job Search Databases

American Association for Applied Linguistics (AAAL) Career Center
http://www.aaal.org/jobbank.cfm

American Council on the Teaching of Foreign Languages (ACTFL) Job Central
http://jobcentral.actfl.org/jobseekers/myaccount/index.cfm

Chronicle of Higher Education Jobs
http://chronicle.com/section/Jobs/61/

Higher Ed Jobs
http://www.higheredjobs.com/

Linguistic Society of America (LSA) Jobs
http://www.lsadc.org/info/jobs-index.cfm

The Linguist List Job Search
http://linguistlist.org/jobs/search-job1.cfm

Modern Language Association (MLA) Job Information List
http://www.mla.org/jil

TESOL International Association Career Center
http://careers.tesol.org/

Articles

Matsuda, A., Dogancay-Aktuna, S., Eslami-Rasekh, Z., & Nemtchinova, K. (2005). Demystifying the tenure-track job search: Stories of four NNES professionals. *The CATESOL Journal, 17*(1), 171–181.

REFERENCE

Samimy, K., Kim, S., Lee, J., & Kasai, M. (2011). A participative inquiry in a TESOL program: Development of three NNES graduate students' legitimate peripheral participation to fuller participation. *The Modern Language Journal, 95,* 1–17.

CHAPTER 3

THE RESEARCH-INTENSIVE UNIVERSITY

Yuko Goto Butler
University of Pennsylvania

On the day when I was granted tenure at a so-called "research-intensive university" in the United States some time ago, an international student from Africa in our master's level Teaching English to Speakers of Other Langauges (TESOL) program came into my office. I was still in the process of digesting what it meant to obtain tenure and hadn't really begun to feel excited about the news. The student, after congratulating me, told me that my tenureship was "special" for him as well. He said that "I have always thought that American universities like this one would never take foreigners and minority people seriously. But after hearing that you've gotten tenure, I realized that I might have been wrong. I began to think that I may have a chance as well. I just started thinking about staying in the U.S. and pursuing a Ph.D." It was by far one of the most rewarding remarks that I had ever received as a teacher and a researcher.

When I started looking for a job after finishing my own Ph.D. program, I had very little real understanding of how research-intensive universities worked. Just like the international student mentioned above, I had a number of misconceptions. Judging from the label "research-intensive,"

Demystifying Career Paths after Graduate School, pages 23–33
Copyright © 2012 by Information Age Publishing
All rights of reproduction in any form reserved.

I simply imagined that this must be referring to institutions where the faculty is expected to produce massive amounts of research, teaching is secondary, the environment is highly competitive, and so forth. Thus, when I was offered a position as an assistant professor in educational linguistics (applied linguistics) and TESOL at such a university, I was nervous about being able to survive in a research-intensive institution as a non-native English speaker (NNES).

It turns out many of my initial perceptions were wrong. In fact, research-intensive universities can allow NNESs to maximize their strengths, at least in my view. A research-intensive university usually provides you with various types of support for you to be successful. In the discussion that follows, I first sketch an outline of the system and culture of the research-intensive university, followed by descriptions of the challenges one may encounter and the strategies needed in order to overcome such challenges. It is very important to note, however, that there is substantial diversity in the systems and practices among research-intensive universities and that the description that follows is inevitably influenced by unique factors that are not generalizable across all cases. As such, readers should bear in mind that some of the descriptions below may have only limited applicability to other institutions.

SYSTEM, CULTURE, AND EXPECTATIONS AT THE RESEARCH-INTENSIVE UNIVERSITY

What is the Research-Intensive University?

What is the research-intensive university? It does not seem to have an agreed-upon definition in the literature. A former president of Stanford University, Gerhard Casper, in a speech given at Peking University on May 3, 1998, indicated that the research-intensive university has to meet the following three criteria: "it selects its students; it is primarily dedicated to the search for knowledge; and it is marked by a spirit of critical inquiry" (Casper, 1998, para. 5). He explained the reason for his choice of the term "research-intensive university" as opposed to the commonly-used term "research university" by saying that research cannot be the sole function of universities and that the intensity of research is part of a university's mission of teaching and learning. In Casper's view, research and teaching are in a mutually stimulating relationship; high-quality research is based on high-quality teaching, and high-quality teaching is seen as originating in high-quality research. The research-intensive university, therefore, can be thought of as an institution where the goal is high quality research and teaching, which is sought based on the mutual pursuit of knowledge by both faculty and students, both of whom are engaged in a process of critical inquiry.

The Student–Faculty Relationship

One can see, therefore, that the common perception that the research-intensive university does not pay very much attention to teaching is not accurate. While it is undeniable that research is a major component of one's tenure review (discussed in further detail below), good teaching has increasingly been recognized as an important qualification for successful candidates. This is not surprising if you accept Casper's notion of the research-intensive university discussed above.

The research-intensive university attracts students with high standards and expectations, and they often are focused on pursuing both knowledge and innovation. Many TESOL and applied linguistics programs in the United States are offered at the graduate level, and the graduate students in those programs often have some teaching and/or other types of work experience prior to starting in such programs. They tend to be older and more mature than other student groups and come from a variety of linguistic and cultural backgrounds. Such programs tend to attract many international students as well as domestic students who have high levels of aspiration and motivation.

Under these circumstances, teaching can be demanding but can also be an intellectually stimulating and exciting opportunity for producing research. Faculty members at research-intensive universities are expected to mentor their students in such a way that they can become critical and independent researchers and/or educators in their respective fields. Through the process of mentorship, scholarship often becomes a joint endeavor between faculty members and their students. The exact practices may differ from one university to another, but the university where I have been working encourages the faculty to co-present papers and co-publish papers with students. Doing so is considered a sign of good mentorship by the faculty and is highly valued by the university. As many of the students advance in their studies during the program, I often see them more as research collaborators or even colleagues, rather than simply as students.

High Expectations for Producing Innovative and Critical Research

There is no doubt that faculty members at research-intensive universities are expected to produce innovative and critical research that can potentially make a significant contribution to the field. Some universities (or departments) may give you a clear description of what constitutes a sufficient quality and volume of research in order to gain tenure. For instance, some universities will let you know which journals are considered to be "flagship journals" and how many publications in such journals are needed in order for you to be considered as having made a satisfactory contribution to the field. At the same time, other universities and departments may not give you such specific guidelines with respect to the requirements for gaining tenure.

In general, it is critically important to have a reasonable number of publications in established peer-reviewed journals in the field. Publishing a book in addition to journal articles may be considered as desirable or even expected to get tenure in certain fields, such as linguistic anthropology. Some universities have established point systems for scoring faculty research productivity. For example, a publication may receive different points depending on the perceived ranking or influence of a given journal it appears in, whether or not the publication is single-authored or multi-authored, and so forth. In my experience, book chapters are usually not as valued as peer-reviewed journal articles. Editing books may be a good way to have your name recognized in the field. At the same time, however, it may require a substantial amount of work and it may be valued only marginally, depending on the university or department. Similarly, publications that are not in the English language and book reviews may or may not be considered as making a significant contribution to the field. Therefore, it is critically important to obtain as much information as possible from your institution about the research expectations for granting tenure at an early stage in your career.

The Tenure Review Process

The exact procedure for tenure review varies from one institution to another, but the process usually is broken down into two stages: a third-year review and a final review. The primary purpose of the third-year review in most institutions is to make sure that you are on the right track and to give you feedback so that you can be sufficiently prepared for the final review. The final review is much more rigorous than the third-year review, and it usually takes place during the sixth or seventh year after your initial appointment, assuming you've remained at the same institution. If you switch institutions, you can expect to have an individual negotiation with the dean of your department with respect to the timing of your final review.

The review covers the following three aspects of your contribution: research, teaching, and service (both inside and outside of the institution). While all three aspects are considered important, research is the most heavily weighted and is evaluated intensively in a research-intensive university. For the final review, you will be asked to prepare a number of documents that span your career. These include, for example, your CV, a statement of academic interest (an explanation of your past, present and future research), copies of your all published works, copies of manuscripts under review, a teaching chronicle, copies of students' evaluations/reports on your teaching performance, a list of advisees and dissertation committees, a description of your services, and any other material relevant to the review such as reviews of your book(s) written by other researchers. In addition, depending on the institution or department, you may be asked to make an oral presentation on your research in front of fellow faculty members and students in your department, a presentation that is sometimes referred to as a tenure colloquium.

The tenure review committee is usually appointed by the dean of the school or college to which you belong and typically consists of three or four tenured faculty members and a student representative. The committee selects external reviewers who belong to different institutions and departments and will send them your documents. These external reviewers are leading experts in the field who can independently evaluate the academic merits and significance of your research. As a result, your dissertation advisor, co-authors, and co-researchers of your published papers typically will not be eligible to serve as external reviewers. The number of such external reviewers differs from institution to institution. My university requires the committee to obtain approximately 10 external reviews. At some institutions, the tenure review committee may ask you to submit a couple of names of the researchers by whom you wish to be reviewed and another couple of names by whom you do not wish to be reviewed. However, it is usually entirely up to the committee to determine whether they wish to adhere to your requests in making the final list of external reviewers. The evaluations conducted by external reviewers are taken very seriously and weigh heavily on the final decision to grant tenure. Your case will also be reviewed by select internal faculty members as well as your advisees and often your students. The committee puts all of the evaluations together and makes a recommendation. Your case then will be discussed and voted on at different levels of the university. The final decision will be made by the Provost's Office (see Chapter 11 for a more detailed discussion of the tenure review process).

After Tenure

The tenure review process is indeed very rigorous and stressful for many candidates. However, it can give you a great opportunity to reflect on your own research and teaching and to have your work known within the field. After obtaining tenure, you are expected to continue to be productive and to keep making contributions to the field. During the pre-tenure period, you might be exempt from some of the heavier administrative duties, but after tenure, you are expected to assume more of a leadership position in program administration, various types of committee work, and other university-wide duties. You are also expected to be active outside of the work you do with your institution, including editing journals, taking leadership roles in professional organizations, providing consultation to other schools and programs, and so forth.

CHALLENGES AND STRATEGIES

Obviously, producing high-quality research is a key component to being successful at the research-intensive university. You need to be constantly productive, and your work has to be recognized by leading experts in the field. For non-native English speaking scholars, producing a sufficient volume of high-quality research papers in English poses an extra challenge. It may also be a challenge to get used to academic customs that can be very different from those in one's home country. The following sections summarize some of the general strategies that may be helpful for dealing with such challenges.

Understanding the Requirements for Tenure at Your Institution

As mentioned above, it is critically important to collect accurate information about the requirements for tenure at your institution as early as possible and to plan accordingly. You may hear rumors or receive mixed information about such requirements. Many institutions will provide you with a mentor who is familiar with the requirements. Some institutions also may have a junior faculty mentoring committee in order to help you with getting tenure. If your institution or department has a support system of this kind, take advantage of it. Talk to your mentor and the dean of your department in order to obtain accurate information about the requirements for tenure at the earliest stage of your career. How many articles do you need to publish? Which journals are considered flagship journals? Does the department have a point system for ranking your publications? Do you need to publish a book? Are you expected to obtain grants? Can you get a leave for a semester or for a year during the pre-tenure period? These are just some of the questions you should ask as you learn the requirements for tenure at your institution.

In general, it is quite important for you to publish your dissertation as early as possible, either in a journal format or in a book format, depending on your discipline. Your dissertation should be your first independent and representative work, and it has to be recognized in the field. As we all know quite well, it takes a long time to publish a paper or a book. If you decide to publish your dissertation in a book format, give yourself sufficient time, since most research-intensive universities require you to have reviews of your book in journals and other publications before your tenure file is submitted. You need to allow extra time for people to review your book and publish their reviews before you are reviewed for tenure.

In addition to your dissertation, you will be expected to have a new line of research, which can be an extension of your dissertation study or can be an independent and new research project. Research-intensive universities want to see that you have not stopped at the dissertation and that you can continue producing high-quality work as an innovative and independent researcher. If your dissertation topic is closely related to your graduate school advisor's research, it may be advisable to minimize the amount of time you spend on co-publishing papers with your former advisor, even if you are the first-author of such papers.[1] You need to prove that you are an independent researcher, and continuing to co-author papers can sometimes be seen as indicative of a lack of independence.

Writing and Publishing Constantly

Once you understand the tenure requirements, you need to work strategically to meet them. It is important to write and publish constantly. It may be fine if you have no publications in the first year of your pre-tenure period, but it generally does not look very good if you have blanks in your publication record. Everybody has his or her own way of writing; some people prefer to write early in the morning, while others can concentrate better late at night. Some can write fast, while others want to invest as much time as possible for writing. You just need to find the way that works best for you. But regardless of how you do this, make sure that you try to write constantly, even if you can write only one sentence some days. Joining or forming a writing circle among junior faculty members can be a good way to regulate your writing schedule and to receive feedback on your writing in a low-pressure environment. If you feel comfortable doing so, you can share your manuscripts with your colleagues and ask them for their feedback before you submit them to journals.

Since the convention is that you should only submit your manuscript to one journal at a time, it is important to send your manuscript to an appropriate journal. You should investigate the journals in your field prior to submitting a manuscript. What are the popular topics and issues that each journal deals with? Who is the targeted audience? Is the journal more geared towards theory-building or is it more practice-oriented? What is the average turn-around period (how long it takes a manuscript to be published), and what is the acceptance rate? What is the required format? If you cannot obtain sufficient information from journals or their websites, you can ask the editors directly. In some cases (but not always), editors may quickly scan your manuscript and tell you whether it fits their journals or not.

Unfortunately for non-native speakers of English, the notion of world Englishes is not uniformly accepted among journals. If you do not feel comfortable with your English, it is advisable to have your manuscript proofread before submitting it to a journal.

Managing Your Time Wisely in Order to be Productive

It is important to secure time for research and to strike a balance between research and other obligations both at work and at home. Committee work and other university-related administrative duties are important components of your work. However, if it gets too overwhelming for you, you may want to make a request to your dean or the appropriate parties to reduce such duties. Similarly, journal editors and grant-funding agencies may ask you to review manuscripts and grant proposals. Reviewing journal manuscripts and grant proposals is a wonderful opportunity to learn about how to successfully publish papers and obtain grants, but be wary of taking on too many such tasks during your pre-tenure period, especially if they influence your own research productivity.

Obtaining grants and fellowships, especially those that are considered prestigious, will usually be a major plus for your tenure review. However, you have to remember that it can require a substantial amount of time and energy to prepare grant proposals and to manage large-scale studies. If your research only requires a smaller amount of funding, you may want to take advantage of smaller in-house funding opportunities. Even if you need to obtain a large grant, starting from smaller grants increases your chance of getting a larger one. Fellowships, such as the National Academy of Education/ Spencer Postdoctoral Fellowships, make it possible for you to buy additional time for research. In addition, fellowship programs often provide you with opportunities to build professional networks, which in turn help to guide your research and to have your research recognized by the field.

Research-intensive universities usually allow you to have a nine month contract, and as a result, you are free from teaching and administrative duties during the summer. You definitely want to take the nine month option if it is available and spend the summer productively. Summer is a great time to focus on your research and writing. In my case, I also try to spend some time exploring something new outside of my own field by attending seminars and reading books during the summer. I often find it very insightful to learn about how other disciplines approach various questions, and how these other approaches might relate to my own research.

Finally, it is also advisable to find something that entertains you outside of your work. I know some colleagues who are semi-professional cooks, musicians, hikers, kick-boxers and so forth. Enjoy spending time with your family. You'll find that you can be more productive if you don't lock yourself in your office all the time.

Creating Intellectually Stimulating Relationships with Your Students

As mentioned above, successful teaching is also an important component of your work and eventually will be helpful for your tenure review. The teaching load differs greatly depending on the institution, but you are usually asked to teach three to five courses per year if you are working at an institution that uses the semester system. Take students' evaluations of your teaching seriously and improve your teaching accordingly. Even if your initial teaching evaluations are not very impressive, it is important to show that you are making improvements. Ask your colleagues to share their teaching tips and seek advice in order to better understand your students' characteristics and needs.

It is necessary to build a trustworthy and intellectually stimulating relationship with your students. Depending on your students' cultural, social and linguistic backgrounds, their beliefs about what counts as a "good" student–teacher relationship may differ. Be cognizant of the fact that you may have your own cultural and social biases of which you may still be unaware. Personally, I feel that non-native English speaking professionals might be in a relatively good position to be sensitive to such cultural and social bias issues. It is critically important to be in close communication with your advisees and your research assistants in order to narrow gaps in expectations and/or to avoid miscommunication.

Students can also help you grow as a researcher. You often get innovative research ideas and insights by interacting with your graduate students. It is important to build intellectually stimulating relationships with your students. In my own case, I hold a weekly research meeting that is open for any students who are interested in my research project. In those meetings, the students are encouraged to express their views freely. I often find gems in their experiences, perspectives and insights, which continue to offer new and interesting ways of viewing the research topics that we are examining.

SUMMARY AND FINAL ADVICE

The key strategies that I discussed in this chapter can be summarized as follows:

- Discovering the requirements for tenure at your institution;
- Writing and publishing constantly;
- Managing your time wisely in order to be productive; and
- Creating intellectually stimulating relationships with your students

The research-intensive university is a very exciting and rewarding place for anybody who is interested in research and teaching, regardless of your native/non-native English speaking status and your majority/minority status. Its primary mission is to advance knowledge through critical inquiry in the intellectually rich environment created by both faculty and students. The bottom line for success in the research-intensive university is the extent to which you enjoy what you do there. An old high school teacher of mine once told me that "no matter what challenges you may face, there is always a ray of light at the forefront of academic inquiry." If you are willing to believe such a statement, you will never get bored at a research-intensive university.

NOTE

1. Note that this may not apply in some disciplines (e.g., neuropsycholinguistics).

RESOURCES

The following is a list of select sources where you can find information about fellowships, grants, and other types of information useful for applied linguistics and TESOL specialists. This is by no means a comprehensive list. You may find funding opportunities via regional foundation websites as well.

American Association for Applied Linguistics (AAAL)
   http://www.aaal.org/

American Council on the Teaching of Foreign Languages (ACTFL)
   http://www.actfl.org/

British Association for Applied Linguistics (BAAL)
   http://www.baal.org.uk/

Center for Applied Linguistics (CAL)
http://www.cal.org/

Educational Testing Service (ETS)
http://www.ets.org/

Institute of Education Sciences (IES)
http://ies.ed.gov/

International Association of Applied Linguistics
http://www.aila.info/

TESOL International Association
http://www.tesol.org/

Fulbright Scholar Program
http://www.cies.org/about_fulb.htm

The Ford Foundation
http://www.fordfound.org/

The MacArthur Foundation
http://www.macfound.org/

The Spencer Foundation
http://www.spencer.org/

REFERENCES

Casper, G. (1998). *The advantage of the research-intensive university: the university of the 21st century.* Talk given at Peking University, Beijing, China. Retrieved from http://www.stanford.edu/dept/pres-provost/president/speeches/980503peking.html

CHAPTER 4

TEACHING-FOCUSED UNIVERSITY

Ekaterina (Katya) Nemtchinova
Seattle Pacific University

I was chatting with another new faculty member at a new faculty seminar. When we started talking about our backgrounds, it turned out that while I was hired straight from graduate school, Todd had held a tenure-track position in a big research university for several years.

"Why did you give it up and come here?" I wanted to know.

"Frankly, I wanted to do less research and more teaching. I was intrigued by a smaller campus and what it has to offer, and an opportunity for more interaction with students."

UNDERSTANDING THE TEACHING-FOCUSED INSTITUTION

As much as higher education settings vary in the United States, one most obvious division is between a large university with a dominant research mission and a smaller college with a primary teaching mission. If you are considering a position in one of the latter, it would be helpful to know about

Demystifying Career Paths after Graduate School, pages 35–47
Copyright © 2012 by Information Age Publishing
35

these institutions' culture, practices, and expectations for faculty. This chapter describes teaching-focused colleges and universities.

Although "teaching-focused" is not a term with a formal definition, it is commonly used to describe institutions that emphasize academic instruction as their principal goal. While there is no exact published number of teaching-focused colleges and universities in the United States, a search of the Carnegie Foundation for the Advancement of Teaching (n.d.) database based on tenure criteria yields 1,625 such institutions. These colleges offer baccalaureate, master's, and a number of doctoral degrees in many fields of arts and sciences. They can be public (administered by the state), private (generating their own funding), residential (offering on-campus housing and student life programs), non-residential, liberal arts (focusing on education of the whole person), comprehensive (granting master's and doctoral degrees), and faith-based (representing a certain religious tradition). Teaching-focused institutions serve a diverse student population in terms of background, age, gender, and ethnicity.

As a rule, teaching-intensive institutions have a small- to medium-sized student body (up to 10,000 students), which results in smaller classes, lower student/instructor ratio, and more face-to-face time with students. Classes are taught by professors (not graduate assistants) whose teaching loads extend to seven to nine courses a year, independent of the quarter or semester system. According to the 1989 National Survey of Faculty, instructors in teaching-focused institutions spent an average of 13.1 hours per week in preparation for teaching, 11 hours teaching undergraduate, and 5.2 hours teaching graduate courses, as opposed to 9.4, 5.7, and 4 hours respectively for faculty in research-intensive institutions (Carnegie Foundation for the Advancement of Teaching, 1991).

INSTITUTIONAL EXPECTATIONS: REVIEW FOR TENURE AND PROMOTION

Similar to those in other higher education institutions, tenure and promotion criteria in teaching-focused institutions are defined by teaching, research, and service, although the distribution of weight for each category is different: teaching-focused institutions place primary prominence on teaching and advising. The faculty is also expected to engage in research and publication, although to a lesser degree compared to research universities. Service to the university and profession is imperative for one's successful academic career as well. Compare, for example, the weight of different criteria for tenure decisions in teaching- and research-focused institutions as illustrated by the percent of the faculty members saying that the indica-

TABLE 4.1   Most Widely Used Indicators for Tenure Decisions

Percentage of faculty considering each indicator "very" or "fairly" important

Research-focused institutions	(%)	Teaching-focused institutions	(%)
Number of publications	95	Student evaluation of courses taught	84
Type of publications (books, edited volumes, articles)	89	Service within the university community	69
Recommendations from outside scholars	86	Number of publications	68
Reputations of presses or journals publishing the books or articles	84	Lectures or papers delivered at professional meetings or at other colleges and universities	67
Research grants received by the scholar	77	Recommendations from faculty within the institution	65

Source: Data is from Carnegie Foundation for the Advancement of Teaching, 1991, p. 24

tor is "very" or "fairly" important (Table 4.1), based on the Carnegie Foundation 1989 National Survey of Faculty.

It is seen from Table 4.1 that while research institutions do not even list student evaluations among "very" or "fairly" important indicators, teaching-focused institutions rank them as having the most influence on tenure and promotion decisions. According to the associate dean of my institution, who has extensive experience with these matters, department chairs in teaching-focused institutions are usually reluctant to support tenure and promotion for faculty members with a poor teaching record. Not only does a poor teaching record discredit the department in an environment where teaching effectiveness is important, she explained, but it also forces administrators to deal with students' complaints.

A tenure review usually starts in the sixth or seventh year of a full-time faculty appointment; most colleges precede it with a pre-tenure evaluation halfway through the tenure-track period. Additionally, department and division administrators conduct annual appraisals of faculty for performance evaluation and rank and salary raises.

To apply for tenure, candidates submit a well-organized report that includes a self-reflective narrative of their achievements in the areas of teaching, research, and service. The achievements in these areas should be clearly documented by a curriculum vitae (CV), teaching evaluations, publications and their pre- and post-publication peer reviews, description of service activities, and so on. The application undergoes several rounds of review by different academic divisions and faculty governance committees. While individual institutions differ in their criteria for success in each category of tenure review, evaluation scales, and guidelines for format and style, it is the candidate's job to carefully follow the college's guidelines in displaying work and presenting himself or herself in the best possible way.

Teaching and Advising

Since teaching is weighted most heavily in evaluation of faculty competence and contributions in teaching-focused institutions, you need to make a convincing case for your excellence in this area. Your narrative in your tenure portfolio should include a self-reflection on various dimensions of your teaching and address challenges by acknowledging a problem (if any), describing it, and explaining its cause and solution. The same reflective approach applies to self-evaluation of advising in which you describe your advising philosophy, the strategies you use, and ways of improving your advising practices. In addition, you may be expected to include syllabi, a course-specific analysis of every class you teach, and a breakdown of student evaluations. Consider including some letters from recent graduates commenting on your teaching and advising in this section.

Research

While teaching-focused institutions prioritize teaching over research, they also expect you to demonstrate a strong commitment to scholarship (e.g., engagement in research, presentations at national and international conferences, and publishing in respectable academic venues). Discuss research requirements with your department chair and ask for sample tenure and promotion files of successful colleagues to find out your institution's expectations early in your career. In your narrative include a clear explanation of your research agenda and its role and importance within the context of a broader field, as your university community might not be familiar with your topic and terminology. Describe your academic achievements, explain dissemination methods (e.g., types of journals you publish in), and discuss possible hindrances to your scholarly productivity such as a low acceptance rate of a particular journal in your field, a heavy teaching load, or numerous new course preparations in a professional way. Also, mention your future plans for scholarship and growth in your discipline as this speaks to your promise as a scholar.

Service

In addition to evidence of sound teaching and a solid scholarship record, you need to demonstrate your accomplishments in serving their department, institution, and a wider professional community. Teaching-focused institutions tend to place higher premium on service than research universities. The Carnegie Foundation survey of 1989 showed that 69% of teaching-focused institution faculty (compared with 26% in research universities) felt college service to be either very important or fairly important in getting tenure (see Table 4.1). University service can be internal (committee and task force appointments in and outside of the department, participation in campus-wide projects, and supervising student organizations) and external (administrative and leadership positions in professional organizations, non-peer-reviewed publications and adjudication for conferences and journals). Not only should your service activity be carefully documented by including dates of service and a description of duties, your narrative should also assess the significance of your appointments for promoting university and professional community. To boost your service record, you might want to include any notes of acknowledgment you received, as well as letters from superiors detailing your specific contribution to the university or profession.

Collegiality

Although not mentioned specifically in any guidelines, collegiality—an ability to work effectively with other faculty members—is a critical factor for tenure and promotion in a teaching-focused university, with its smaller and more closely-knit community. While in a research university collegial interactions lie predominantly within one's department, new faculty members in a teaching institution should aim to establish working relationships with a broader institutional community. Collegiality can be described as "cooperating with colleagues and taking initiatives for progress," demonstrating "a basic understanding of department and university culture" (Hu-DeHart, 2000, p. 28) and "support for and sympathy with the statement of purpose of the college" (Gibson, 1992, p. 214). Others mention "displaying good academic citizenship," or "contributing to a collegial atmosphere" (Connell & Savage, 2001, para. 1) as important measures of collegiality. To put it another way, to be a collegial colleague means to get along and work well with others, to interact with faculty inside and outside of your department both academically and socially, and to solve interpersonal conflicts with colleagues and staff, should they arise, before they escalate into irresolvable matters. For those who are not sure how to begin the socialization process, Boice (2000, pp. 221–222) outlines a number of useful strategies and specific behaviors junior faculty members could adopt to increase their collegial appeal.

CHALLENGES, STRATEGIES, AND SUCCESSES

Becoming a Master Teacher

Since the principal responsibility of faculty members in a teaching-intensive institution is teaching, honing one's teaching skills becomes a priority. And yet it is a widely held opinion that graduate institution provides little preparation for teaching, focusing instead on research in an academic discipline (Boice, 2000; Gibson, 1992). Faced with a teaching task with minimal or no teaching skills, new faculty members tend to imitate their favorite instructors; they rely too much on the way they have been taught, or the way they are most comfortable with. This often results in favoring a certain type of learners (e.g., visual) or activities (e.g., whole class), thus ignoring other students' learning preferences or needs and failing to vary instruction. Another common teaching mistake novice professors make is focusing on their own grasp of the course material, assuming that good knowledge of the subject means good teaching. This often results in over-preparation for classes, excessive lecturing, and emphasis on delivery of material at the expense of student learning (VanZanten, 2011).

How does one develop into an expert teacher? While it is not feasible to come up with a single recipe for brilliant teaching because of the multitude of such variables as one's teaching philosophy, subject matter, and student population that come into play in any given teaching situation, Chickering and Gamson (1987) in their influential study described seven teaching practices that proved to successfully ensure student learning. According to Chickering and Gamson (1987), effective teachers:

1. encourage contact between students and faculty,
2. develop reciprocity and cooperation among students,
3. encourage active learning,
4. give prompt feedback,
5. emphasize time on task,
6. communicate high expectations, and
7. respect diverse talents and ways of learning.

While these principles may seem rather evident, relating to common sense, having them in front of you and reflecting on how each could be implemented in your class might be a good start along the road to effective teaching. In terms of classroom practice, the following suggestions may be helpful:

Establish rapport with students. Establishing rapport with students is a crucial condition for building trust and promoting successful learning, so start working on it as early in the course as possible. On the first day of class, make an attempt to learn students' names and let them get to know each other in an ice-breaking activity. Convey your passion about the subject by talking about why you are excited to teach this course. Tell students a little about your linguistic, cultural, and educational background so that they know you as a person. I also use the ice-breaking phase to address non-native English speakers' (NNES) issues as they relate to students' field of study and the subject at hand. By talking about my challenges and successes as a NNES professional, I hope to present a role model for NNES and an authentic voice for native English speaker students.

Continue to work on the rapport with students throughout the course by showing a genuine interest in your students, learning about their enthusiasms, and listening to their concerns. Be flexible, approachable and respectful of your students while setting firm boundaries and clearly communicating your expectations for students' conduct and learning outcomes. Above all, keep in mind that "believing that students are able to learn—even if they achieve different levels of mastery and have varying strengths—is a fundamental requirement for an effective teacher" (Van-Zanten, 2011, p. 90).

Teach from a student-centered stance. In a student-centered classroom, students actively participate in their own learning by constructing knowledge rather than merely accepting it from the teacher. This is achieved by interspersing a traditional lecture (a favorite mode of teaching by novice professors) with class discussions, question-and-answer exchange, pair and group work, problem solving, and so on. The benefits of a student-centered approach are known to increase students' motivation, as they are more challenged and can have a certain amount of control over class activities. This approach also promotes deeper understanding and better retention of the material, and develops higher-order thinking skills and confidence. Trying these techniques even on a small scale will help create a constructive learning and teaching experience in your classroom.

Learn from peer observations. Observing more experienced colleagues of yours and inviting them to your classes can help you improve your teaching practices. While it may feel uncomfortable to have someone else in your class, particularly at the beginning of your teaching career, consider such benefits of peer observations as collegial support, constructive feedback, and assistance that ultimately will enable you to become a better teacher. In addition to advice on your teaching behavior, you will also receive confirmation of your existing instructional strengths and gain self-confidence (Donnelly, 2007). To make the most of a peer observation, focus on several aspects of your teaching that you think might need improvement, ask the observer to monitor them during the observation, and follow up with a discussion of your own reflections as well as your observer's feedback on the class. Also, ask a senior colleague to review your syllabi and teaching materials. Use his or her comments to modify your organization of materials and clarity of instructions, improve the means of assessment, and so on.

Another equally productive way of gleaning insight into teaching is observing someone else's teaching. By sitting in on a veteran teacher's class, you can explore elements of teaching from a student perspective and pick up some useful tools of the trade. Examine both the "how-to" and "why" of teaching as you focus on instructor-student interactions, specific strategies for asking and answering questions, encouraging student participation, and managing small group and whole class discussion. While everyone develops their own unique teaching style, strategies used by the senior faculty members could help you develop your own successful teaching.

Use course evaluations to improve your teaching. While course evaluations are often viewed as unfair and ego-damaging, they can become a valuable tool in reflecting on and improving one's teaching. The key is in the attitude: instead of taking comments personally, treat them as a formative assessment. Students' insights into the strengths and weaknesses of the course will help you refine its content, activities, and assignments. If student feedback seems irrelevant or contradictory, seek help of a senior colleague in interpreting the data.

In addition to formal end-of-the term assessment, you might want to conduct an informal mid-term evaluation, particularly if you are teaching a course for the first time. By asking anonymously a few open-ended questions (e.g., "What do you like about the course so far?" and "What do you think could be done better?") you will be able to get feedback and make the necessary adjustments before the course is over. You might want to share your summary of the feedback in class—not only does it show that you take note of their opinions, but it can help improve final course evaluations as well.

To increase student response rate of course evaluations, keep reminding students about the importance of their evaluations in class and by e-mail. Consider offering extra credit points to the whole class if a certain percentage of students (e.g., 80–85%) participates in the evaluation.

Enhance Presentation Skills

College professors, native and non-native English speakers alike, are expected to have excellent public speaking skills. Do you keep good eye contact, a relaxed posture, and a smile while you talk to students? Do you move around the class as you speak, addressing different groups of students? Did you master the art of speaking, rather than reading, only occasionally consulting your notes, while being organized and spontaneous at the same time? What do you do when you cannot answer a student's question on the spot? Observing yourself as you teach in regards to these questions, practicing presentation techniques, rehearsing and even memorizing parts of your talk will help you develop your own public speaking style and become a confident and effective speaker.

Staying Organized

One of the biggest challenges for new faculty in a teaching-intensive institution may be finding the time for writing and research. Although multiple responsibilities of teaching, research, and service on the one hand and family and social obligations on the other do seem to be overwhelming at times, you will find that careful planning and time management help you structure your professional and personal life. Stay organized by keeping your files and records in order and making "to do" lists. Prioritize your projects, set deadlines for the most important ones, and abide by them. Restrict your service engagements to the ones that really interest you and fit into your schedule without disrupting interaction with students or research time.

To carve out some time for scholarship on a regular basis, arrange your schedule so that you have a block of "research time" once or twice a week, or write for an hour or two every day. Regularity helps to form an academic writing habit and increase productivity; it also turns out to be more effective than "bingeing" on writing over the summer (Boice, 2000) or waiting for the strike of inspiration. Focus on feasible projects at the beginning of your scholarly career. Because teaching-focused institutions have less stringent requirements for publication venues, consider writing book reviews, professional newsletter contributions, and shorter articles as well as publishing in second-tier journals to generate a publication record and develop confidence.

A busy schedule with a multitude of tasks can make you feel strained. Make time for yourself to unwind. Spending time with friends and family, pursuing a hobby, and enjoying nature will help you to relieve stress. Do not forget about the physical and mental benefits of exercise; make a workout of some type a part of your to-do list if you have a tendency to neglect these activities.

Building Confidence

It is natural for any new teacher to feel nervous and insecure. The feeling may be exacerbated for NNES by their self-perceived insufficiency in fluency, accuracy, vocabulary, and/or pronunciation (Ding, 2000; Kamhi-Stein, 1999). Because of the combined pressure of language and teaching anxiety, novice teachers sometimes try to establish their authority by being too firm, even domineering, and setting excessively high expectations, whereas students interpret such behavior as unfriendly, distant, or condescending (Boice, 2000). If you feel apprehensive about your competency, do not apologize for your accent, admit your self-doubt about teaching, compare yourself to your colleagues, or dwell on your failings. Instead, make a conscious effort to treat your missteps as an opportunity to grow as a professional, to develop a positive attitude and to learn from them. Focus on your successes; make a list of your achievements and create a personal mantra that plays in your head every time you feel low (mine was "I am a doctor; I am a professor"). Striking a balance between an authoritative profile and a pro-student outlook is key. In class, conveying that you are in charge even if you do not feel it and at the same time being supportive and friendly will make students recognize your authority as a professor, while working with a mentor and having a support network (e.g., a new faculty group on campus or an online forum) is bound to increase your confidence.

A certain degree of confidence is needed not only in teaching, but in dealing with colleagues as well. Being able to say "no" is one of the most important skills for a junior faculty member to develop (Garcia, 2000). Be assertive when you need to decline yet another service request or express your point of view, even if it goes against the opinion of senior faculty members. Decide what you want to say in each case and stick with it by acknowledging the situation and stating your position in a respectful yet decisive way. Confidence, like any other skill, can be practiced, and it is in your power to pursue it.

SUMMARY AND FINAL ADVICE

Working in a teaching-intensive institution means spending most of one's working hours with students in and out of the classroom while producing publishable research and serving the university and profession. Although interacting with students is an extremely rewarding experience, new faculty members are often intimidated by the challenges of teaching. Other common concerns include finding time for scholarship in the face of a large teaching load, building confidence, and navigating the college's policies. As you are planning your career at a teaching-focused institution, consider the following suggestions:

- *Learn about tenure and promotion requirements early on in your career.* Familiarize yourself with your institution's tenure and promotion criteria in a timely fashion; find out tacit expectations in the area of research and service and plan accordingly. Talk to your chair and senior colleagues and attend workshops to ask questions and seek resources.

- *Become an effective teacher* by observing and being observed by more experienced colleagues. Analyze student and peer feedback on your teaching and take action to remedy areas that need improvement. Work on your presentation skills. Be positive, enthusiastic, friendly, and patient while maintaining fairness and holding students to your expectations.
- *Increase your collegiality and visibility on campus.* Network with colleagues in and out of your department to establish social and academic ties. Get actively involved in your institutional community by attending campus functions, being a candidate for a faculty governance committee, and speaking up at gatherings.
- *Manage the multiple demands of your new career by being organized.* Decide on your priorities and concentrate on accomplishing them one small task after another. Use your time-management skills to set aside regular time for family, friends, and leisure activities as well as research.
- *Work with a mentor to help you navigate the new environment.* Many institutions nowadays have mentoring programs in which new faculty members are paired with more seasoned colleagues for academic and social support. In the absence of such a program in your institution, ask your chair to refer you to someone who could help you overcome challenges of teaching and scholarship, address your emotional issues, help you develop collegiality and visibility, and provide informal advice, information, and an inside view of the institutional culture.
- *Enhance your confidence in interacting with students and colleagues.* Challenge yourself to accomplish professional and personal goals despite the fear of failure. Be consistent in your confidence building and remind yourself of your successes and achievements to foster positive thinking.

Hopefully these suggestions will help you on your way to excellence in your career. Teaching is a very enjoyable experience; it is also a tremendous learning experience as you strive to attain mastery and become a full-fledged member of an academic community.

ADDITIONAL RESOURCES

American Association of University Professors
    http://www.aaup.org/aaup

Carnegie Foundation for the Advancement of Teaching
http://www.carnegiefoundation.org/

Consortium of Liberal Arts Colleges
http://www.liberalarts.org/

Council of Independent Colleges
http://www.cic.edu/

Enhancing Education: Solve a Teaching Problem
http://www.cmu.edu/teaching/solveproblem/

National Council for Higher Education
http://www.nea.org/home/32959.htm

REFERENCES

Boice, R. (2000). *Advice for new faculty members.* Needham Heights, MA: Allyn & Bacon.

Carnegie Foundation for the Advancement of Teaching. (n.d.). The Carnegie Classification of Institutions of Higher Education [database]. Retrieved from http://classifications.carnegiefoundation.org/

Carnegie Foundation for the Advancement of Teaching. (1991). Research-intensive vs. teaching-intensive institutions. *Change, 23*(3), 23–26.

Chickering, A. W. & Gamson, Z. F. (1987). Seven principles for good practice in undergraduate education. *American Association for Higher Education Bulletin, 39*(7), 3–7.

Connell, M. A. & Savage, F. G. (2001, November-December). Does collegiality count? *Academe Online, 87*(6). Retrieved from http://www.aaup.org/AAUP/pubsres/academe/2001/ND/Feat/Conn.htm

Ding, D. (2000). Another multicultural classroom: Non-native teachers of native students. In T. L. Good & L. B. Warshauer (Eds.), *In our own voice: Graduate students teach writing* (pp. 146–152). Needham Heights, MA: Allyn & Bacon.

Donnelly, R. (2007). Perceived impact of peer observation of teaching in higher education. *International Journal of Teaching and Learning in Higher Education, 19*(2), 117–129.

Garica, M. (Ed.). (2000). *Succeeding in an academic career: A guide for faculty of color.* Westport, CT: Greenwood Press.

Gibson, G. W. (1992). *Good start: A guidebook for new faculty in liberal arts colleges.* Bolton, MA: Anker.

Hu-DeHart, E. (2000). Office politics and departmental culture. In M. Garcia (Ed.), *Succeeding in an academic career: A guide for faculty of color* (pp. 27–39). Westport, CT: Greenwood Press.

Kamhi-Stein, L. D. (1999). Preparing nonnative English-speaking professionals in TESOL: Implications for teacher education programs. In G. Braine (Ed.),

Non-native educators in English language teaching (pp. 147–160). Mahwah, NJ: Lawrence Erlbaum.

VanZanten, S. (2011). *Joining the mission: A guide for (mainly) new college faculty.* Grand Rapids, MI: William B. Eerdmans.

CHAPTER 5

COMMUNITY COLLEGE

Yilin Sun
South Seattle Community College

Ke Xu
Borough of Manhattan Community College, CUNY

Ji-eun Kim, a recent Ph.D. graduate in Teaching English to Speakers of Other Languages (TESOL) from a U.S. university, was so excited to start her first day at an urban community college. How could she not be? She was told that she was chosen as the final candidate for this tenure-track assistant professor position out of more than 150 candidates!

She e-mailed her friends back in Korea and told them about her new position. One of her friends shot back a string of questions: "What is a community college? Are they private schools? Be careful! I heard many bogus colleges in the United States cheat people out of their money. Don't be trapped, Ji-eun! You have a Ph.D.; you should teach at a real college..."

Ji-eun didn't know where to start to explain to her friends—"*Yes*, a community college is a *real* institution of higher education and it *is* a *real* public college! Community college is a great place for Ph.D. graduates to start a career both as a teacher and a researcher..."

Demystifying Career Paths after Graduate School, pages 49–61
Copyright © 2012 by Information Age Publishing
All rights of reproduction in any form reserved.

UNDERSTANDING THE COMMUNITY COLLEGE SYSTEM

What is a community college? What should a new doctoral graduate be prepared to teach at a community college? What are the expectations for faculty members at a community college? For many graduate students who have not studied in a U.S. undergraduate program, community college sounds foreign. In fact, graduate students who major in TESOL, adult education, or applied linguistics will find a community college a wonderful place to teach in the area of TESOL or foreign language. This chapter focuses on teaching English as a Second Language (ESL).

In the United States and Canada, community colleges are publicly funded higher education institutions characterized by a two-year curriculum that leads to either the associate degree, which prepares students for the workforce, or transfer to a four-year college. Many community colleges also offer four-year degree programs in certain areas. Another prominent feature of community colleges is the diverse array of adult education and continuing education programs they offer. There are almost 1,200 community colleges in the United States, from small rural colleges in remote areas to multi-campus college districts in large urban settings (Rowh, 2011). Community colleges now enroll 44% of America's undergraduate students in higher education and the enrollments continue to rise (Rowh, 2011).

In recent years, community colleges have become the "college of choice" for an increasing number of students (Rowh, 2011) for a variety of reasons: low tuition, local setting, smaller class sizes, and easy entrance requirements.

Adult Basic Education and ESL Programs at Community Colleges

Adult Basic Education (ABE) and ESL Education programs are often among the largest programs in many community colleges. A vast majority of adult ESL learners are served at community colleges, and ESL programs are the fastest-growing programs at many community colleges (Crandall & Sheppard, 2004; Kuo, 2002). Today one in four students in community college is an immigrant, and the number of immigrant students is increasing rapidly. While the majority of adult ESL learners in the community college system are immigrants, international students learning ESL also increasingly prefer community colleges due to their lower cost and easier access. Some colleges also provide short-term TESOL certificate programs for those going abroad to teach English. Due to such active involvement in ESL education, community colleges provide leadership in developing

ABE learning standards and curriculum guidelines to address the needs of increasing numbers of adult ESL students.

The types of instruction and services that community colleges provide for adult ESL learners vary. Many community college ESL programs provide a wide spectrum of courses from non-credit, beginning literacy courses to credit-bearing courses, while others focus only on credit-bearing or more advanced academic ESL courses leading to admission to regular college courses.

Class Size and Student Profile

The average class size in community college ESL programs is 15 to 30 students. Some programs may offer smaller classes under 15. At many colleges, in any given class, you might find more than 10 countries represented among your students. Many immigrant students work and study at the same time; others are new immigrants or refugees without a job. Many, especially those in literacy classes, had no formal education or only little schooling in their own country. Thus, developing literacy skills in English can be a real challenge for them.

Others who have completed high school or higher education in their native countries before immigrating tend to progress much faster in their English learning. There are also a large number of so-called "generation 1.5" students who immigrated at an early age and went through the American public school system before entering college. They enroll in developmental English or college preparation courses to build up their English skills before going to regular college programs. Once ESL students achieve intermediate-level English proficiency, a majority enters the workforce, but many may return to their studies once they have earned sufficient income. In recent years, community colleges have been making greater efforts to help ESL students' transition into tuition-based, college-level programs.

One of the advantages of teaching at a community college is working with students who are appreciative of and passionate about learning. Many students are highly focused on their goals and demand quality education, while others find community college a place of discovery and awakening. Of all the students we have taught in various contexts, the adult ESL students at community colleges have been the most gratifying group to work with.

Institutional Expectations

Since community colleges focus primarily on teaching, the average teaching contact hours varies from 12 to 20 per week (Sun, 2010). Although research and publication are not required, they are always considered a plus. Most community colleges take research, conference presentations, and publications into account for faculty promotion and tenure.

Tenure System and Tenure Review Process

A tenure-track position at a community college requires at least a Master's degree plus some relevant teaching experience. Candidates with a doctoral degree are often preferred.

The pre-tenure period at community colleges is typically three years. The tenure review committee normally consists of three tenured faculty members, one student representative, and the dean or the unit administrator. In most cases those committee members are assigned by the head of the department. Some colleges allow the pre-tenure instructor under review to provide input on the selection of tenure-review committee members.

The criteria for tenure may vary from college to college. In general, the following aspects are included: teaching, committee work, professional development, and communication with colleagues. Teaching effectiveness weighs more than the other three aspects. Every quarter or semester, your tenure review committee members individually observe your teaching and write an observation report. You may have pre-observation and post-observation discussions with your committee members.

The pre-tenure faculty member is usually required to submit a statement with short-term (quarter/semester) and long-term (annual) goals for instruction, professional development, and committee work. The committee reviews the statement and identifies specific areas for improvement. At the end of each quarter or semester, the pre-tenure faculty member and the committee meet to determine whether the goals have been met and set new goals. Each year at the end of the second quarter or semester, the committee votes to continue or terminate the tenure process based on its evaluation of the achievement of the goals. If the committee recommends continuing with the tenure process, the tenure candidate submits a detailed self-review of professional achievements and a plan for continued development. The unit administrator prepares a tenure file that includes all the teaching observation reports, meeting minutes, and the candidate's short- and long-term plans and self-review reports.

Typically during the third year, the tenure review committee meets in order to make the final tenure recommendation. The decision is made by vote without the presence of the candidate. The committee's recommendation is then reviewed by the Vice-President for Instruction, President, Chancellor, and the Board of Trustees. It normally takes at least one quarter or semester to get all the documents prepared and reviewed by these individuals. The final decision is made by the Chancellor upon a review of the file and an interview with the candidate.

CHALLENGES, STRATEGIES, AND SUCCESSES

Teaching and Working with Adult Students

If you teach advanced ESL reading and writing courses at the developmental or transitional level, the students may have specific expectations. In many programs, over 50% of the students enrolled are generation 1.5 students, and their writing skills vary greatly. Many of them are fluent in spoken English but weak in writing. Maintaining academic standards while providing comprehensible instruction to students of varying abilities and objectives can be a real challenge.

To meet the challenge, the best approach is to build trust with students and inspire them by providing a role model. What you may try would be sharing your personal journey as a second language learner, the challenges you have faced, and strategies you have used to meet them, inspiring students with your own success story. You can also utilize a variety of group activities and online resources to guide students to take charge of their own learning—in other words, moving from teacher-directed to self-directed learning. These strategies have certainly worked with us.

In teaching students with insufficient skills in writing, comprehension, and grammar, non-native TESOL educators who have experienced similar learning curves have a great advantage in helping students. We know the non-native speaker's learning process better than native English-speaking teachers and can explain complicated ideas effectively. We can explain the grammar in a way our students can understand by using examples that are appropriate at their proficiency level.

You may occasionally encounter a few disrespectful students, some even from the same cultural heritage as yours, making negative comments about you just because you are a woman, a non-native speaker, and/or a person of color. When this happens, don't be disappointed or upset. You need to realize that many students may come to your classes with limited knowledge and understanding of gender and racial inequalities that exist in their homeland, the host society, or the institution of higher education. It is our responsibility to inform them and raise their awareness of how such power structures may have an impact on their everyday lives and their interactions with professors who do not fit in their familiar gender, racial, or linguistic expectations (Kubota, 2002). By building themes and topics on race, gender, and non-native identities as well as global issues into your course instruction, you can create an environment in which students can explore such questions in relation to their own life experiences. You may consider building the following questions into your class discussions and writing assignments: Who are we? What are we? Whose descriptions define us? Why are our identities important and why should we explore them at all?

These questions foster a supportive relationship between the instructor and students in the classroom. Citing Darling and Mulvaney (2003), Li (2006) advocates the need "to work toward 'reciprocal empowerment' that aims to 'foster mutual attention, mutual empathy, mutual engagement, and mutual responsiveness'" (p. 131). Achieving such reciprocal empowerment requires both non-native professors and non-native students to interact in ways that increase connections and trust. Indeed, they need to support each other as members of minority groups (Li, 2006).

As English language teaching professionals, we need to bear in mind this fundamental question: Why do we teach English? Teachers cannot claim success if students, no matter how fluent they are in English, are ignorant of world issues, lack social conscience, or use their communication skills for illegal activities, oppression, or environmental destruction.

Curriculum, Instructional Methods, and Materials

Adult ESL education programs at community colleges often need to follow the state adult education learning standards. Curriculum is based on these standards. There is also a standardized assessment instrument that the state mandates that all programs use in assessing student learning for reporting purposes. Along with the standardized test, formative assessment tools developed by instructors are used to measure students' learning.

As a new faculty member, you might find it overwhelming to develop your own syllabus and select teaching materials to meet the learning standards and assessment requirements. The best way to learn how to implement those standards in your teaching is to review the program curriculum guidelines and sample syllabi developed by other faculty members.

Instructors in many programs can select instructional materials, while others need to use specific textbooks. In either case, there is still a lot of flexibility for creative use of instructional materials. Recent advances in technology have changed the way we prepare our lessons and instruct our students. Appropriate integration of technology in the classroom encourages students to use language in many different ways and bring world issues into the classroom.

Professional Development, Research and Publication

Having set the teaching goals straight, you need to engage in professional development activities to stay current in the field. Full-time faculty members are expected to be actively engaged in professional development activities including attending and presenting at professional conferences and workshops, conducting research projects, and publishing. Although not required at community colleges, research and publications are often considered a plus. Colleges provide grants and funds to promote scholarship of teaching and learning and to support faculty members to present and attend conferences and workshops to keep up with the current trends in the field.

Research projects on assessment and classroom-based action research are much needed and supported at community colleges. Many granting agencies look for proposals from under-represented institutions, including community colleges. Therefore, community college instructors with solid research backgrounds have a fair chance in the competition.

Here are some effective strategies to promote your research (Sun, 2010): 1) watch for calls for proposals from the state, the college research department, or other sources that offer research grants or funds; 2) bring research ideas to your Dean or Vice-President for Instruction and get their support first; 3) collaborate with other faculty members within your college or from another institution to increase the chance of receiving a grant; and 4) build in release time from teaching and a plan to present at a conference in the proposal whenever possible. Once you receive a grant and complete your project, update the college community via newsletters and workshops on key research findings and how they facilitate students' learning, institutional transformation, and faculty development. Finally, publish your research.

One significant challenge in working in the community college is to get release time to attend professional conferences. Here are some strategies for your consideration:

- Build good working relationships with your mid-level administrators and help them be aware that faculty's active participation and presentations at conferences will help boost the program's reputation at national and international levels.
- If the request gets denied for no apparent reason, talk to the unit administrator directly to find out the reasons for rejection.
- If the institution has a faculty senate or union, check with the representative and follow the policy. It is important to get prior approval from the mid-level administrator for professional development activities.

- If you feel strongly that you were treated unfairly, talk to the Vice-President of Instruction directly, or file a grievance through the faculty union or via another channel.

Workplace Communication

Most colleagues and administrators are very supportive and will offer assistance to new colleagues. Occasionally, however, as a non-native English speaker from another country, you may experience some unpleasant encounters and hear comments like these:

"Those immigrants take away jobs from part-time instructors here."

"Your English is so good, but you have a cute accent..."

What can you do then? One way to rebut the former is to state calmly, "The United States is made up of immigrants, and the jobs are also created by immigrants. Don't you agree that the hiring committee is smart enough to hire a faculty member for qualifications, not for their appearance or accent?" A possible response to the latter would be "Thank you, so is yours. I can hear your accent, too. So where do you come from?"

It is often easier to manage overt discriminatory behavior and comments than to deal with subtle discrimination. When you suspect something is happening, you should review the situation carefully before acting on it.

E-mail Communication

E-mail has become an essential part of our daily communication with colleagues and students. In e-mail exchanges, it is sometimes difficult to gauge the writer's tone, which can result in misunderstandings. Once you click the send button, you cannot redo your message, so pay attention to spelling, grammar, and punctuation marks. Double-check your typed messages before sending them. For an important message, sleep on it before you send it. Using a proper register and greetings always works better than being too casual.

Tenure Review

Since your tenure case is initially reviewed by a committee, it is important to make sure the professional goals you list are realistic and achievable. Start with two specific ones for each of the four areas: teaching, committee work, professional development, and communication with colleagues.

Set up the teaching observation dates early with your committee members to avoid observation visits happening all at once at the end of the term. Give observers a copy of your lesson plan and other materials prior to their observation. Ask them to make a general observation for their first visit and then focus on a particular area later on, such as how you set up group work, deliver lectures, and balance teacher-talk and student-talk. Also, remember to set up a post-observation meeting after each visit to receive feedback. Every year, the Vice President for Instruction also observes your teaching.

In addition to class observations, your tenure committee also reviews your professional development activities and committee work. Take the opportunity to serve on division-, college- and/or state-level committees or professional organizations. Committee work often gives you opportunities to network with faculty and administrators from other disciplines so that you can gain new experience in budgetary and curricula decision-making processes at divisional and institutional levels.

It is important to keep an open mind and a positive attitude towards the tenure process. Most likely, your tenure process will go smoothly because you already demonstrated excellence in the rigorous hiring process. However, it is not uncommon that committee members make critical comments or express concerns about some aspects of your teaching or professional development. If this happens, try to be self-reflective without being defensive. Explain your perspective and write your responses to the observation reports in an objective manner. Also, take the suggestions for improvement seriously. Be sure to document your improvements and achievements before the next meeting. Review the minutes from each meeting carefully and make revisions as necessary. It is also helpful to find a mentor outside your tenure committee who is knowledgeable about the program in order to seek his or her perspectives and suggestions for professional growth.

Student evaluations need to be taken seriously because committee members and the Vice-President for Instruction review them regularly. If there is a bad evaluation for a particular course, you may explain the challenges you encountered in the teaching process and the steps you took to resolve the issues and make improvements. Do conduct on-going needs assessment for each course and gather feedback from the students before the mid-term, so you will have time to address the concerns that students may have before the end of the course.

Make sure you document all your participation and presentations at conferences and workshops. Keep a list of all the workshops, webinars, and other professional development activities you attended as well as the descriptions and abstracts of all the presentations you gave. If you have publications, that definitely is a plus!

Getting to Know the System and Getting Voices Heard

We would strongly urge you to learn the college system and get involved in its operation. Colleges love faculty members to get involved with different committee work. Start with small steps and gradually build confidence and skills. Once you have participated in committee work, try to volunteer to chair a committee. This will allow you to develop a meeting agenda and learn how to run meetings effectively.

Develop good listening skills and seize the opportunity to voice your ideas during meetings. Academic, professional, and social networking and management skills are important for non-native speakers to build confidence, develop competent communication skills, and understand how the higher education system works.

As non-native speakers and professionals of color, we need to get involved in as many activities as possible, making sure that our professional experiences and contributions are well-recognized and that our voices are heard in decision-making processes.

Balancing Multiple Roles

Working at a community college may not be as stressful as working at a research-intensive university, where you publish or perish. One can easily be overwhelmed, however, by creating new courses or participating in endless committee work. Knowing when and how to say "no" without sounding irresponsible certainly pays off.

It is also recommendable to spend time and make lunch dates with your colleagues and get to know them at a personal level. Appreciate and acknowledge your office staff members, as they are the ones who help you resolve issues and make your work life easier.

Remember you also have a life outside classrooms and committee meetings. Make sure you spend at least one full day a week with your family or friends, and plan a trip to somewhere during the summer or holidays.

SUMMARY AND FINAL ADVICE

Community colleges provide a challenging but rewarding work experience. The workplace challenges may include getting to know the working environment and leadership; understanding cultural nuances and etiquettes; building human relationships and using effective communication strategies; dealing with conflict, stereotypes, and institutional prejudice; and balancing work and personal life. Here is a summary of the advice we shared:

- *Build confidence and learn the workplace culture and system.* Be a good observer, learn the system, and build trust with colleagues and leaders. Serving on committees and having lunch dates with colleagues can help you learn the system and workplace culture.
- *Build supportive relationships with your leaders and colleagues.* Convince your supervisor and colleagues that you are a cooperative team player and an asset to the department. Show interest in your peers' work, sincerely acknowledge their experience and seniority, and listen to their professional feedback on your work.
- *Find mentors who can guide you through your journey.* Choose someone who guides, encourages, and challenges you; someone who advocates for you and protects you; someone who tells you the truth and listens well; and someone you respect and trust.
- *Maximize professional development opportunities.* Watch for grant or release time opportunities. Attend and present at conferences, workshops, and brown-bag lunch sessions to exchange ideas. Read current professional publications and stay current in the field. Get involved in your local and national professional organizations and make your voice heard.
- *Publish and develop materials.* Take small steps and build confidence and skills in this area. Write for the college newsletter or a local professional association. Always seek feedback and editing advice from your mentor or a native speaker before submitting a manuscript for publication.
- *Utilize strategies and technologies in teaching to meet the students' needs.* Stay aware of your students' changing needs. Take workshops on instructional technologies to build a toolbox of innovative techniques and resources. Vary teaching strategies and learn from students who may know more than you do in some areas.

We hope the above advice will ensure you a smooth transition into your new career. Last but not least, always remember that successful navigation of the higher education system cannot be done by a single person—it needs support from the whole community!

RESOURCES

This selected list of websites is not intended to be comprehensive but suggestive.

Community College Organizations

American Association of Community Colleges
http://www.aacc.nche.edu/

American Association for Women in Community Colleges
http://www.aawccnatl.org/

Association of Canadian Community Colleges
http://www.accc.ca/

League for Innovation in the Community College
http://www.league.org/

National Alliance of Community and Technical Colleges
http://www.nactc.org/

The Rural Community College Initiative
http://srdc.msstate.edu/rcci/

Research-Related Websites about Community Colleges

The Chair Academy
http://www.chairacademy.com/

Community College Research Center
http://ccrc.tc.columbia.edu/

Council for the Study of Community Colleges
http://www.cscconline.org

Institute for Community College Research
http://www.sunybroome.edu/iccr/

REFERENCES

Crandall, J., & Sheppard, K. (2004). *Adult ESL and the community college.* (Working Paper 7, CAAL Community College Series.) New York, NY: Council for Advancement of Adult Literacy. Retrieved from http://caalusa.org/eslreport.pdf

Darling, P. S. E., & Mulvaney, B. M. (2003). *Women, power, and ethnicity: Working toward reciprocal empowerment.* Binghamton, NY: Haworth Press.

Kubota, R. (2002). Marginalization as an asset: Toward a counter-hegemonic pedagogy for diversity. In L. Vargas (Ed.), *Women faculty of color in the white classroom:*

Narratives on the pedagogical implications of teacher diversity (pp. 293–308). New York, NY: Peter Lang.

Kuo, E. W. (2002). English as a second language: Program approaches at community colleges. Retrieved from http://www.eric.ed.gov/PDFS/ED447859.pdf

Li, G. (2006). Navigating multiple roles and multiple discourses. In G. Li & G.H. Beckett (Eds.), *"Strangers" of the academy: Asian women scholars in higher education* (pp. 118–133). Sterling, VA: Stylus.

Rowh, M. C. (2011). *Community college companion: Everything you wanted to know about succeeding in a two-year school.* Indianapolis, IN: JIST Works.

Sun, Y. (2010). Standards, equity and advocacy: Employment conditions of ESOL teachers in adult basic education and literacy systems. *TESOL Journal, 1,* 142–158.

CHAPTER 6

WRITING CENTER

Lucie Moussu
University of Alberta

Among the fifteen different responsibilities and duties listed on the job description for "Applied Linguistics Coordinator" I held in my hand was "writing center consultant." Everything else on the list concerned teaching English as a Second Language (ESL) students and coordinating ESL instructors. As a nearly graduated Ph.D. student in ESL, I had applied for this position because I was passionate about ESL, but I knew nothing about writing centers! Fortunately, I was able to borrow a book about tutoring ESL students in writing centers and read it on the plane on my way to the job interview. This book proved very useful and I got the job, but I never actually did any consulting for the writing center.

A year after I was hired though, I was suddenly appointed director of the writing center, whose policy was, ironically, to assist only native speakers of English.

DEFINITION OF THE "WRITING CENTER"

The above story typifies how many writing center (WC) directors begin their careers. Such unusual beginnings are due to the relative novelty of WCs, the paucity of writing center administration programs, and also the

Demystifying Career Paths after Graduate School, pages 63–75
Copyright © 2012 by Information Age Publishing
All rights of reproduction in any form reserved.

lack of a typical WC director job description. As a result, WC directors may hold a wide variety of degrees, ranging from literature, ESL, or journalism to dance, history, or nursing, to offer just a few examples.

My 2011 informal survey of WC directors in the United States and Canada revealed that very few of them were non-native speakers of English (NNESs), although the situation might be different in WCs around the world. WCs outside of English-speaking countries are still uncommon, but there are some bilingual and multilingual WCs. For example, Marie-Lise,[1] the WC director at the bilingual University of Ottawa and a native speaker of French, feels privileged to work and live in two languages and cultures and hires native speakers of both French and English to tutor and deliver workshops in their mother tongues.

If you look at a list of WC job ads, you will notice that "WC director" has several meanings. Especially in Canada, many of these positions are purely administrative (that is, non-tenure track) and have staff status, with WCs typically housed in Student Services, a Learning Center, or an Academic Skills unit. Other positions are academic, sometimes tenured or tenure-track, with WCs being part of an academic unit.

Some WCs are housed in specific faculties or departments, while others serve the whole university. Furthermore, some WCs serve only students, others serve faculty and staff too, and still others serve members of the community at large. Several WCs have also been created in high schools and even in elementary schools. With these institutional and structural differences come significant funding and budgetary variations, as well as diversity in staffing and hierarchy.

A few WCs employ only professional writers as "tutors" (or "consultants" or "coaches"), but most employ graduate and/or undergraduate students. Tutor selection and remuneration processes also vary greatly from one WC to another. For example, Carlton University in Ottawa Canada employs only graduate students assigned and funded by their own departments while I, as director of my WC, choose and hire graduate and undergraduate tutors and manage my own budget. Sometimes, tutors are paid for their work or receive course credit, while others are volunteers.

Tutors generally have diverse linguistic and academic backgrounds, and may be trained in various ways: through credit or non-credit courses, through intensive orientation days before the semester starts, and/or while they are working as tutors. In some WCs, tutors work with clients[2] at all levels of study and from all departments. In other WCs, individual tutors specialize in specific topics (such as business writing or ESL) and only offer help in these areas. A few WCs serve only ESL students.

Aside from tutoring, the services offered by WCs also vary greatly. Harris (1988) cites the following typical services, but not all of them are offered by all WCs:

Workshops, resource libraries of books and handouts, word processing, self-instruction in computer-assisted-instruction (CAI), and a variety of other media, writing assessment, grammar hotlines, conversation groups for English-as-a-second-language students, writing contests, tutor training practicums, and credit courses. While most writing centers work only with writing skills, some also offer help with reading, study, and/or oral communication skills. (n.p.)

Historically, my current WC has focused on one-on-one tutoring for writing skills. However, we are currently moving towards creating writing groups and developing students' reading skills as well.

ADMINISTRATIVE RESPONSIBILITIES

WC directors' main duty is administration, which involves the management of resources (money, furniture, etc.) and staff. Simpson (1985/2006) summarizes these responsibilities:

- to provide and preserve a sense of direction for the writing center
- to shape the curriculum of the writing center
- to teach in the writing center's programs
- to prepare and/or purchase materials needed in the writing center
- to consult with writing center staff and with faculty on writing instruction
- to select and train tutors
- to supervise tutors
- to evaluate tutors regularly
- to keep careful records that are made available as required to students, teachers, tutors, and administrators
- to administer budget allocations responsibly
- to ensure continuous funding of the writing center
- to publicize the writing center
- to maintain communication with the institution's other writing programs
- to work with faculty in writing across the curriculum programs
- to continue professional growth through appropriate reading, courses, studies, research, and participation in professional organizations and workshops
- to organize all activities of the writing center
- to provide for regular reports on the activities, progress, and problems of the writing center
- to provide for regular and thorough evaluation of the writing center's program. (n.p.)

As director of the University of Alberta's WC, I do all these things (and more—for example, I am also responsible for supervising our administrative assistant), but not all WC directors have responsibilities such as teaching or controlling a budget.

On a daily basis, these duties translate into a number of meetings (e.g., with the University Writing Committee), a number of hours spent answering tutor and client questions, and much time spent solving other issues (e.g., How many hours can tutors work this semester given our budget? Who should do this presentation to the political science class?). While doing all this, I am also teaching and trying to do research (getting ethics permissions, applying for grants, planning projects with my research assistant, reading articles and books, submitting and revising articles, communicating with co-authors, attending grant writing workshops, etc.).

In order to stay on top of things as director, you must first learn about the specific policies and regulations of your university, your state/province, and your country. For instance, some universities offer vacation pay to tutors while others don't, states/provinces have different regulations regarding the number of hours students are allowed to work, and the United States and Canada have different regulations regarding hiring procedures.

Also, learn about your community: What types of students attend the institution? Do they mostly live in dorms? How many libraries are on campus? Do you have a large "distance education" school? How many international students attend your institution? What kinds of first-year English/composition courses do all students take, if any? What other student support systems are available on campus? What do faculty members and students know about and think of the WC?

Answers to these questions will allow you to make informed decisions about the services your WC should offer (e.g., online tutoring for distance education students, satellite WCs in libraries), the marketing of your services, and the management of resources and staff. For example, after trying different marketing strategies, Helena, a native speaker of Swedish and WC director at Loras College, noticed that the best method for her small campus was to talk constantly about her WC with faculty members and to stay in touch with current and potential clients through Facebook.

When you make decisions, people working in your immediate surroundings will appreciate feeling that their opinions are taken into consideration. It is particularly important to include WC staff in regular discussions about your WC's daily operations and new projects. Students, staff, faculty members, and the administration will also welcome newsletters and regular reports about client statistics, successes and challenges, services offered, new projects, and so on. They will also enjoy and benefit from occasional pizza parties, potlucks, and other enjoyable activities that help build a close community of writers.

Finally, remember that the position of director is a very public one, unlike the more common positions of regular faculty members. As a NNES, you will have to be exceptionally careful when you write anything that can be read by large numbers of people. Write important emails a day before you send them and have a second reader double-check them. Verify drafts of reports as many times as possible.

TEACHING

If you are hired as a faculty member, you will likely be required to teach a few classes every year (although your assigned workload and course releases may vary even within institutions: I teach two courses per year but the previous WC director taught only one). You might teach courses in your original field (e.g., philosophy) or writing courses. You could also create a tutor-training course if one doesn't already exist (which I did at my previous institution), or revise an existing course (which I did when I arrived at the University of Alberta). You might be able to create new writing courses, too, such as the course on second language writing I created and will teach next winter.

Whatever you teach, remember these important points. First, make sure that your students understand you. Use different techniques (PowerPoint, handouts, discussions, presentations, etc.) to communicate your message. People in general and NNESs in particular have a difficult time assessing how clearly they speak. Record yourself while teaching (with your students' permission) and analyze how you speak, how your students react to what you say, and how you react to what they say. Listening to a recording of my own teaching made me realize that I say "Do you know what I mean?" too often.

Second, do not assume that you communicate what you actually mean to communicate. Expressions of praise or disapproval vary greatly in different countries and cultures. Unlike in many other countries, students in North America are used to receiving high grades and regular praise. I once received a terrible evaluation from a WC tutor who said that I never told my tutors that I cared about them. Needless to say, I do now.

In order to take "some of the air out of the balloon of those who might otherwise make [her non-nativeness] into a problem," Jette, who comes from Denmark and is the WC director at Wartburg College, always lets her students know that she is foreign. And although she believes that working in a bilingual WC helps remove the "sort of stigma of being a non-native speaker," Marie-Lise always tells WC clients that French is her first language.

Finally, get as much feedback from students and colleagues as you can. Ask colleagues to observe your classes and to write reports for inclusion in your annual evaluation. Collect student feedback *before* the regular end-of-term teacher evaluations and act on it.

SERVICE

Department chairs often see administration and service as identical, but it is rarely the case when it comes to directing a WC. At research universities, most WC directors who are also faculty members are expected to spend 40% of their time teaching, 40% doing research, and 20% doing service to the department, the institution and the community. These expectations may vary if you work in a college or high school, or if your position is strictly administrative, but most institutions expect educators to be engaged in activities outside the classroom (e.g., serving on committees, becoming involved in local and international professional associations, etc.). For example, I am an occasional guest reviewer for *TESOL Quarterly* and was, for four years, a member of the Teachers of English to Speakers of Other Languages (TESOL) book publication committee.

Whatever the expectations are, make sure to keep track of your "service" and "administrative" activities carefully. At the end of the year, these distinctions might make a big difference in how your work is evaluated.

At my previous university, all my work as WC director was counted as service. Because I was spending 80% of my time doing administrative work and "service" was supposed to be only 20% of my load, I was reprimanded for doing too much service and not enough research and publishing. At my new university, I was told that my work as WC director would be understood and recognized better, but after my first annual review, I realized that this was not the case. Since my salary and progression through the ranks (tenure and promotion) depend on this recognition, I quickly brought up the problem to my Chair, who agreed to revise my contract (I now have a 20% research, 20% teaching, and 60% administration load).

RESEARCH

Research expectations can be very different depending on your institution and the type of position you hold. By way of illustration, Helena shares the following: "Because my job is not tenure-track, there are no expectations that I do any research. However, I love doing research, so I am working on a couple of projects. It is very hard to carve out time to do research due to all my responsibilities. The research projects I do are normally fairly small—my goal is to present my findings at conferences. One day I hope to have time to write many articles."

Meeting research and publishing expectations in research universities can be very difficult for tenure-track NNES. If you don't like doing research or are insecure about your English writing skills, you will struggle. There is also the expectation that because you are a *writing* center director, you should be a highly productive and proficient writer.

You need to develop your own strategies. Jette identifies people on campus who can be her "allies" and work with her on different projects. When writing articles, Agnes, WC director at Carlton University, thinks only in English and never switches to her native tongue, Hungarian. A friend of mine reads academic articles and makes lists of words and expressions that "sound smart." Shu-min, a native speaker of Mandarin Chinese from Taiwan and co-ordinator of the University of Victoria's WC, reflects that "I think my less positive experiences have more or less been self-inflicted, in that most of them resulted from my own perception of other people's possible perceptions of me as a visible minority and nonnative English speaker. I often question and second-guess myself, even in times when I know that I am using English correctly. I often worry about not being able to exert authority because others may question my qualification or ability as a non-native speaker."

When I get discouraged or lack inspiration, I remind myself of what *my* skills and strengths are. For example, I am interested in second language writing and can easily create projects around this topic that tap into my knowledge and personal experience as a NNES.

LEADERSHIP AND PROFESSIONAL DEVELOPMENT

For me, a WC director's most agreeable responsibility is leadership. You have the potential to influence and help thousands of students and faculty members and to inspire your tutors to become great educators and future WC directors. As a NNES, you can be a role model for ESL clients, hire multilingual tutors who will show ESL clients that it is possible to become good writers in English, and do research about ESL students that will be useful to other WC directors.

You can also show your clients and tutors that you, too, are always learning and improving your writing skills. For example, you can ask tutors to provide feedback on your articles or involve them in research projects, create and deliver ESL workshops, be an advocate for ESL students, bring your personal experience about international issues to the discussion when appropriate, and so much more.

I have combined leadership and professional development into one section because I believe that they go hand in hand. Show your tutors what it means to be a good WC director by developing skills that will enhance both your personal life and your career. For example, learn about new theories, take advantage of academic and administrative workshops, share knowledge at conferences, collaborate on research projects, attend institutes for WC directors, engage with a community of practice, network with other WC directors, and mentor tutors and students.

This is what I love about my job: learning, teaching, leading, and directing are deeply intertwined with one another.

TENURE AND PROMOTION

As a tenure-track assistant professor, I have not yet been tenured or promoted, but experience has taught me a few things that I wish I'd known before I signed contracts.

First, once you have a job description and before you accept the offer, find people familiar with WCs and ask about the job description and your contract. Interpreting job descriptions and contracts can be tricky, especially if this is your first job after graduate school. Don't hesitate to talk with your hiring committee, too, if certain things seem unclear, and *always* negotiate your salary, even if you feel uncomfortable doing it.

Once you have signed a contract, go over it with your new chair or supervisor until you know exactly what is expected of you. If things don't go as planned, talk to your Chair immediately and listen carefully to what he/she says. The path to tenure and promotion is normally quite rigid for typical faculty members, but this position is atypical in that there are very few WC directors out there compared to "regular" faculty members. You will need to learn what rules apply to you, how far things can be changed to fit your unique situation, and how to stand up for your work. Don't hesitate to ask other WC directors for suggestions and support.

Finally, start planning for tenure from day one. Keep a folder with everything: thank you notes, reports, course syllabi, invitations, conference papers, course evaluations, teaching reflections, articles you wrote, letters related to service, grant proposals, and so on. If you are organized, your annual reports and "tenure and promotion binders" will be easier to put together.

PROFESSIONAL PREPARATION AND JOB-HUNTING

As you can see from the above sections, the job of a WC director is a multifaceted one. Simpson (1985/2006) offers guidelines for developing the skills you will need if you want to become a WC director. First, you should be familiar with materials development and evaluation, research methods, and the theories of teaching, learning, and rhetoric/composition. Second,

Simpson strongly recommends experience in some of the following areas: accounting, basic business administration, psychology, personnel management, information systems, computer technology, records management, decision making, grant writing, curriculum design, and ESL pedagogy.

A third dimension is your knowledge of U.S./Canada writing standards and genres across disciplines. For example, if your primary field of study is literature, you are familiar with the typical English essay (and MLA style citation), but you may not be familiar with lab reports (and APA style citation), a common form of writing in science departments. As a NNES, you might also come from cultures where writing doesn't have the same status that it has in North America. Emmy, the WC director at Wilfrid Laurier University, comes from Denmark and explains that she felt very unprepared when it came to understanding the U.S. academic writing culture. She says, "The Germanic academic tradition that shaped my own studies was not writing-based."

It is rare to find applicants for WC directorship who possess knowledge and experience in their primary fields (e.g., communication) *and* pedagogy *and* administration (e.g., accounting) *and* rhetoric/composition *and* WC theory. Hence, the more unique and broad your educational background is, the more "marketable" you become.

One tactic that I used as a graduate student was to look at a wide range of job descriptions during my early years of study. These gave me a good indication of what my future employers might expect me to know and gave me enough time to learn these expected skills.

While still a university student, I also taught for many years, which made me realize that I love to be "in charge." Based on this understanding of my own skills, I took courses in higher education administration to be ready for any administrative job that might present itself.

Working as a WC tutor can also be a great introduction to the field of WCs. While in graduate school, Helena worked in a WC for five years. Caroline, the WC director at Upper Iowa University and a native speaker of Dutch, also worked as tutor in a WC and taught ESL as well. These experiences, in addition to her NNES status, provided Caroline with an in-depth knowledge of the language learning process and a better understanding of "the organization of college papers, the presentation of ideas, and how to lead clients to see how these function in their papers."

As discussed in the first section of this chapter, you can come from any educational background and still become a writing center director. In times of depressed job markets, be creative and search for opportunities that come up in odd places. While TESOL graduates usually look at the TESOL job list and literature graduates search the MLA job database, a large number of other resources exist (e.g., the *University Affairs* website advertises job openings in Canadian institutions). Conferences can also provide information about different job openings, and listservs, such as WCenter, the International Writing Centers Association (IWCA) listserv, often distribute information about job openings. On its website, the Council of Writing Program Administrators posts openings for administrative positions in a wide variety of educational contexts. And an online search with creative keywords can reveal hundreds of unexpected opportunities.

Finally, as more and more international students and scholars come to North American educational institutions, and as these institutions work to foster diversity, NNESs who studied TESOL/TESL already have a background in an area that employers increasingly seek. Not only do you possess the academic knowledge to create valuable support for ESL clients, but you also understand the needs and challenges ESL clients might be facing while studying in a new language. Many universities heavily recruit international students and need educators who understand these students' struggles and needs. Today, hiring committees in any educational context greatly value any knowledge of and experience with international issues (second language acquisition, immigration regulations, second language writing, etc.).

Therefore, while searching for a job, you should always emphasize your international background as a NNES as a positive facet of your experience. As Agnes explains, "My experiences [as a NNES] enabled me to empathize with fellow writers wresting with the all-too familiar challenges when facing a blank page in need of being filled." Shu-min adds, "I feel accepted and valued as an important member of my workplace and as a role model by clients who are non-native speakers of English. My manager and colleagues are aware and appreciative of the diversity of cultures and languages that are represented at the university."

WHY SHOULD YOU WANT TO BECOME A WRITING CENTER DIRECTOR?

As shown throughout this chapter, WC work is complex and unpredictable—and never boring. Working for a WC can be challenging for the following reasons. First, WCs are dissimilar in their structures (which makes it difficult to predict anything based on other WCs' histories). Second, university administrators rarely identify WCs as budgetary priorities. And finally, the university community often sees WCs as remedial places that edit weak students' papers instead of places that *teach* all students how to become more successful and independent writers.

Nevertheless, WC directors typically love their jobs and are proud to face budgetary and pedagogical challenges and to fight misconceptions. They are also proud to stand for the art and value of writing, students' individual needs, ESL students' support, one-on-one work (which is harder and harder to preserve in a tight budgetary environment), and educational excellence.

Furthermore, since tutors don't assign grades to their clients' papers and are often students themselves, clients feel safe in WCs and frequently say that WCs are the only place on campus where someone really cares about them as individuals. In fact, some clients come to our WCs not only to get help with their papers but also to find emotional support in a non-threatening environment.

Together with the mandate to foster excellence in student writing and the belief that WCs are safe havens for their clients, the uniqueness of the challenges that WCs face give their directors (and tutors) a rare and rewarding sense of pride. As a regular faculty member, I never experienced this kind of gratification.

SUMMARY AND FINAL ADVICE

I never planned to direct a WC, but I know that I was meant for this career. Whenever I feel discouraged after hours of budget meetings or frustrating discussions with people who don't understand WCs, I sit in the middle of our tutoring space and observe my tutors and our clients. After listening to my tutors explain for the fiftieth time—but still with a smile—what a thesis statement is, and seeing our clients light up when they finally understand something difficult, I remember that my work changes many lives for the better. As Jette concludes, "my road to the WC community has not been a predictable one, but I love every minute of it."

Here are a few points to remember:

- Learn about your skills and strengths both as a professional and as a NNES. Keep developing these strengths while overcoming your weaknesses.
- Emphasize the value of your non-nativeness in educational and research contexts. Don't be afraid to use it to your advantage.
- Don't limit your job search to well-known channels. Be creative, and remember that every WC is unique.
- Make sure your responsibilities are clearly delineated in your contract. Don't be afraid to talk to your chair or dean if things seem unclear or unfair.
- Learn about the policies of your department, institution, community, province/state, and country. The faster you learn about them, the less likely you are to make costly or embarrassing mistakes.

- Keep the lines of communication open between the WC and its stakeholders. Write regular reports and let everyone know what you are doing in your WC.
- Evaluate your own administrative, teaching, and communication skills often. Do it early and act on it, too, so that you won't be unpleasantly surprised during your annual review.
- Remember that in research universities, getting research grants and publishing articles is paramount. Work constantly on your research and writing skills.
- Attend conferences, workshops and institutes for writers, ESL teachers, and WC directors. Network with other professionals, start research projects with them, and support their work when they need it (e.g., during tenure reviews).
- Learn to prioritize and organize your time well. Don't let administrative work overwhelm you.
- Never stop learning and sharing what you have learned.

NOTES

1. When I conducted my informal survey (through WCenter, the IWCA listserv), I also asked the NNES WC directors who responded if they wanted to help me write this chapter, since every WC is unique.
2. Although most WCs offer free services to university students, I use the term "client" rather than "student" in contrast to "tutors" who are also often students. In some WCs, clients can also be staff and faculty members.

RESOURCES

Council of Writing Program Administrators
   http://wpacouncil.org/

International Writing Centers Association
   http://writingcenters.org/

High School & Middle School Writing Centers
   http://guest.portaportal.com/wcenters

The Writing Center Directory
   http://web.stcloudstate.edu/writeplace/wcd/index.html

University Affairs
   http://www.universityaffairs.ca/

FURTHER READINGS

Harris, M. (1997). Presenting writing center scholarship: Issues for faculty and personnel committees. In C. Gerhardt & B. Gerhardt (Eds.), *Academic advancement in composition studies: Scholarship, publications, promotion, tenure* (pp. 87–102). Mahwah, NJ: Lawrence Erlbaum Associates.

North, S. M. (1984). The idea of a writing center. *College English, 46*, 433–446.

Swales, J. & Feak, C. (2004). *Academic writing for graduate students.* Ann Arbor, MI: University of Michigan Press.

ACKNOWLEDGEMENTS

Thank you to WC directors/coordinators Agnes Nemeskeri (Carlton University), Caroline Ledeboer (Upper Iowa University, Fayette Campus), Emmy Misser (Wilfrid Laurier University), Helena Hall (Loras College), Jette Odgaard Irgens (Wartburg College), Marie-Lise Bain (University of Ottawa), and Shu-min Huang (University of Victoria) for their invaluable contributions to this chapter. Special acknowledgement to Agnes Nemeskeri who passed away on February 6, 2012. I would like to extend my condolences to her family, colleagues, and students.

REFERENCES

Harris, M. (1988) SLATE (Support for the Learning and Teaching of English) statement: The concept of a writing center. Retrieved from International Writing Centers Association, http://writingcenters.org/resources/writing-center-concept/

Simpson, J. H. (2006). What lies ahead for writing centers: Position statement on professional concerns. Retrieved from International Writing Centers Association, http://writingcenters.org/resources/starting-a-writing-center (Original work published 1985)

CHAPTER 7

MOVING FROM NORTH AMERICA TO OVERSEAS

Noriko Ishihara
Hosei University

In a class teaching English as Foreign Language (EFL), I start the class as always. There's something wrong about the audio—it doesn't play for whatever reason. I call the technology department and someone comes in the middle of my teaching. I switch to Japanese to explain the problem and the class bursts into laughter.

"Do you speak Japanese?"

"How strange to hear you speak Japanese!"

Hello everybody, this is my native language, I say to myself. This is the moment I realize I've come back to a largely monolingual community in Japan where being bilingual is an anomaly. Many students hardly ever hear bilingual language users code-switching back and forth.

RELOCATING FROM NORTH AMERICAN TO OVERSEAS

What does it mean to move from North America to overseas? For some, it means going home after years of academic and/or professional training

---

Demystifying Career Paths after Graduate School, pages 77–87
Copyright © 2012 by Information Age Publishing

in higher education; for others, it means moving to another culture for career or other opportunities. In either case, if you are now socialized in North American academia, there await different hiring practices, new expectations in the workplace, socialization or re-socialization into the communities you belong to, culture shock (or reverse-culture shock) along the way, the forming or re-shaping of support communities in the new context, maintaining a membership in the North American communities, and possibly even reuniting with or separating from some of your family members. This chapter focuses on these experiences.

While considering relocation, it is essential to be familiar with career options overseas and preferably have secured employment in advance. The career options in higher education overseas are as various as in North America, including teaching and researching at a graduate school, university, or college, or a community, technical, vocational, or junior college. Some of the programs may be administered in a more or less North American style or in a more traditionally localized manner. Some instructors in higher education also double as EFL teachers for private businesses or English schools. Regardless of our professional experiences in North America, we may be asked to teach rudimentary EFL courses or provide pre-service or experienced local EFL teachers with EFL teacher development through the medium of English or a local language.

For many of us without dual citizenship, employment overseas may also involve cumbersome considerations over the working visa, which could "make or break" the relocation. To work in a new country, it is important to secure a position and the necessary visa ahead of time. For those returning to their native country, expiration of a current student or working visa in North America could even be the main logistical reason for returning home.

Part-Time Employment

Many professionals work part-time as adjunct professors when they relocate overseas after earning a degree. Some universities expect their full-time instructors to have teaching experience in the country, at least a few publications, and some level of proficiency in the local language. To qualify as an adjunct professor, language, teaching, and research requirements are typically less demanding. To obtain a part-time position, it may also help to know someone who already works in the institution, someone who would know you personally and professionally and vouchsafe for the quality of your work. Some institutions offer a monthly salary for the summer and spring months when there are few or no classes offered; this may be a point to investigate in applying for a part-time position. The nature of the part-time status can be complex and highly variable, as it may or may not include a specific appointment term, an obligation to attend administrative meetings, an opportunity to extend the appointment, and so forth.

In order to secure a sufficient income, many adjunct professors engage in "university hopping," teaching many hours at multiple institutions. This could be a challenge, since it involves commuting and dealing with different institutional practices on top of having to put in many hours of teaching. On the other hand, adjunct professors are typically not required to attend often lengthy administrative meetings and can therefore focus on teaching. For this reason, some instructors take advantage of the part-timer status and continue to teach a small number of specific courses tailored to their expertise even after landing a full-time position.

While there are benefits in teaching part-time, especially in terms of flexibility and time, compensation and benefits are usually limited and the teaching load can fluctuate depending on student enrollment or the outcome of student evaluations. If a more stable full-time position is considered more desirable, it may be important for applicants to enhance their research profile and develop a professional network as well as (re)gain proficiency in the local language. The following section details an illustration of full-time employment overseas.

Full-Time Employment, Tenure System, and Institutional Expectations

Hiring conventions, employment terms, and institutional expectations vary greatly across countries, cultures, and even across similar institutions in a given culture. Because it is difficult to generalize over such diverse employment situations abroad, let us review typical cases in Japan to illustrate how a system can resemble or differ from that in North America.

Unlike the tenure system in North America, full-time faculty members are almost automatically employed for life in many universities in Japan. Although this convention has begun to change in some of the universities that have adopted the tenure system from North America, the traditional practice still prevails in many institutions. Although research is encouraged, "publish or perish" pressure is almost non-existent even for new full-time faculty members, who can choose to conduct the types of research they prefer at their own pace. Some promotional reviews can be rigorous but others are almost a formality. This naturally results in variation in the degree of rigor with which faculty members pursue research. While much of the pressure is missing, most universities offer monetary support for conducting and disseminating research to the extent of their economic capacities. The highly competitive governmental grant-in-aid is available each year, and many universities offer in-house administrative support for applications.

It is not hard to imagine that the status of tenured full-time instructors is highly stable in terms of job security and compensation. Perhaps because this stability is given, there typically is no negotiation, nor even information about salary during the job interview. It is common among local employees not to know their salary until the first paycheck. Furthermore, it may be surprising by North American standards that salaries are sometimes simply based on the employees' age, rather than on their highest degree or their teaching or research accomplishments. Salaries are usually offered for 12 months and during sabbatical years. There often are in-house health benefits and pension systems that employees can opt to join.

The downside of the stability mentioned above may be the level of administrative contribution expected of the employees by the university. Since full-time faculty members are likely to be tenured, there usually is no release time from teaching for the purpose of furthering research. While the importance of conducting research may be less strongly emphasized, the teaching load may be heavier, and administrative involvement is likely to be more extensive than in equivalent institutions in North America. Many administrative meetings are arranged only with a starting time and can continue for hours without a break until participants have nothing more to volunteer.

CHALLENGES, STRATEGIES, AND SUCCESSES

Finding New Pedagogies

One of the most important responsibilities after joining a new institution is to become familiar with local practices in learning and teaching and to strike a fine balance between those practices and the alternative approaches we have to offer. In each institutional context, what is expected of a teacher, a student, a colleague, a researcher, and so forth, may be different (see, for example, Cortazzi & Jin, 1999). It is crucial not to readily over-generalize, as institutional practices vary across learning communities. However, it is sometimes true that our students' learning experiences and expectations differ from those in North America. For example, communicative language teaching may not necessarily be a context-appropriate methodology if it is applied in the same way as in many North American classrooms (e.g., Holliday, 1994). Additionally, class size may be considerably larger and the student-faculty ratio can be challenging. Students may also take 15 other classes a week in addition to working part-time and being busy with club activities, which means that they tend to come to class with little preparation. Students may be accustomed to taking notes in the grammar-translation method that is still prevalent in some countries. They may never have been encouraged to ask questions or discuss any topic with others in class even in their native language. Writing by hand may be valued or commonly practiced, and some students may not know how to type in English. Some lack basic sociolinguistic and technological skills in sending e-mail or attachments to faculty members using a computer, even though they are keen on text-messaging their friends on their cell phones. (All of these examples were my experiences in metropolitan Tokyo in the 2010s.) These are the times when we may wish to consider adapting our teaching strategies, even though they served our purposes effectively in North American institutions.

In your efforts to find new pedagogies, you may not have to alter everything profoundly, though some small adjustments may be an appropriate starter. For instance, for students with little experience with discussing topics in class, you might start with an introduction to what a discussion is, what the ultimate purpose of it is, and what an effective classroom discussion looks like. Then you might facilitate, volunteering through various supportive means, and eventually withdraw some of those scaffolding steps to help learners become more independent. For students who do not review materials outside of class, specific tasks or assignments may be necessary, at least at an initial stage. You may decide to collect the assignments and incorporate them into final grades. Even if you believe in learner autonomy, some handholding may be a useful strategy until students learn to take responsibility for their own learning.

(Re)socializing into a New Community

Needless to say, it is sometimes required or at least desirable to be functional in the local language in teaching and administration. In teaching a content-based class in applied linguistics, for example, we may be asked or even expected to write a syllabus and deliver the class in the students' first language. If your academic and professional training is conducted in English in North America, you may need to find new academic resources in the new language to accomplish this teaching assignment, even if you share your students' first language or if you are already highly proficient in basic interpersonal communication in the local language. This may also be true for research or other professional communication. Even though English may prevail in many academic contexts even outside North America, being able to function academically in the local language may also help you increase your professional opportunities. If you are a native of the language and culture and were hired on the basis of that status, it may be taken for granted that you will function effectively, both academically and culturally, in the local language.

(Re)socializing into the new community also means learning about institutional conventions and administrative rules. Sometimes, these conventions are implicit and unwritten, and it may take some time to realize that different norms exist, which can be frustrating at times. For example, there may be different discourse structures and writing conventions for e-mail as well as different norms for speaking in faculty meetings. Understanding culturally appropriate behaviors and nuances can be crucial in building amicable rapport. Also, having an open mind implies being flexible about what is unexpected and refraining from taking for granted what appears obvious to you. A supportive colleague or mentor with similar experiences may also share insights and perspectives with you along the way.

As you eventually gain status as a central participant in the local community, you may wish or be expected to play an increasingly large role in shaping or revising the curriculum, institutional policies, aspects of university administration, and the like. While it may take time and patience to understand the institutional structure and its operations, it will be important that you act as an ethnographer, so to speak. Observing the current system and understanding it through participant observation will be a crucial strategy if you are to become a competent member of this community (Lave & Wenger, 1991).

Balancing Global and Local Professionalism

As your affiliations in the new community develop, there will be a wider range of options for professional activities, including publishing papers and attending academic conferences. There are likely to be active associations of all sizes for local language teachers, researchers, and teacher educators at various academic levels, especially if you happen to be working where applied linguistics researchers are active. It would be crucial to select the professional communities that fit your needs locally so that you can interact with stimulating colleagues. As a result of your academic training in North America, you may be seen as having greater expertise than many others in the community and asked to play a leadership role in these associations.

As your responsibilities and network expand locally, maintaining your North American or international network may become a challenge. There may be international centers and programs affiliated with North American or other Western institutions, such as a local campus of a North American or British university (e.g., Columbia University Teachers College Japan Campus, Texas A&M University at Qatar, and the University of Nottingham campuses in Malaysia and China). Such institutions will most likely assist you in keeping updated with developments internationally, and you may find it refreshing to participate in their professional development opportunities or to offer such opportunities yourself at those institutions.

While some research or educational topics are more suitable for publishing in the local language and through local professional associations, writing in English for international journals or books will tend to give you a higher profile and wider readership. Developing effective strategies may be important in determining what to write, in what language, and for what venues. Similarly, attending local and international conferences will have different sets of benefits and commitments.

Even with the most efficient strategies for juggling multiple professional communities, keeping up with multiple sets of communities locally and internationally can be quite overwhelming simply in terms of the time and energy the task demands. Attempts to keep up with changes in North America while learning about local developments may seem a daunting task, like trying to shoot at a moving target. At times it may be important not to overburden yourself. For example, you might consider attending some conferences without presenting a paper yourself so that you can focus on learning from others and enjoying it. If your current position is already tenured, it may be important to pace yourself so that professional development does not burn you out. In addition, you could select and prioritize your commitments carefully and learn to say "no" or "later" in a tactful manner when necessary.

Collaborating with a mentor or colleagues is another strategy. Collaboration can work domestically and internationally, allowing you to access developments and negotiate ideas that you may not come across while working by yourself. A collaborative writing group (see Motha, 2011, and also Chapter 17, Collaborative Communities) or a mentor you can trust can be truly inspiring. Occasional visits abroad with these collaborators can be exciting and refreshing, and these collaborative researchers may also be interested in personally and professionally visiting you or your institution. In staying updated with your collaborators, various forms of technology will facilitate communication with your colleagues near and far. Even though e-mail has become an essential tool for professional communication, there are other means that assist our different modes of communication (e.g., Skype, Facebook, and LinkedIn).

Dealing with (Reverse) Culture Shock

As there could be quite a few unfamiliar conventions in the new community, you may occasionally encounter (reverse) culture shock. There may be occasions where you may feel that things are unfair or unreasonable and become frustrated when it seems difficult or next to impossible to change the status quo. One example is the apparent distinction that sometimes exists in hiring native rather than non-native speakers of English. Though the distinction may be becoming less common, it remains a die-hard practice in many institutions (Mahboob, 2010). Another case may be the disappointing reality of unequal distribution of male and female instructors in higher education. Still another is the red tape that may well be a universal characteristic of academic institutions around the globe.

In cases such as these, it is important not to use a North American yardstick to make a hasty judgment over the local practices. Instead, it may be productive to develop listening skills to first understand the local logic and local values. Then you may wish to negotiate your point of view and initiate dialogue for possible change. In fact, you may not be alone, as others may share similar backgrounds or values. In such a case, it would be encouraging to collaborate with like-minded colleagues to discuss how you understand the issues and to consider what could be done to deal with unsatisfactory conventions or institutional prejudice. You may wish to make sure that your voices are heard, especially in key decision-making processes.

SUMMARY AND FINAL ADVICE

Relocating to a new or native culture after obtaining a degree or working in North America requires effort, diligence, and patience, yet this journey can be a valuable and eye-opening experience. The challenges include finding a part-time or full-time position overseas, (re)socializing into local institutional practices, dealing with (reverse) culture shock in the process of (re)socialization, (re)shaping supportive communities domestically and internationally, maintaining networks in North America, and balancing work and life. Below is a summary of the suggestions I discussed above.

- *Value your bi-/multi-cultural background and maintain the identities you cherish as much as possible.* Regardless of whether you are working in a new culture or returning to your original one, your knowledge and experience in North America should be highly valued by yourself and by your colleagues. Let it not be a deterrent in the (re)acculturation into a local community. Instead, use it in a constructive manner as a way of contributing to the local institution.
- *Learn about similar as well as different local expectations in the workplace.* Be a careful observer and learn about local practices and values through participation. Having a supportive and informative guide will help you in this process.
- *Maintain affiliations in the local and North American communities as much as possible.* This will broaden your professional opportunities

in research and keep you updated about developments worldwide. This will also help to maintain your bi-/multi-cultural experience and networks. Use a range of technologies to facilitate this process.

- *Work with collaborative mentors and colleagues domestically and internationally.* Some valuable information or networks are simply unavailable through books or online. Be ready to travel near and far for conferences, workshops, lectures, and other professional development opportunities. Build constructive rapport by learning from others' work, sharing your work, and listening to feedback.
- *Avoid burn-out and enjoy your professional opportunities.* The task of keeping up with multiple communities may be overwhelming at times. Do not overburden yourself but try to strike a fine balance between work and life. In keeping in touch with family or friends you left behind in North America, the technologies mentioned above can also be of tremendous help. At the same time, remember that you always have the option to move back to North America or elsewhere, as many do in our profession.

I hope that this chapter will help you to feel excited about relocating overseas rather than discouraged or overwhelmed. Just as in any other context, a career outside of North America can provide an enriching and fulfilling experience. You will feel rewarded when your expertise is valued and you will become an asset to the local and international communities.

RESOURCES

The list of resources below is not intended to be exhaustive but only illustrative of what is available.

Job-Hunting Resources Overseas

American Association for Applied Linguistics (AAAL) Job Bank
http://www.aaal.org/jobbank.cfm

The Chronicle of Higher Education Jobs
http://chronicle.com/section/Jobs/61

Japan Research Career Information Network (JREC-IN)
http://jrecin.jst.go.jp/seek/SeekTop?ln=1

Linguist List (online international linguistics community) Jobs
http://linguistlist.org/jobs/index.cfm

Teachers of English to Speakers of Other Languages (TESOL) International Association: Career Center
http://careers.tesol.org/

The *Times* Educational Supplement Jobs:
http://www.tes.co.uk/jobs/

Applied Linguistics Resources Outside of the United States

Applied Linguistics Association of Australia (ALAA)
http://www.alaa.org.au

Applied Linguistics Association of Korea (ALAK)
http://www.alak.or.kr

Applied Linguistics Association of New Zealand (ALANZ)
http://www.alanz.ac.nz/conferences

Asian Association of Teachers of English as a Foreign Language (Asia TEFL)
http://www.asiatefl.org

British Association for Applied Linguistics (BAAL)
http://www.baal.org.uk

Canadian Association of Applied Linguistics (CAAL)
http://www.aclacaal.org

Hong Kong Applied Linguistics Association (HAAL)
http://www.haal.hk

International Association for Applied Linguistics (AILA)
http://www.aila.info

Irish Association for Applied Linguistics (IRAAL)
http://www.iraal.ie

The Japan Association for Language Teaching (JALT)
http://www.jalt.org

Singapore Association for Applied Linguistics (SAAL)
http://www.saal.org.sg

South African Association of Applied Linguistics (SAALA)
http://www.saala.org.za

REFERENCES

Cortazzi, M. & Jin, L. (1999). Cultural mirrors: Materials and methods in the EFL classroom. In E. Hinkel (Ed.), *Cultures in second language teaching* (pp. 196–219). Cambridge, UK: Cambridge University Press.

Holliday, A. (1994). *Appropriate methodology and social context.* Cambridge, UK: Cambridge University Press.

Lave, J. & Wenger, E. (1991). *Situated learning: Legitimate peripheral participation.* Cambridge, UK: Cambridge University Press.

Mahboob, A. (Ed.). (2010). *The NNEST lens: Nonnative English speakers in TESOL.* Newcastle upon Tyne, UK: Cambridge Scholars Press.

Motha, S. (2011). Suhanthie Motha: NNEST [Non-native English speaking teacher] of the Month, May, 2011 in *NNEST of the Month Blog.* Retrieved from http://nnest.blog.com/2011/04/30/suhanthie-motha

CHAPTER 8

WORKING IN CANADA

Ling Shi
University of British Columbia

It was at the end of my three-year contract teaching in the University of Hong Kong. My colleagues were taken by surprise when the boss announced that I had "snapped up" a job in the University of British Colombia (UBC), a research-intensive university in Canada. Many Canadians would probably use the phrase to refer to, for example, bargains in a store. To me, the phrase "snap up" suggests a surprise, and certainly a positive one. I heartily rejoiced because I was coming home to where I had studied for my Ph.D. One of my nonacademic Canadian friends thought UBC needed Chinese-speaking professors like me to attract students with a Chinese background and also to represent the Chinese population in Vancouver. Another friend who was working for the Canadian government said that I, being a female and a visible minority,1 was a good statistic for employment equity that UBC claims to adhere to in its hiring. The reactions of my friends made me feel sensitive to my Chinese background. I found myself lost in wonder: Was my Chinese background an asset or a drawback in Canada? What were my challenges as a female Chinese minority working in a Canadian university? Was I hired just to improve the statistics for UBC's employment equity? With all these questions, I started to learn about the Canadian system after coming to UBC.

Demystifying Career Paths after Graduate School, pages 89–101
Copyright © 2012 by Information Age Publishing

DESCRIPTION OF THE SYSTEM, CULTURE, AND EXPECTATIONS

Universities and Colleges in Canada

Generally speaking, post-secondary education in Canada can be separated into two types: university education and college education. While colleges mainly offer diplomas, universities grant bachelor's degrees, master's degrees, and doctoral degrees. Canadian colleges are also called community colleges that " typically provide a more job-related curriculum than universities" (EI Group, 2012, para. 2). Since most Canadian universities and colleges are publicly funded and operated under the provincial legislation, there are some differences in how universities and colleges are run across provinces. For example, colleges or Cégeps in Quebec offer high school graduates a two- or three-year program for general and vocational education before going to a university. There are also university colleges in provinces such as British Columbia and Nova Scotia where students can study for a college diploma with credits that can be transferred to some university degree programs. In Ontario, York University also has an agreement with Seneca College that their students, after two years of a college program, can transfer to York and receive credit for one year of university.

Canadian universities can be divided into major, medium, and small universities based on the size of student population. They can also be divided into public and private universities. All major universities are publicly funded, whereas private universities are usually smaller in size. According to Nishizaki Information Services (n.d.), major universities in Canada include University of Toronto with an enrollment of 73,016, McGill University with an enrollment of 36,351, University of British Columbia with an enrolment of 35,000, and Western University (formerly University of Western Ontario) with an enrollment of 33,823. These major universities are also known as research-intensive universities, as they obtain most of their research funding through competitions from the federal government, which provides about "$3 billion annually for direct cost of research, institutional costs of research, infrastructure and salary support" (Association of Universities and Colleges of Canada, 2012, para. 6). Based on the total amount of sponsored research income universities received in 2009, University of Toronto was ranked the first ($858,182,000), followed by University of British Columbia ($524,560,000) (Research Infosource Inc., 2010). Like major universities, medium-sized universities offer both graduate and undergraduate programs but may not have a medical school. Examples of these universities include University of Waterloo with an enrollment of 26,451 and Simon Fraser University with an enrollment of 23,480. In comparison, small public universities focus only on undergraduate education and are also known as teaching universities.

Types of Faculty Appointments

There are commonly three types of faculty appointments in Canadian universities: tenure-track faculty members, instructors, and sessional instructors (also called sessionals). Some institutions also reserve a lecturer rank as a conditional appointment for faculty who are still working on a terminal degree (Gravestock & Greenleaf, 2008). The primary responsibility of instructors and sessionals is teaching. While instructors can be hired with tenure, sessionals work on contracts that need to be renewed every 12 months; however, those with seniority are guaranteed some teaching assignments. Compared with sessionals, who may only have a master's degree, instructors are often Ph.D. holders and can teach graduate courses. Since instructors are not required to do research and supervise graduate students, they typically teach a full load of 30 credits each year.

Faculty positions require a Ph.D. degree, and faculty members are expected to do research, provide services (e.g., serve on committees), supervise graduate students, and teach graduate and undergraduate courses. Most tenure-track faculty members in the Faculty of Education at UBC teach 12 credits (a three-credit course contains about 36 teaching hours) per year. Apart from teaching and working on research projects, faculty members serve on various committees. In the department where I work, there are seven committees, focusing on curriculum, research and awards, graduate advisory (dealing with graduate matters such as admission, graduation, and scholarships), department head's advisory (providing advice for the head on important matters), merit, social, and Digital Literacy Centre advisory. Each faculty member typically serves on two of these committees each year.

How Faculty Members are Hired

In screening the applications, Canadians and permanent residents of Canada must be considered first if everything else is equal, because Canadian immigration requires a rationale for international hiring. In the department where I work, candidates who demonstrate solid training in research methodology are preferred, and reference letters written by well-known professors/scholars are highly weighted. Special attention is also paid to the candidate's academic capacities, his or her ability to teach the existing courses in the department, and some indication of whether the candidate will be a good colleague or citizen. Each candidate shortlisted will then be invited to visit the university for two days during which s/he will be interviewed and do a presentation on his/her research to the whole department. Based on my experiences, typical questions for the candidate are: What types of research (e.g., qualitative or quantitative) can you supervise? What graduate or undergraduate courses can you teach if you are hired? What research plan(s) do you have if you come? After meeting all of the candidates, a department meeting will be held to vote for a hiring decision. When an offer is sent to the first-ranked candidate, rejection letters to other candidates are held until the offer is accepted.

Employment Equity

In all university job advertisements, there is a statement about employment equity such as the following statement in the UBC job ad:

> UBC hires on the basis of merit and is committed to employment equity. All qualified persons are encouraged to apply. However, Canadians and permanent residents of Canada will be given priority. We strongly encourage applications from members of underrepresented groups, including women, people of color, people of aboriginal origin, and people with disabilities.

According to the Equity Office at UBC (http://equity.ubc.ca/employment/), the Canadian government created the Employment Equity Act in 1986 with the purpose of enhancing diversity and removing barriers to equitable opportunities for women, visible minorities, aboriginal peoples, and persons with disabilities. As one of the universities covered by the Federal Contractor program, UBC must follow the government criteria and set its own goals and timetables to achieve employment equity. In Canada, employment equity is both an academic and public discourse, monitoring employment discrimination in mainstream institutions against historically marginalized groups (Singh & Whittick, 2006). To prevent discrimination based on factors such as ethnic origin, religion, and gender, Canada has human rights statutes at both the federal and provincial levels. There are also federal awards to encourage employment equity. York University, as Furedy (2001) noted, won a federal Equity Award in 1994. Seven of the ten provinces in Canada (British Columbia, Manitoba, Saskatchewan, Quebec, Nova Scotia, New Brunswick and Prince Edward Island) have an employment equity policy, although only Quebec extends its mandate beyond the public service (Bakan & Kobayashi, 2000). However, despite the policies, according to Bakan and Kobayashi (2000), "visible minority women are remarkably absent from most public service workplaces in Canada" (p. 46). Based on relevant ethno-cultural background information in 2006, about 84.2% of all full-time university teachers in Canada are white (Canadian Association of University Teachers, 2010). After coming to UBC, I also noted I was only the second visible minority faculty member (out of about 25) hired at the time by the Department of Language and Literacy Education at UBC. I will comment later on my experiences and challenges of working as a female faculty member of color. Soon after I arrived, like all new employees at UBC, I completed an employment equity survey to help determine the representation of women, visible minorities, aboriginal people, and persons with disabilities in the university workforce. There is evidence that universities in Canada are pushed to implement employment equity and diversity, but there is a still a long way to go.

Tenure and Promotion

Canadian universities typically expect the newly hired faculty to be long-term productive members. Most faculty positions require a pre-tenure review in the third year to help identify areas where the person needs to improve before applying for tenure between the fifth and the seventh year. When granted tenure, assistant professors in Canadian universities are normally promoted to the rank of associate professor. However, there are cases of people getting tenure without promotion if their research productivity is limited. Individuals can choose to apply for tenure early, for example in the third or fourth year, if they have worked as a faculty member previously in another university. Unless the person has been extremely productive, the advice is not to go up early. However, one must apply in the seventh year at the latest and, if the application is not successful, the job is terminated in the ninth year. Individuals who are granted tenure secure the position until retirement unless gross negligence or criminal behavior is exhibited.

According to the Agreement on Conditions of Appointment (July 1, 2010 to June 30, 2012) for Faculty at UBC, tenure review takes into account "the interests of the Department and University in maintaining academic strength and balance" (Article 4.01) and is based on whether the individual has maintained and also shown promise of continuing to maintain a high standard of performance in meeting the criteria of teaching, scholarly activity, and service. There is no specific weighting for the three components. Satisfactory teaching performance is based on a peer review and students' evaluations. Good service is defined as "willingness to participate and participation in the affairs of the department and the university" (Article 3.06). In comparison, the criteria for research contributions in many Canadian universities are normally more stringent (Gravestock & Greenleaf, 2008). However, without specifications for the number of scholarly publications, the implication is the more the better. Many people find such uncertainty worrisome, so they will ask old-timers in the department for advice. For example, I asked my colleagues and was told that an average of two refereed journal articles each year was expected.

When ready to apply for tenure and promotion, the applicant submits to the department head his or her CV with publication samples, a teaching dossier (a collection of evidence of teaching contributions and effectiveness), and a list of three external reviewers. The suggested reviewers must not be the person's supervisor or someone with whom the applicant has collaborated in the past. In normal situations, the department will seek three reference letters. One of the referees will be selected from the candidate's list, and the other two will be chosen by the department. Preferably, the referees are distinguished scholars in the field who are also known to be good reference writers. After receiving the reference letters, the application will be reviewed first at the department level, then at the faculty level, and finally by the university board or president/chancellor before a final decision is made. Most applicants find the whole process stressful, although, according to Furedy (2001), the rate of granting tenure at Canadian universities is as high as 80 to 90%. People who fail the process can also seek legal assistance through the faculty association, a union organization that represents faculty on employment matters.

CHALLENGES, STRATEGIES, AND SUCCESSES

Although there is the policy on employment equity, it does not mean that working in Canada as a visible minority woman is without challenges. I remember how a statement from a graduate student reminded me that I was different from other professors because of my ethnic origin. The student was from mainland China, finishing her master's program under my supervision. She told me one day that she wanted to apply to study for a Ph.D. Since she had done good research for her MA, I asked whether she was planning to continue to work with me in the same area. She said no, because, as she put it, "To tell you the truth, I don't want to travel far away from China just to be supervised by another Chinese." I felt surprised at the remark and told her that it was unacceptable in the Canadian context. She then approached a Caucasian professor, though she had no research plans that matched the professor's interest or expertise. The student eventually moved on to another university, but her words lingered in my mind for a long time. "It's like reverse racism," said one of my colleagues, in alarm. In the following sections, I will comment on some related challenges and strategies based on my experiences of working at UBC.

Working with Students Who Expect High Grades

New faculty members, especially those who are from visible minorities, might experience culture shock when teaching in an undergraduate teacher-training program. In my first term at UBC, I taught an undergraduate Teaching English as a Second Language methodology course. At the end of the term when students received their course grades, several complained with their eyes cast up in astonishment, "I am an 'A' student. How can you give me a 'B'?" I did not know how to respond because in both Hong Kong and mainland China, I had never encountered any students who questioned a teacher's evaluation to argue for a higher grade. In addition, I was used to a grading system with an average of B after working in Hong Kong. When I explained that B was a good grade, the UBC students did not believe it. I could not make sense of the situation until I talked to another faculty member. I learned that grades had been inflated and the average grade that many instructors gave to their students in the same program was A. I wished I had known earlier, but it was too late. The evaluation that the students gave me matched the course grades I gave them. It was below five on a seven-point scale. The average course evaluation in the faculty was at the high end of five. To adjust myself to the local culture, I learned to focus more on the positive side of students' work and raised the average grade in the class. Subsequently, my course evaluations improved to match the average scores in the faculty.

Working with Students with a Troubled Family History

Making an adjustment to the local culture was not always smooth. In my second year at UBC, I taught an undergraduate training course in the teacher-training program. At the beginning of the course, I asked the students, who had just come back from a long teaching practicum in the elementary schools, to reflect on their experiences and exchange teaching ideas that worked well in the classroom. One student caught my attention when she talked about how she taught writing. The children in her class were asked to write on a topic she assigned. While writing, she encouraged the children not to write at their desks but on the floor, on a chair, under the table, behind the door, or even in the cupboard. In this way, she explained, she enabled the children to learn how to write from different perspectives. "This is an important writing skill," she claimed. She then presented a peer evaluation checklist that focused on grammar items. When commenting on her presentation, I questioned her about her technique of teaching students to write from different perspectives, and I also suggested adding items in the peer review checklist to, for example, focus on organization and the needs of the readers. She looked at me with furious eyes and said, "No. There is no need to consider other people's needs. One should only write for oneself just like one should only live for oneself." Her voice pierced the air. I lost my words and suggested that we talk after the class.

She restated her view in my office after the class. She said she never considered readers' needs in her own writing and believed that it was important to teach elementary students to do the same. She then gave examples of how she only considered her own needs when writing to a government agency to fight for her rights. She explained that she grew up on the street in Toronto after she left home in a small town in Ontario at the age of 13. It was hard to believe that she had managed to complete her secondary education when living on the street and then had moved to Vancouver to escape from her abusive boyfriend. I sat motionless with both sadness and admiration in my heart. She was obviously very tough. Her hard life had resulted in her being aggressive with others but also defensive of her own person. Having been brought up with a tradition of Confucianism that regards teachers as models for their students to emulate, it was hard for me to imagine how a person who had grown up on the street could become a teacher in a regular school. She was, however, an inspiration for other students or young people who struggled in a similar situation.

I told her that I admired how she had managed to come to UBC in spite of a troubled life. I then explained my belief that most parents would object to the possible lack of discipline in the class when children were allowed not to write at their desks. I also shared with her how my own writing had benefited from readers' feedback. Perhaps because of my understanding of her life and also my willingness to share my own experiences, she listened, in contrast to her defensiveness in class. Later, I invited her to my office a couple of times to talk about not only the class but also the challenges in her life. As we understood more about each other, I noticed that she was more willing to listen and consider my views. She also became cooperative in class and volunteered to lead group discussions. My experience suggests that mutual understanding and trust are key to successful teaching. Although I have never heard about the student since she completed the course, I often wonder if she is teaching and serving as a role model in an alternative school for troubled children.

Publishing in Refereed Journals

Apart from challenges in teaching, new faculty members face challenges to publish in refereed journals in order to meet expectations for successful progress toward tenure. In many ways, getting peer-reviewed publications is a challenge for both junior and senior faculty members. At a dinner party at the home of a senior professor shortly after I arrived in Vancouver, the wife of the professor, knowing that I was new, said abruptly, "You have a problem." When she saw the puzzlement on my face, she explained, "You must publish as much as possible in order to keep your job." The authoritative tone in her voice suggested stories she had heard about the challenges of getting published. I soon learned that publishing was not just a problem for me but also for other faculty members, including senior professors.

The key to getting published is to revise one's work based on review comments. It took me some time to learn how to deal with negative review comments for my papers. When I first wrote a paper based on my Ph.D. thesis, I sent it to a refereed journal. The three reviewers were all very critical of the study. One said that there was something publishable but the paper needed a major revision, including a reanalysis of some of the data. The editor agreed with the reviewers and suggested that I revise and resubmit it. However, I decided to give up because I could not believe that my Ph.D. research, having survived the examination by the thesis committee and external examiner, could still have so many problems.

I later learned that most published papers actually go through substantial revisions, so I readjusted my attitude to review comments. I took each negative comment seriously and regarded it as valuable advice to help improve the paper. When I did not agree with the reviewer, I would introduce the relevant idea as a different or alternative perspective. For a negative comment that undermined the whole study, I would add the relevant point as a limitation of the study. By addressing all of the comments in the revision, my papers did improve. As a result, most of my papers survived the review process and were published in refereed journals. Over the years, I learned how to follow the review comments to revise papers to meet the specific needs of different journals and readers.

Getting Research Grants

Another key to ensure tenure is to get research grants. The process of getting a research grant is slightly different from publishing a paper. Compared with writing journal articles, which can be revised and resubmitted based on the reviewers' comments, grant applications must be close to perfection before submission. In my first year at UBC, I started to write a research proposal for the Social Sciences and Humanities Research Council of Canada (SSHRC), a prestigious federal funding agency providing research grants to scholars in Canada. To take advantage of my insider's knowledge about the Chinese culture, I focused my research on the challenges of second language writers with Chinese or Asian backgrounds. I felt less pressure when I learned that several professors in the department got the grant only after many years of trial. I attended workshops organized by the Faculty and the university on how to write research proposals. Because the proposal would be reviewed by experts from both inside and outside the field, I invited professors not only in my own but also from other departments to read the draft and provide feedback. The proposal was revised many times before submission. My hard work paid off when the news came that I got the grant. One colleague said that it was a big deal, because it would then be very difficult for the university not to grant me tenure.

SUMMARY AND FINAL ADVICE

Working in Canada as a visible minority university professor is a challenging but rewarding experience. The Canadian policies on employment equity provide a healthy working environment, though people from minorities still need to adjust themselves to the local culture. For example, I had to face students who argued for high grades and who had troubled lives. I also learned to deal with negative comments and revise papers to meet the specific needs of individual journals and readers. The following is my advice for Ph.D. graduates, especially those who are visible minorities, who wish to work in a Canadian university:

- *Before applying for a tenure-track position at a research-intensive university, try to get a contract job to gain some experience.* You become more competitive if you have taught in an English-medium university and have one or two papers based on your Ph.D. research either published or in press.
- *It would be a help if you were a Canadian citizen or had immigrant status, but international applicants should not be discouraged.* The university search committees are required to go through the list of Canadian applicants first, but the balance between merit and equity considerations is tilted in favor of academic merit or individual achievement. In other words, an international applicant with more academic merit is more likely to be hired than a local applicant with less achievement.
- *If you are in humanities and social sciences, you need to apply for a SSHRC as soon as you are hired.* A SSHRC grant indicates you have an established a research program recognized by experts in the field. It is very competitive, so getting a SSHRC grant is a big deal for Canadian professors.
- *Once you are hired, you are expected to hit the ground running, so don't wait too long to write up your research for publication.* Make sure that you have papers in refereed journals because they are counted more

favorably than other publications such as book chapters. Learn to deal with negative review comments for your journal submissions. Address each of them in revising the paper before resubmitting it.

- *Always ask for advice if you are not sure about any procedures in teaching.* Most colleagues would be happy to help when approached, but may not offer unsolicited suggestions or information themselves. Do not complain about why people do not tell you anything. This is because they might think you already know.

- *Try to understand the backgrounds of the students.* It is important to develop mutual understanding and trust to ensure students' maximum engagement in learning and to win their collaboration with you.

NOTE

1. The Canadian Employment Equity Act defines visible minorities as "persons, other than Aboriginal peoples, who are non-Caucasian in race or non-white in colour" (Statistics Canada, 2012, para. 2).

RESOURCES

Canadian Universities

Association of Universities and Colleges of Canada
http://www.aucc.ca

Academic Job Ads

University Affairs job database
http://oraweb.aucc.ca/pls/ua/ua_re

Academic Keys
http://www.academickeys.com/search?q=Canada

Employment Equity in Canada

Canadian Human Rights Commission
http://www.chrc-ccdp.ca

Human Resources and Skills Development Canada
http://www.rhdcc-hrsdc.gc.ca

Diversity! in the Workplace
  http://www.diversityintheworkplace.ca

Examples of University Hiring Policies and Procedures

McMaster University
  http://www.mcmaster.ca/vpacademic/

York University
  http://www.yorku.ca/univsec/policies/

Simon Fraser University
  http://www.sfu.ca/avppolicy/

University of British Columbia
  http://equity.ubc.ca/employment/

REFERENCES

Agreement on Conditions of Appointment for Faculty, July 1, 2010 to June 30, 2012. (n.d.) Retrieved from http://www.hr.ubc.ca/faculty-relations/collective-agreements/appointment-faculty

Association of Universities and Colleges of Canada. (2012.) *Research, discovery, and innovation.* Retrieved from http://www.aucc.ca/policy-issues/research-and-innovationhttp://www.aucc.ca/policy-issues/research-and-innovation/ http://www.aucc.ca/policy-issues/research-and-innovation/http://www.aucc.ca/policy-issues/research-and-innovation/

Bakan, A. B., & Kobayashi, A. (2000). *Employment equity policy in Canada: An inter-provincial comparison.* Ottawa, ON: Status of Women Canada. Retrieved from http://publications.gc.ca/collections/Collection/SW21-46-1999E.pdf

Canadian Association of University Teachers (2010). *CAUT almanac of post-secondary education in Canada.* Retrieved from http://www.caut.ca/uploads/2010_CAUT_Almanac.PDF

EI Group (2012). *About community colleges in Canada.* Retrieved from http://www.campusstarter.com/AboutCommunityColleges.cfm

Furedy, J. J. (2001). Employment "equity" steamrolls conservative government. Retrieved from http://www.conservativeforum.org/EssaysForm.asp?ID=12097

Gravestock, P., & Greenleaf, E. G. (2008). Overview of tenure and promotion policies across Canada. Retrieved from http://www.mtroyal.ca/wcm/groups/public/documents/pdf/aptc_canada_tenurepolicies.pdf

Nishizaki Information Services. (n.d.). Universities in Canada. Retrieved from http://www.university-canada.net

Research Infosource Inc. (2010). *Canada's top 50 research universities 2010.* Retrieved from http://www.researchinfosource.com/media/2010Top50List.pdf

Singh, H., & Whittick, G. (2006). Hiring and recruitment. Retrieved from http://legacy.oise.utoronto.ca/research/cld/events.htm

Statistics Canada (2012). *Visible minority of person.* Retrieved from http://www.statcan.gc.ca/concepts/definitions/minority-minorite1-eng.htm

CHAPTER 9

WORKING IN THE UNITED KINGDOM

Constant Leung and Tracey Costley
King's College, London

Pinar[1] is originally from Spain and has spent the last 10 years in Britain completing graduate school and working in a number of university applied linguistics departments during that time. She is currently finishing a post-doctoral research program and is looking for a teaching post in applied linguistics and/or Teaching English to Speakers of Other Languages (TE-SOL). The vignette below is part of Pinar's weekly routine in her search for a lectureship (equivalent of assistant professor in North American universities).

> Making use of a bit of free time Pinar logs on to jobs.ac.uk to have a look at any new vacancies. The headline banner on the website says "2,834 vacancies," and she smiles to herself. She knows that out of that only very few will be related to applied linguistics. After refining her search she is down to four new posts. There are a number of others, but she has already looked at them. The first is for a professorship at a research-intensive Russell Group university that she looks at out of curiosity... what do you need to have in order to get that post, how many publications and what is the salary... she quickly scans the ad and thinks maybe one day she will be in a position to apply for such a

Demystifying Career Paths after Graduate School, pages 103–114
Copyright © 2012 by Information Age Publishing
All rights of reproduction in any form reserved.

post. The other three are more promising; one is for a temporary lectureship at another Russell Group university, and the other two are permanent positions, both of which are at post-92 universities...she pauses for a moment to weigh her options...should she apply for any of them...she has to keep focused on her post-doctoral work, but she also needs to think of looking for a permanent post for when her contract ends...does she want to work in a newer university...would she have an opportunity to continue her research there or would it be only teaching...should she apply for the Russell Group post knowing that it is only temporary...she downloads all three applications and returns to the book chapter that she is working on for publication.

This is very typical of the routine efforts that early-career academics have to make in order to find openings in universities in the United Kingdom (UK). Drawing on our own individual experiences, as a professor from a minority ethnic background and as a white woman from a working class background on a professional non-academic contract respectively, as well as our knowledge of the fields of language education and applied linguistics, we offer an account of our experiences and understanding of some of the processes that an early career academic may go through in order to secure a full-time academic post in the UK.

HIGHER EDUCATION IN THE UK

There are 115 institutions holding the title of "university" in the UK (Universities UK, 2011). The term "university" identifies institutions that have the power to award degrees, and this status is conferred by the UK government. Of these 115, 89 are in England, with the remaining number located in the other "home" nations: Wales, Northern Ireland and Scotland. It should also be mentioned that among this figure are two "federal universities"—the University of London and the University of Wales. In this system one governing body presides over the quality and standards of a number of constituent colleges; for example, University College London and King's College London are part of the University of London.

In general, universities in the UK are public institutions and receive funding from the central government. At present, there are two private universities within the UK. Public funding meant that historically student fees were heavily subsidized. However, in the past few years, political devolution in the UK has meant that university systems in the different home nations have adopted different funding arrangements. One consequence of this is that English and Welsh universities will increase their fees for "home" students (resident UK and European Union nationals); students can be charged a maximum of £9,000 (approximately $14,600 U.S.) per year for programs starting in 2012. This has been increased from £3,375 per year (approximately $5,530 U.S.). In contrast, the Scottish government has kept tuition free for all Scottish students studying in Scotland and will support Scottish students wishing to study in other UK institutions.

There are other organizational differences across the UK universities. For example, in Scotland all undergraduate programs are four four-year courses, whereas in England the standard length of an undergraduate degree is three years. There are no legal or social barriers preventing English students from studying at a Scottish universities and vice versa, and this is the same in regards to staffing and other areas of professional interaction such as conferences, working groups and publications. It is our experience that, although devolution results in a certain amount of localized legislation, colleagues working in the different parts of the UK tend to see themselves as working in the same professional environment.

UNDERSTANDING THE DIFFERENT TYPES OF UNIVERSITIES

Universities in the UK are generally seen to belong to three groups: "post-92" universities, "Redbrick" universities, and "Russell Group" universities. These are important terms in regards to understanding the socio-historic landscape of higher education in the UK; they denote a perceived hierarchy in that they are often used to confer status and prestige on universities and, perhaps by extension, also to mark and place those who work within them.

The term "Russell Group" refers to a group of 24 research-intensive universities in the UK. It is a voluntary grouping of universities that have banded together to maintain "the very best research, an outstanding teaching and learning experience and unrivalled links with business and the public sector" (The Russell Group, 2012, n.p.). One might say that the Russell Group is the equivalent to the Ivy League schools in the U.S. context.

The term "Redbrick university" is primarily associated with the institutions that were founded around the turn of the 20th century in cities such as Liverpool and Manchester. In the early days these institutions tended to focus on science and engineering subjects. The term "Redbrick" has been widened in public parlance to include other university institutions that were founded in the 1950s and 60s, such as Nottingham.

The "post-92" universities (also known as "new universities") have a more recent provenance. Prior to 1992, degree-level education took place in two types of institutions: polytechnics and colleges of higher education, and universities. Very generally, polytechnics tended to provide degree courses associated with applied disciplines such as engineering and business studies, although many of these institutions did offer degree courses in "traditional" subjects such as mathematics and English. Until 1992 the polytechnics did not have individual institutional powers to award degrees; their degrees were awarded by an external body.

The Further Education and Higher Education Act of 1992 unified the higher education system and granted the polytechnics full and equal university status. Although the policy changes succeeded in creating one single system, the extent to which the system is a level playing field is a different matter. In practice, it is still quite common to hear references to "new universities" or "ex-polys" in which the histories of these institutions are invoked and their specialization in practical application highlighted. Almost 20 years after the 1992 Act, the terms such as Russell Group and post-92 universities are widely used in public discourse, which suggests that in the public imagination the status differences between different institutions have not really disappeared. These status differences are also reflected in the self-ascription by universities themselves and is often a crucial part of the way in which an institution constructs its identity (for example, see The Russell Group, 2012). The opening vignette of Pinar's job search touches on some of these status differences.

FACTORS SHAPING EMPLOYMENT IN HIGHER EDUCATION

In terms of employment, the process of moving from being a Ph.D. student and/or an early-career academic to securing a permanent academic post is likely to be broadly comparable to that in North America and Europe. The general structuring of posts in England is as follows: lecturer, senior lecturer, reader and professor, in an ascending order of seniority. Some senior academics may take on administrative roles such as deans of faculties. All levels of posts can be offered on a permanent or time-limited basis in full-time or part-time modes. Individuals holding part-time positions are likely to be teaching one or two courses (or parts of these courses) at a particular institution, and some (if their specialization is in demand) may have a number of these contracts across different institutions.

In terms of getting a foothold in the profession, a part-time or visiting lecturing position could be construed as a good starting point for new Ph.D. graduates or early-career academics. It would allow them to begin to develop their experience as lecturers at the same time as familiarizing themselves with the demands and challenges of life within academia. For many recent graduates the hope is to pick up work in the department in which they studied, but it is not uncommon, in our experience, for new graduates to follow work opportunities in institutions across a broad geographical area. Traveling to different institutions for one to two hours of work a week is not an uncommon experience.

In the UK there is generally no standardized teaching load for the different levels of academic appointments. The actual amount of teaching, research and administration that individuals are expected to do varies a good deal within the different types of universities. Broadly speaking, in research-intensive Russell Group universities, academics are expected to devote a good deal of their energies to research and publications, and this is expected to take place alongside their teaching and administrative duties. Academics are subject to a lot of pressure to produce at least four high-quality research publications in international journals every four years. In less research-intensive institutions, generally post-92 universities, while research has an important place, in the main it is fair to say that they tend to prioritize teaching. Academics in these institutions are encouraged to conduct research, but in general the level of support in terms of time and material resources may be more limited than in research intensive-institutions.

Applications for promotion either within one's institution or in another institution are normally expected to be supported by a strong track record in teaching, research, and administration. For instance, a relatively early stage career lecturer will have to demonstrate the following when seeking to be promoted to senior lecturer: research-based publications that would be recognized as of high national and international quality (see details in later discussion of the Research Excellence Framework), effectiveness as a teacher as evidenced by student evaluations (see below for discussion of the National Student Survey), and contribution to curriculum and institutional development. We would like to stress that it is normally the case that promotion is not usually conferred; individuals are expected to show their interest in promotion, and they have to apply for specific posts.

THE RESEARCH EXCELLENCE FRAMEWORK AND THE NATIONAL STUDENT SURVEY

A UK-specific factor influencing employment opportunities is the Research Excellence Framework (REF). The REF is a central government-organized scheme of assessment of research quality and impact. In various manifestations it has been in operation since 1986 and takes place once every five years or so. In this exercise, all university-based research units in all disciplinary areas are evaluated mainly in terms of the quality of their output as represented by their publications. Research publications are generally gathered at a departmental or research unit level, and a selection is sent forward to be externally evaluated. Under the current dispensation, research assessed and given a numerical grade on a scale of 1* (one star) to 4* (four star). 1* is work that is assessed as being original and important at a national level, whereas 4* is used to describe work that is considered to be world-leading in regards to its originality, significance, and rigor. Research-oriented academics would want to be included in their units' submission to the REF.

A university's REF performance is factored into its ranking in the various league tables that are produced annually (see, for example, The Complete University Guide, at www.thecompleteuniversityguide.co.uk/league-tables/rankings). Universities may risk losing research support funding if their REF ratings fall below a certain level. All research-intensive institutions would want to enter a high percentage of academics who have produced high-quality work in order to maximize research income. There is, however, no sector-wide standard requirement or norm in terms of the percentage of academic staff[2] included in the REF submission. In practice this means that the percentage of academics being entered into the evaluation exercise varies across different institutions and subject areas.

Another aspect of the performance of universities is evaluated through a different exercise. The Higher Education Funding Council for England (HEFCE) organizes the annual National Student Survey (NSS), which is administered to final-year undergraduate students. Students are asked to rate and comment on issues such as quality of teaching, assessment arrangements, learning resources, and so on with reference to the courses they have studied. It is quite common that the student comments refer to specific course content and quality of teaching and assessment. The results of the survey are published and also used as part of the data for university league tables.

Along with the national evaluation exercises, individual institutions also have their own internal systems for gathering data and feedback from students for evaluation purposes. At King's College London, for example, most departments seek feedback from students when they complete individual courses as well as their degree programs. Students are asked to provide feedback on the quality of teaching on specific modules as well as suggestions for improvement. Departments also have staff-student liaison meetings in which student representatives attend face-to-face meetings with staff to give feedback on behalf of their peers. Student feedback is sometimes published and circulated at a departmental level as well as more formally at an institutional level. Staff often use this feedback to shape and refine programs.

The combination of the REF and the NSS exert pressures on departments and staff; therefore they are both somewhat high stakes processes. While both of these evaluation exercises have career implications for established staff, they also amplify the need for new-career academics to develop a research and teaching profile that is "attractive" to potential employers.

APPLYING FOR A JOB

All academic vacancies are generally advertised in three ways: 1) through a university's own website (both internally and externally), 2) through public websites such as www.jobs.ac.uk, and 3) through print media such as *Times Higher Education* and other newspapers. Pinar, as we described in the opening vignette, regularly checks these sources to find information on new posts and vacancies. Advertisements will usually give a short description of the department in which a vacancy exists, and often this will be accompanied by a brief profile of the university to which the department belongs. The advertisement will also contain, in the form of a job specification, a list of specified duties and essential qualifications and qualities that a candidate is expected to have. This information is useful not only in terms of understanding the nature of the vacancy but also in terms of offering clues to applicants in terms of how to "shape" their applications.

When making an application, an important point for any candidate is to tailor his or her application to fit as closely as possible to the details given in the job specification. All advertised posts are likely to provide a specified staff contact for interested parties in order that any questions may be addressed directly to a person who has relevant knowledge of the post and the department concerned. It is often helpful to make use of this contact, as well as any other individuals who may have relevant information, so that a "good fit" application can be developed. The ability to address specific post-related expectations would set a candidate's application in a good light and may help that candidate to be short-listed. Successful short-listed applicants will be invited to attend an interview, and often these interviews include a requirement to prepare and deliver a short presentation on a set topic to members of the interview panel. The interview panel would normally comprise faculty members, subject specialists, and senior administrative staff. In the case of senior posts (such as a professorial post) the panel may include an academic from outside the institution. In addition to showing a "good fit" with the advertised post, it would be advantageous for job applicants to indicate how they would contribute to the department as a whole in terms of scholarship, running programs, and curriculum development.

Although it has long experience of ethnic and linguistic diversity, the UK has something of a checkered history in terms of race relations and racial equality. A report by the Commission for Racial Equality (2007) suggested that the last 30 years or so have seen significant changes in approaches to and awareness of equality and diversity in the workplace and society more broadly. However, it also states that although "much has been done over the last three decades to tackle discrimination in employment... we do not yet have a truly level playing field when it comes to work" (Commission for Racial Equality, 2007, p. 18). The Race Relations Act, a key piece of legislation in enforcing equal opportunities and non-discriminating practices on grounds of race and ethnicity, was first introduced in 1976 and has been refined over the years to act as a set of statutory requirements for all sections of society. In 2000 the Act was revised to bring the need for all public institutions to promote racial equality to the foreground. Universities, as public institutions, are therefore expected to make explicit how they are enacting statutory requirements and how their policies can ensure that individuals are afforded equal opportunities. A 2009 review by the Equality Challenge Unit found that while these kinds of institutional policies are having a positive impact in terms of equality and diversity,

> BME[3] staff, however, remain significantly underrepresented in more senior positions in both the academic and professional workforces...[they also cite] experiences of marginalisation in the higher education sector. (Equality Challenge Unit, 2009, p. 4)

Institutions vary in their approaches to publishing their policy statements. For instance, the online information on the London South Bank University (LSBU) (see www.lsbu.ac.uk/diversity/race.htm) provides an interesting comparison to that provided by King's College London (KCL) (see www.kcl.ac.uk/equal-opps). KCL's page provides a link to its policies on diversity and equality and what the college is doing to ensure that these are embedded in all areas of activity within the institution, whereas LSBU provides a more detailed account of ethnic diversity in the UK, national policy on equality, and the college's code of conduct. It is not our intention here to make judgments on the policies and practices of these institutions; we simply wish to highlight how institutions differ in terms of the type of information they provide and the policies and strategies they employ. Job applicants can use this information to tailor their applications in a way that highlights the range of skills, experiences, and linguistic and cultural capital they would bring to the department, as well as the university more broadly.

OUR EXPERIENCES AND CHALLENGES

In preparing this chapter we held focused discussions with two female applied linguists, Pinar (in the opening vignette) and Niki[4]. Niki is of Iranian origin and Pinar is Spanish. Both are working in a university in London. As long-term residents they are committed to professional careers in the UK. Although both of them are similarly qualified, one of them is at a relatively early stage of career building. They feel that although English is their professional language, it is not necessarily their first or preferred language for all domains of their lives. We discussed and explored their experiences of academic life in England with them in two separate informal individual interviews. The following account reflects their expressed views, embroidered with observations drawn on our own experiences. We will first turn to the idea of race and ethnicity and its proximity to our everyday professional experiences.

Although both Niki and Pinar are aware of broader social issues to do with discrimination in society, race and ethnicity are not something that, in their perception, have impacted their experiences within academia in the UK generally. This is broadly consistent with the present authors' own experiences. Perhaps working in applied linguistics, particularly in departments where English language teaching is a strong element, we tend to be part of teaching and research teams that have multicultural and multilingual outlooks; in many instances the teams are multiethnic. Collectively we (informants and authors) do not recollect instances of direct discrimination along the lines of race and ethnicity in our immediate experiences. Interestingly, Niki made a point to mention that she felt that she had been afforded a greater degree of both personal and academic freedom in choosing her area of specialization in England than in her previous working experience. While for all four of us, there is a sense that in a good deal of our everyday professional work, race and ethnicity are not frontline issues. Colleagues working in different departments and in other institutions may have different experiences and views on these issues. It is also important to note that gender inequality is not entirely absent in British higher education, requiring us to work toward more equity.

All of us—our informant colleagues and ourselves—agree that an important strategy in career development, in terms of securing employment, whether temporary or permanent, is to get yourself seen and known in the field. All of us have experienced periods of instability in the process of finding work in an earlier career phase. Niki and Pinar describe the period of hard work that they had put into finding different opportunities before securing their permanent positions as an "apprenticeship." Niki, for example, spoke of a time before her permanent appointment when she was working at three different universities across London where she taught courses on both undergraduate and postgraduate programs. She spoke of the demands of needing to quickly become familiar with the different institutional practices she encountered as well as the need to shape her ideas and materials to effectively communicate these to the range of different students and colleagues she was working with. She spoke of how this challenged her to reflect on her own experiences and institutional practices, as well as requiring her to be flexible and to adapt both herself and her work to a range of different audiences. Another point Niki made was how this experience helped her understand the transition from being a Ph.D. student to being a member of the academic staff.

There is a sense for all of us that "timing," in the sense of being in the right place at the right time with the requisite expertise, is important in terms of securing employment. Niki, for example, secured two of her temporary posts through meeting colleagues at conferences, and the third came as a result of her being recommended by her Ph.D. supervisor. In practice, to hit the right timing means being persistent with our efforts and also with our "hanging around" and not giving up.

Our two informant colleagues, one on a permanent lectureship contract and the other on a time-limited researcher post respectively, spoke of how they were increasingly under pressure to not only publish work but also to show they have the ability to "bring in money." As is likely to be the case for all academics, there is a certain expectation that we are able to bid successfully for grants from research councils and other funding agencies, and to show the "impact" of our research both in terms of the dissemination of ideas through publications and active participation in academic conferences and professional activities. An individual with a strong publication record and a demonstrated ability to obtain research grants is an attractive asset for an institution. Both of our informants feel that a good track record in being able to secure research income is important not only in terms of making a success of their current positions, but it would also strengthen their case for promotion and career advancements in future years.

SUMMARY AND FINAL ADVICE

We would like to offer two broad observations that may be of interest to any early career colleagues interested in developing a career in the UK:

- *It is important to develop a strong research and teaching profile*, which suggests that teaching is informed by research, and that one's research contributes to disciplinary and professional knowledge and has impact in the world beyond academia.
- *It is important to maintain a focus on both teaching and research as a medium-to-long term career development strategy.* As universities become ever more eager to offer high quality teaching and to produce top-ranking research, academics have to be able to show that they have several strings to their bow.

We close with a perceptive and tell-it-as-it-is comment from Niki: "Accept the reality that as a newcomer to any community of practice you have to be hardworking, accept what is on offer, and possibly work harder than other more established colleagues...but that there are opportunities out there and those opportunities are open to us all."

NOTES

1. Pseudonym.
2. Hereafter, "staff" refers to "academic staff," which is equivalent to instructors and faculty members in North America.
3. The term BME (Black Minority Ethnic) specifies "African-Caribbean black" ethnicity; the broader term "ethnic minority" covers all minority groups including Asians and newly arriving EU groups. The term "staff" here includes both academic and professional (e.g., personnel or human resources professionals) employees.
4. Pseudonym.

RESOURCES

Job Vacancies

www.jobs.ac.uk is a free, open source database that lists current vacancies in higher education in the UK. This website is updated on a weekly basis and individuals can receive email updates on all posts of interest to them.

Times Higher Education (http://www.timeshighereducation.co.uk/) is a monthly publication that not only includes information on vacancies but also has a range of articles and news stories pertaining to higher education in the UK and is a useful source of information in terms of what is taking place in higher education in the UK.

National newspapers such as the *Guardian* (http://www.guardiannews.com/) and the *Times* (http://www.thetimes.co.uk/) have dedicated education sections where colleagues will find information about vacancies as well as more general updates about what is taking place across the UK.

Legal Information

Information about the Race Relations Act 1976 and its amendments can be found at http://www.legislation.gov.uk/.

REFERENCES

Commission for Racial Equality. (2007). *A lot done, a lot to do. Our vision for an integrated Britain.* London, UK: Commission for Racial Equality.

Equality Challenge Unit. (2009). *The experience of black and minority ethnic staff working in higher education.* London, UK: Author.

The Russell Group. (2012). The Russell Group: Creating opportunities. Retrieved from http://www.russellgroup.ac.uk/

Universities UK. (2011). An overview of the higher education sector. Retrieved from http://www.universitiesuk.ac.uk/UKHESector/Pages/OverviewSector.aspx

CHAPTER 10

WORKING IN HONG KONG

Xuesong (Andy) Gao
University of Hong Kong

Yan, a recent doctoral graduate in applied linguistics from a university in Hong Kong, was thrilled to receive a job offer from a very prestigious university in Hong Kong. She finally found a faculty position after spending a couple of years as a post-doctoral fellow in one of Hong Kong's universities. However, she was surprised to see that most of her friends were worried. They told her that the university she was going to work in was the one of the best universities in the region but it was also a place of tension and stress. She would be expected to do so much that she might destroy her health. As there was no tenure system like that in North American universities, she might have to keep struggling for contractual renewal before she was offered a permanent position. Nevertheless, universities in Hong Kong do offer extremely competitive remuneration packages. It is also a great place for doctoral graduates to prove themselves as competent academics.

Asia is an extremely heterogeneous and diverse context, which cannot be covered in one chapter. On the one hand, it has highly open higher education systems such as Hong Kong and Singapore, in which non-local and local scholars are treated the same in recruitment and retention. On the other hand, it also has closed tertiary education systems such as China, which mainly recruits its own doctoral graduates or overseas returned

Demystifying Career Paths after Graduate School, pages 115–125
Copyright © 2012 by Information Age Publishing
115

graduates and treats expatriate scholars only as additional but welcomed help. The diversity of socio-political systems and economic development levels in the region also compels universities to adopt different employment and promotion practices. For this reason, I can only use this chapter to describe the situation in Hong Kong where I am currently based. Even with this task, I find it extremely difficult to generalize diverse practices and policies in Hong Kong's private and public universities. Therefore, this chapter draws on my personal experience as a non-local, non-native English-speaking doctoral graduate in two University Grants Committee (UGC) funded tertiary institutions in Hong Kong.

TERTIARY INSTITUTIONS FOR DOCTORAL GRADUATES IN HONG KONG

In comparison with countries like the United Kingdom and the United States, Hong Kong has a relatively small tertiary education sector with no more than eight public tertiary institutions generously subsidized by the government through the UGC. Apart from the government's subsidies, the Research Grants Council (RGC) operates under the aegis of the UGC and allocates research funding to all UGC-funded institutions, which constitutes a considerable proportion of the universities' total income. For this reason, all the UGC-funded institutions in Hong Kong have been placing increasing emphasis on their staff's research performance, such as their successful applications for external research grants. Hong Kong also has quite a number of private tertiary institutions, many of which are professional training and lifelong learning colleges associated with the UGC-funded universities such as the University of Hong Kong School of Professional and Continuing Education. There are also independent universities or colleges such as Hong Kong Shue Yan University and Chu Hai College of Higher Education. As these private colleges and universities run self-funded programs and rarely receive any funding support from UGC or RGC, they mostly offer teaching positions with relatively unattractive remuneration packages and insecure contracts in comparison with those in UGC-funded institutions.

Academic Positions in Hong Kong's Tertiary Institutions

In UGC-funded institutions, there are three types of openings for applicants with postgraduate degrees (doctoral degrees inclusive), including academic, teaching and research positions. Academic positions, equivalent to faculty positions in North American universities, include professors and lecturers at different levels such as assistant professors or senior lecturers, who are often referred to as "academic staff" or "staff of professorial rank" in Hong Kong's universities. Academic positions are now only open for application from doctoral graduates, preferably with a good track record of publications. Academic staff are expected to do research, teach undergraduate and postgraduate courses, and provide services as required by the university and academic communities. The employment of academic staff is normally funded by the financial support that UGC gives to undergraduate and postgraduate degree studies (including both Master of Philosophy and Doctor of Philosophy) in UGC-funded institutions. It is often said in one of the institutions I worked in that those who teach in the above-mentioned programs may have better job security than those who teach in self-funded programs such as Master of Arts or Master of Education. This said, universities that have long-standing and reputable master's programs do also use their surplus income from these programs to employ academic staff.

In most UGC-funded institutions, academic staff, if they are not permanent ones, may receive renewable three-year or two-year contracts with 10% or 15% contract-end gratuity. Although there is no standard practice of offering academic staff permanent positions in these institutions, academic staff can usually apply for permanent positions after six years' service. The process of getting a permanent position is sometimes called "substantiation" in Hong Kong. Substantiated academic staff do not need to renew their contracts once every few years, and they remain employed until they are given a few months' notice of termination by their employers. Such termination is unusual, but it becomes a reality for many academic staff when academic restructuring in universities makes their positions redundant or they are found to be incapable of rendering service to their employers for medical reasons. Some universities in Hong Kong also claim that they offer tenure-track positions, but it must be noted that these so-called "tenure" positions are different from those in North American universities. At present, failure in getting permanent positions or tenure does not necessarily lead to automatic dismissal. It is quite possible for some academic staff to keep applying for contract renewal until their retirement in a few universities in Hong Kong. However, a North American style of tenured employment is likely to be the norm in the near future.

Master's and doctoral graduates can apply for teaching positions such as teaching consultants, teaching fellows, or language instructors in Hong Kong's universities. Staff in these teaching positions ("teaching staff") teach language or subject courses to both undergraduate and postgraduate students. They may receive one-year, two-year, or three-year contracts with or without any contract-end gratuity. They are expected to undertake heavy teaching duties and they are often considered lower in the universities' academic hierarchy. In one university, academic staff are classified as "teachers" and teaching staff labeled as "non-teachers" in the university staff handbook. Master's and doctoral graduates may also look for research positions such as post-doctoral fellows, research fellows, or research assistants. Some universities in Hong Kong also offer fresh doctoral graduates positions such as research assistant professor. These positions are most likely to be project-based, research-intensive, and, apart from research assistantship, most of these positions are not renewable.

Non-Local Applicants and Retirement Age

Like in many other parts of the world, there have been ongoing efforts to promote Hong Kong and its tertiary institutions internationally (Fok, 2007; Mok, 2003, 2007). As mentioned by Kubota and Sun in the introductory chapter, this internationalization drive means that Caucasian native English-speaking academics as well as those with American or British educational backgrounds often find themselves more sought after by tertiary employers than other candidates. University academics in Hong Kong are comparatively better paid than their counterparts in other countries, attracting many expatriate scholars to its universities. A survey of the websites for departments of English and educational studies in seven UGC-funded universities in Hong Kong revealed that all the departmental heads or chairs for these departments have Caucasian (European) names. This phenomenon can be interpreted as the departments' desire to affirm unmistakably their "international" image. In one department, over half of the academics are, judging by their names, Caucasian. However, although "45% of the academics were drawn from overseas" in the same university, "the non-local student population was only 4% in 2004, of which 88% were from the Chinese mainland" (Fok, 2007, p. 188). In the light of these figures, one can assume that doctoral graduates with non-local and non-Caucasian backgrounds are at a distinct disadvantage in their pursuit of academic careers in Hong Kong.

In addition, successful non-local applicants must prepare themselves for a retirement age that might be younger than in other parts of the world. The retirement age for all academic, teaching, and research staff is 60, though universities in Hong Kong sometimes give special permission to particular individuals to stay on beyond the official retirement age.

WORKING IN HONG KONG'S UNIVERSITIES

As mentioned earlier, Hong Kong's universities are places of tension and stress for those who work in them. This is particularly so for academic staff as they are expected to be multi-tasking and productive in a variety of areas including research, teaching, and service.

Research

All the UGC-funded institutions in Hong Kong expect their academic staff to have a high level of research performance, including publications in international peer-reviewed journals and successful applications for external research grants. It is a major achievement for an individual academic to receive a General Research Fund (GRF) grant, a competitive research grant scheme operated by RGC. The number of GRF grants is a crucial indicator of performance for UGC-funded institutions with regards to their research activities. As a result, one institution even has GRF funding as one of the most important criteria for promotion and substantiation. In addition, the emphasis on research pushes university academics to publish more in high-impact, internationally refereed journals, in particular those listed in high-profile journal citation indexes such as the Social Sciences Citation Index (SSCI) or the Arts and Humanities Citation Index (A&HCI). At one department of English in a Hong Kong university, individual academics reportedly have to publish one SSCI or A&HCI journal paper each year in order to have their contracts renewed, and probably two each year so that they can be promoted and become substantiated after six years. As a result, publishing in these international journals has put enormous pressure on university academics and also presented a great challenge for them since, as scholars often considered to be based in a periphery context, they endeavor to publish in high-profile journals located in the academic center, or in North America and Great Britain (Flowerdew, 2000, 2001).

Teaching

Apart from doing research, teaching is also highly valued as part of performance appraisal for university academics in Hong Kong's universities. Academics may teach classes of various sizes according to the nature of courses and classes. In lectures, one may have to teach some 100 to 200 students in a lecture hall. In tutorials, an academic or teaching staff member teaches some 20 to 40 participants. Their commitment to teaching excellence is often assessed by performance indicators such as student evaluations. Junior academics will find that their teaching evaluation constitutes a substantial part of performance appraisal for their contract renewal. In the performance appraisal process, they also need to produce evidence that they have made efforts to provide a quality learning experience for students, such as making constant improvements in course delivery. Moreover, teaching in a course often entails other duties such as course co-ordination and development, especially when a course is taught by a group of lecturers, including academic and teaching staff. Because of the aforementioned superiority in the university's academic hierarchy, junior academics with their professorial ranks are sometimes given the role of coordinating the teaching of different staff members in a course so that students receive similar content instruction. As course coordinators, they also need to chair the moderation meetings with the teaching team where grading of students' assignments is standardized. In such meetings, sample student scripts with good, middle, and poor grades from each member of the team are discussed to ensure consistency in the application of assessment criteria in marking. Recently appointed academic staff can find themselves in quite awkward situations when they are asked to lead a teaching team that has teaching staff much more experienced in these course-related matters.

Service

In addition to research and teaching, academic staff are expected to play various service roles in the departments, institutions and the wider academic community. They may be required to join various committees at the department level (such as the departmental research and development committees), which are responsible for promoting research culture within the department and acting as the departmental gatekeeper for staff research grant applications, respectively. They may also be elected as members of governing bodies such as the academic board at the institutional level. Many of them are asked to take up roles such as reviewers or members of editorial boards for journals. They may also work in executive committees for local professional organizations or contribute to the well-being of the wider community with their professional knowledge. The tertiary institutions in Hong Kong appreciate and encourage academic staff's efforts to provide these services, as some of them help spread the good name of the institutions.

A TYPICAL DAY IN HONG KONG

So far I have outlined a general picture of what is like to be on an academic staff in Hong Kong's universities; I shall now present a vignette of my typical day's work as an assistant professor at the department of English in a teacher education institution. This highly individualized account adds substance to what might be considered abstract in the above description. In spite of the difficulties in generalization, this vignette illustrates how an individual university academic copes with his work and discharges his professional duties in Hong Kong.

My duties at the Institute include teaching, research, administration, and other professional services, all requiring me to constantly manage exchanges and maintain contact with others, notably departmental colleagues, students, and colleagues in other institutions. I normally start the day like many other colleagues by reading and responding to various work-related e-mails. Many of these e-mails require further commitment of my time and efforts, such as those from students asking questions concerning course content or those from my departmental colleagues about a meeting arrangement for a particular committee that I am a member of. There will also be messages in relation to my recent submissions to journals and those from journals requesting me to be their manuscript reviewer.

After I finish reading and responding to the e-mails, I start preparing for the lectures and tutorials I need to give in the coming days and weeks. I normally teach in the evenings from 6:30 to 9:20 for part-time postgraduate courses (including those for Master of Education, Master of Arts, and Postgraduate Diploma programs). Undergraduate classes usually take place in the mornings and afternoons. As a norm, I am expected to teach nine hours or more each week (three courses) and five courses in one academic year (two semesters). The preparation for teaching these courses involves reading materials relevant to the topics for particular lectures and tutorials, drafting lecture handouts, and developing tutorial tasks that enhance students' understanding of the lecture content. One lecture and one tutorial (three hours in total) invariably require six to nine hours of preparation, which has to be carried out on two or three different days. After students submit their work to me, I often find myself buried with piles of student essays. One of my colleagues once estimated that she had to read and comment on a total of 400,000 words from her students over a two-month period (excluding draft submissions). I have never had to read so many words from my students, but I often spend more hours marking than doing the actual teaching for a course.

Apart from preparing for teaching, I need to make arrangements concerning my research projects, especially as research is the core of my professional duties at the Institute. At any time, I find myself in different stages of different research projects. I may be completing one research project as principal investigator and, for this reason, have to focus on data analysis and writing up the project. I may also be in the stage of collecting data for a project I am collaborating on with my colleagues and, consequently, need to coordinate with them and work out the schedule for data collection. As mentioned earlier, successful application for major external research grants from funding agencies, including the RGC, is highly valued as an important achievement in individual staff members' research efforts. I need to work with my colleagues to draft and submit such grant proposals regularly.

In addition to my teaching and research activities, I need to attend meetings of various working groups, committees, and project teams that I belong to. Upon joining the Institute, I decided to identify myself as an academic researcher and, as a result, I joined the Faculty Research and Development Committees. I was also assigned to be a member of the Development Committee for a new Bachelor of Arts degree program in the Institute. Meanwhile, I work in the Faculty as a member of the working group for student recruitment and admissions, whose task is to coordinate the recruitment efforts and admission of potential applicants. Moreover, as a committee member for a local association of applied linguists, I help organize seminars or conferences for its members. All this work is considered part of my administrative duties and services to the Institute and the wider community.

SUMMARY AND FINAL ADVICE

The above-mentioned contextual conditions and descriptions suggest that any doctoral students who are interested in working as academics in Hong Kong need to engage with the academic community strategically as early as possible. As our professional duties have become much more complex, we also need to continuously make our best efforts in coping with the increasingly multi-faceted nature of our professional obligations. Indeed, it is never easy for us to survive and thrive as university academics in contexts such as Hong Kong. Reflecting on my own professional experiences, here are a few concrete suggestions that might help would-be academics in their pursuit of academic careers and professional excellence:

- *Have a clear picture of what it is like to be a university academic.* Identify an academic from a target university and do a thorough analysis of various aspects of his or her professional duties. We may get this information from their self-descriptions on their personal webpages. By examining these academics' portfolios, we may conclude that we can no longer just claim that we have great potential as academic researchers when applying for academic positions in Hong Kong. Such claims will have to be substantiated by a record of publications, ideally articles in prestigious journals in the field. Moreover, it is important for us to pay attention to the courses they teach and services they offer in their universities and beyond.
- *Allocate time to different aspects of professional activities.* We are expected to do so much in different areas, including research, teaching, administration and service, all requiring time and effort. It is impor-

tant for us to divide our days into small portions of time devoted to different professional activities. In the first few years as an academic, one may spend 40% of the day on research, another 40% on teaching (and its preparation) and the rest of the day on administration and service.

- *Publish as early as possible and as much as possible.* No matter whether we are still in the process of doing our doctoral studies or have recently completed our doctoral research, we need to write for publication as early as possible and as much as possible. The best articles may come out as a result of completed studies, but preliminary findings can be shared with the research community while the study is still in process. In order to publish our writings, we may seek help from our supervisors or senior academics and even collaborate with them in co-authoring our first few articles. We may also closely observe the ways writing is done in academic publications we encounter in their studies and refine our own writings as we go through the pitfalls and rejections in the process of getting our manuscripts accepted for publication.

- *Become a disciplined and committed writer.* In order to achieve a strong track record of publications upon graduation, the most important thing for the doctoral student to do is start writing as soon as possible. Publishing will be a huge challenge for most recently appointed academic staff, especially for those who just completed their doctoral studies. As our professional duties become more diversified after becoming academic staff, we need to cope with various interferences such as teaching preparation and grading student work in our efforts to write and produce academic publications. While teaching and service are important in our performance appraisal for contract renewal or substantiation, research publications are often the determining factor for our survival and success in our academic careers. As a result, we need to be disciplined readers and writers, who always plan and complete a certain amount of academic reading and writing each day. As an example, I have been insisting on writing 500 to 1,000 words each day. Although I have found this rule increasingly difficult to abide by, I still believe in the critical importance of being a disciplined and committed writer.

- *Get involved in international and local professional networks.* Achieve a balance of participation in international and local professional networks to address particular weaknesses of our professional backgrounds in contrast to what is expected of a university academic in a particular context. In the case of Hong Kong, local Ph.D. students may establish their professional connections within international networks so that they can make their doctoral research relevant to the needs and interests of members in international academic networks. Non-local academics outside of Hong Kong may socialize with academics from Hong Kong to have some understanding of the context and prepare their research and teaching for a local audience.

- *Acquire local knowledge.* We need to pay attention to the newspaper reports and academic articles on the target contexts we want to find academic employment in. In the case of Hong Kong, being a multilingual context with great importance being attached to English, Cantonese, and Mandarin Chinese, we may deepen our engagement with local situations in our professional practices through acquiring locally important languages including Cantonese and Mandarin Chinese. Moreover, as we establish local connections, we also develop an understanding of the local professional context through socializing with our local contacts.

- *Gain teaching experience.* In order to develop their pedagogic skills, both doctoral students and recently appointed academics are strongly recommended to take courses on teaching and student supervision, if available, so that they can develop their professional competence in university teaching and supervising doctoral students. Doctoral students are also strongly encouraged to take any teaching duties so that they can have first-hand experience of teaching university-level courses, preparing teaching materials, and contributing to course development. Doctoral students may even volunteer for all sorts of teaching opportunities, such as starting short courses on particular subjects for their fellow doctoral students. They may also start to gain teaching experience through observing and assisting their supervisors in teaching. It is also desirable for doctoral students to familiarize themselves with curriculum theories and program development well before they complete their doctoral programs.

It must be noted that the above-mentioned suggestions give us a starting point to pursue what we want to achieve. To sustain our pursuit of professional excellence, there is an absolute necessity for us to have a high level of commitment, and there can be no doubt that we also need support from various sources in our community.

RESOURCES

The selected list of websites may give readers some ideas of working in Hong Kong as university academics.

Career Preparation (University of Hong Kong Graduate School)
http://www0.hku.hk/gradsch/web/student/career.htm

Hong Kong Association for Applied Linguistics
http://www.haal.hk

Linguistic Society of Hong Kong
http://www.lshk.org

Research Grants Council
http://www.ugc.edu.hk/eng/rgc/

University Grants Committee
http://www.ugc.edu.hk/

UGC-funded Institutions
http://www.ugc.edu.hk/eng/ugc/site/fund_inst.htm

REFERENCES

Flowerdew, J. (2000). Discourse community, legitimate peripheral participation, and the nonnative-English-speaking scholar. *TESOL Quarterly, 34*, 127–150.

Flowerdew, J. (2001). Attitudes of journal editors to nonnative speaker contributions. *TESOL Quarterly, 35*, 121–150.

Fok, W. P. (2007). Internationalisation of higher education in Hong Kong. *International Education Journal, 8*(1), 184–193.

Mok, K. H. (2003). Globalization and higher education restructuring in Hong Kong, Taiwan and mainland China. *Higher Education Research & Development, 22*(2), 117–129.

Mok, K. H. (2007). Questing for internationalization of universities in Asia: Critical reflections. *Journal of Studies in International Education, 11*, 433–454.

CHAPTER 11

GETTING TENURE

Manka M. Varghese
University of Washington

In the same way as many other women, my road to starting a tenure-track position was uneven. I received my Ph.D. in educational linguistics in the summer of 2000 from the University of Pennsylvania after having worked long-distance since 1997, analyzing my data and writing the manuscript in Cincinnati, Ohio, where I had moved to be with my partner. Next, I moved with my partner who had been offered an academic position at the University of Washington in Seattle in the fall of 2000. I then started a temporary position in the College of Education in 2001 and only started a tenure-track position in 2004 after they opened up a national search.

This short anecdote provides an important context to my perspective on getting tenure, which I provide below, and also to show that being offered—let alone starting and pursuing—a tenure-track position is not always as linear as one may initially think.

INTRODUCTION

Tenure-track positions can be very fulfilling. It is also helpful to keep in mind that a tenure-track position, especially for a woman faculty of color,

Demystifying Career Paths after Graduate School, pages 127–139
Copyright © 2012 by Information Age Publishing
All rights of reproduction in any form reserved.

can be a complicated enterprise. The following are key statistics related to tenure at four-year universities in the United States (Snyder & Dillow, 2011). Before 1970 most tenure-track positions were teaching-intensive, and only three quarters of all faculty positions were tenure-track. Currently, most positions are still teaching-intensive but the percentage of tenured faculty is now about 49% of all faculty positions. Of those positions, roughly 41% are occupied by women, 18% by people of color, and about 6% by women of color. Moreover, as in other professions, women across rank earn less than men (roughly 80%), and the number of women and women of color represented decreases over each rank; the least are, therefore, found at the full-professor level. What is especially noteworthy is that although there has been relative success at hiring underrepresented minority faculty in these positions, retention has been significantly challenging. Therefore, becoming promoted to associate and full professor can be more challenging for women of color.

It is important that you are aware of these numbers as you move forward through the process. For example, the fact that there are not that many tenure-track positions and the number of these is decreasing nationally means that if you do get an offer for a tenure-track position and this is very important to you, you should seriously consider it, even if some of the other factors related to it, such as the geographical location of the institution, are not ideal for you. The numbers I shared also reveal that when you are in a tenure-track position, your larger institution and your college and/or department may not be as diverse as you would like these to be.

In this chapter, I first describe what tenure and promotion are, mainly in a tier I research institute, such as the one I am in, but also include information for those who are in other types of institutions. This includes a short history as well as the criteria, the process and the system that exists around tenure and promotion. Then I devote more space to the challenges and strategies that I believe have been useful to me and others in my position in getting tenure. As other authors of chapters have done, I also would like to share the same words of caution, that the information I present here has only limited generalizability since there is significant variation among institutions and individuals.

A HISTORY OF TENURE AND PROMOTION

Tenure is a system of guaranteeing someone permanent employment. This is a system that mainly exists among university professors and teachers in schools rather than in other professions, and its more specific name is academic tenure. For the purposes of this chapter, the focus will be on faculty in universities. Universities have tenure-track and non-tenure-track positions for faculty. During what is usually a seven-year probationary period, an individual in a tenure-track position has an average of five years to come up for promotion. The sixth year is when the promotion materials are reviewed, and if a person is not awarded tenure, the individual has usually one more year in their job when he or she can look for another position. Although external reviewers are invited to evaluate a candidate's record, academic tenure is an internal process for an individual within a particular institution.

A Short History of the Tenure System in the United States

The academic tenure system was fought for and officially granted in the period between 1900 and 1940 for university professors in the United States (Amacher, 2004). Tenure as a system was devised because of the perception that academics and their research were being influenced unduly by large donors on boards of trustees at universities, and such donors and trustees could terminate the employment of faculty for political reasons. The idea was that by providing tenure, universities could allow faculty members greater academic freedom to pursue teaching and research interests and come to conclusions and decisions that are not necessarily influenced by money or politics. In 1915, the American Association of University Professors (AAUP) put forth a declaration of principle, which provided the traditional justification for academic freedom and tenure.

Although the system of tenure had been in existence for a while, it was only in 1945 when it triggered into full swing because universities were being expanded as a consequence of the GI Bill and there were faculty shortages. Currently, the percentage of tenure-track positions is decreasing in the United States and the United Kingdom as well as in Australia, New Zealand and many European countries, with notable exceptions being Germany, France, and Italy. The international context is important to keep in mind, as many of you may be looking for faculty positions around the world. Tenure, overall, is a still a critical aspect of academic positions in that it provides a certain amount of academic freedom without being as influenced by corporate interests as may happen with other types of jobs.

THE PROCESS AND SYSTEM OF TENURE AND PROMOTION

It should be noted that other chapters in this book touch on this topic. For example, many contributors mention that during the average seven-year period before tenure (which can vary according to institutions and other reasons), there are two critical junctures—the third-year review and the final review. These are, of course, in addition to yearly reviews that often are linked to merit and increased pay.

The Third Year Review and Final Review

The mid-career or third-year review process usually starts at the end of the second year. You will usually be asked to provide at least your updated CV. At this point, senior faculty and the dean provide feedback to the candidate about how they think she is doing and what she should be focusing on for the next few years. But again, the seriousness and intensity of the third-year review can vary tremendously. For instance, I was asked to put together a statement of purpose and similar materials that I would prepare for my tenure file, but other individuals, even in the same department, were asked to do less.

The second critical juncture is when an individual is considered for tenure and promotion, usually at the end of the fifth year of his or her appointment. The number of years can vary depending on the institution, whether one was in the middle of a tenure-track position elsewhere, or other factors. Therefore, if you decide to move to another institution during your tenure-track position elsewhere, an important question to ask is whether the years spent somewhere else can be counted towards the period at the new institution. Other factors that can extend the tenure review period are personal reasons, such as childbearing (one can extend the tenure review process by a year for each child at many institutions), or professional reasons such as a prestigious fellowship.

How Do You Get Tenure?

The most important question that is asked about the tenure system is *how one gets tenure.* The easy answer is that it is based on a record of three aspects of work: that is, research, teaching and service. However, the process and system of tenure and promotion is one of the most puzzling ones at a university and obfuscated by implicit and often unarticulated rules, which can cause much frustration and anxiety. Therefore, a critical question to ask during an on-campus interview or before starting a tenure-track position is for some clarity and institutional documents that describe the process in detail. This is important because there are specific materials to gather along the way. For instance, in our tenure file, we have to include at least one peer evaluation of our teaching every year as well as at least one course evaluation every quarter.

The emphasis on research, teaching, and/or service will depend on the institution, and it will also vary by department within the same institution. It is usually the case that at a research-intensive university, the focus will be more on the research in comparison with a teaching-intensive university where the record will be judged more on one's teaching. Many departments, such as mine, expect good teaching. This does not mean that tenure would be denied if you did not get positive evaluations about your teaching on average, whereas tenure would be problematic if your publication record was not positive. Advising and mentoring students, especially doctoral students, are considered part of your teaching activity and an important record for tenure and promotion. Not only can this be an intellectually and emotionally stimulating experience, it can also lead to productive research and publication partnerships.

Overall, in my department, the general rule of thumb, like in many other colleges of education at research-intensive universities, is that the research record should consist of at least two peer-reviewed articles a year. The emphasis on articles is because I am at a College of Education (social sciences); however, my counterparts in the English department (humanities) are usually reviewed based on the publication of a monograph rather than articles. The monograph that is considered is usually sole-authored and not an edited volume. Again, the type of publications (article or books; prestige and type of journals or name of press for monograph) will depend on your department and institution. Being in a College of Education, I was encouraged to aim for mainstream education journals, such as *Teachers College Records* and *American Educational Research Journal* rather than English Language Teaching (ELT) and Applied Linguistics (AL) journals, such as *TESOL Quarterly* and *Applied Linguistics*. However, I did not eventually publish much in these education-based journals before coming up for tenure. This connects to the next important statement I would like to make about the scholarly production for tenure. When one comes up for tenure, it is critical that your scholarly record is defined and within a well-established field (e.g., mine was examining identity in language teachers and investigating language teacher education), and that senior external evaluators who write letters about your record are able to see this and evaluate this. Therefore, when evaluators were writing letters about me, they could recognize my scholarship as contributing to specific inquiry areas within a broader discipline. Book chapters and edited volumes can help to make one's name known in a particular research area. At the same time, they are often not considered to be substitutes for the peer-reviewed articles or a sole-authored book.

The last area that is considered for tenure and promotion is service. This includes both local service as well as national service. Local service can include serving on departmental or university committees, such as a faculty senate or a diversity committee, and any work that you do in your geographical region such as doing workshops for schools or a school district. National service would include reviewing proposals for conferences or manuscripts for journals, being a member of a committee for a professional organization, and serving on an editorial board of a journal.

What is Included in a Tenure File?

Another important question that is asked is *what is included in the final materials for the tenure file.* Where these materials are located could be an actual physical file or an electronic file depending on the institutional requirements. This file is usually divided into three main sections: namely, research, teaching, and service. The materials usually included are at least 1) your CV, 2) a tenure statement of your research, teaching and service, 3) copies of published works, 4) copies of works that are under review, 5) syllabi of all the classes you have taught, and 6) copies of teaching evaluations. Other materials or activities will depend once again on institutional requirements, such as yearly peer evaluations, in my case.

The Tenure Review Committee and its Role

The other critical component in the review process is the tenure review committee. This committee is mainly in charge of making an argument for the whole faculty about your case, by being in charge of choosing or helping choose the external evaluators for your file, writing a letter based on the external letters, and presenting your case. Once again, the composition of this committee varies by department and institution, although it will always consist of three or four tenured faculty members in your department. In some cases, there is also a student member. The committee can be appointed by the dean of the school or college that you belong to or different members can be selected by different bodies. In our college, I was able to choose one member, the second member was chosen by the head of my department, and the last member was chosen by the larger faculty body. Of the three committee members, I was also encouraged to have each member be from different departments of our college. It is extremely helpful to have at least one member who has knowledge of your discipline. This is because, as mentioned earlier, the committee must understand the scholarly contribution of your work. If this is not possible in your department, it will be important for you to find a way to educate your dean or chair and other faculty members about your scholarship.

The committee either selects all the external reviewers or chooses a few and includes others from a list that you provide. In some cases, you can also indicate if there is someone who you do not want to serve as an evaluator, such as a person you have had a significant professional disagreement with. These external reviewers are usually from another institution; they are experts in the larger discipline or your subfield who can evaluate the significance of your scholarship in an unbiased way. The documents sent to these reviewers are normally your CV, your tenure statement, and three or four sample publications that have had the most impact and/or are in the most prestigious journals. Although your co-authors and co-researchers generally cannot serve as external evaluators, in some cases they can. Your former advisor or former dissertation committee members can never serve in this role. The number of external evaluators can vary from three to 10. The tenure review committee then considers these evaluations in composing a letter of the committee's recommendation for your case. In some institutions like mine, the junior faculty must be shown this letter in order to have the chance to clarify anything problematic in the letter. Finally, your tenure file, including the letters from the external evaluator and the tenure review committee, will be reviewed by other tenured faculty members in your department or college. Your case will then be presented by the committee at a meeting only for tenured faculty, and voted on internally. The dean of your college or chair of your department will compose a letter based on the faculty vote with a recommendation, and this will be sent along with your file to the Provost's Office, where the final decision will be made. Normally, the Provost's Office will act on the recommendation of your dean, but not always.

Timeline and Outcome

The typical timeline is the following: In the spring of the fifth year, you should be putting together the file so that documents can be sent to external reviewers during the summer. However, planning for this and talking to others should be initiated at least at the beginning of that year. The letters from the evaluators will be sent back in the fall of the sixth year, or the beginning of the year when you are considered for promotion. At the end of that quarter or semester, the departmental or college faculty vote will take place. The final decision at the university level will be communicated to you typically in the spring of your sixth year, most often by your dean, via written communication or phone. If your tenure case is successful, you will then receive a letter from the university congratulating you and announcing your promotion.

With tenure and promotion comes a change in title to associate professor and a salary raise. In some institutions, this raise can be negotiated with the dean, especially if you have had competitive offers that year from other places. By getting tenure you will also be able to help make significant decisions in your department or college, such as tenure for other junior faculty. Often, you will be asked to take more administrative and leadership positions that you may have not been asked to do before tenure.

Before moving to the next section on challenges and strategies to get tenure, I would like to conclude by underscoring the importance of viewing tenure and promotion as a process. Therefore, one should not look at the fifth year as the year when everything happens. The process of having a timetable, writing consistently, educating others about your work, and submitting your manuscripts for publication needs to be considered continuously, even before starting your position.

CHALLENGES AND STRATEGIES

Since many general challenges and strategies are already touched on in other chapters, the focus of my chapter will be more on some of the unspoken challenges and strategies, especially for women faculty of color, in my experience.

The first and most significant challenge is not only understanding the requirements and timeline for tenure but also having your institution be explicit about them. When I started my position in my college, the requirements and timeline were not written about in formal documents, and most of what was told to me was based on conversations with senior faculty. Now, there are more official documents available for junior faculty to peruse and be guided by. A number of institutions provide mentorship within the department or college. It is up to you to also make an effort to seek support, show mentors your CV, and receive their feedback. You may also receive constructive feedback during the yearly review from your dean or chair. At the same time, there are always confusing or contradictory pieces of information that one receives. For instance, one strategy to clarify the requirements (e.g., how much needs to be published and in what journals) is to look at the records of recently tenured faculty. In my case this was somewhat confusing because the records of these faculty seemed to vary widely. But I eventually understood that my department and college did value different types of files. At the same time, I decided it was safest for me to go the traditional route of attempting to publish two articles in peer-reviewed journals each year in addition to the other components of tenure.

Another perennial challenge is how much time needs to be devoted to teaching and scholarship in addition to research. The easy answer is that it depends on how much weight each is given to in your department or college and institution, but it is not always clear-cut. There is not a single strategy for addressing competing requests but one has to make a decision about what kind of person and what kind of academic one wants to be, and then try to establish routines and strategies based on that. Therefore, if research is something you want to be identified with and your department or college also values it, it is probably important to try to gain some leave and time for it (e.g., by possibly asking for it in a start-up package or applying for a grant to give you that release time). I also found it helpful to be as honest as possible with some students and explain to them or have someone else more senior explain that I had to focus on getting tenure and how after tenure, I would be able to serve more leadership roles, including graduate student supervision.

A significant goal and strategy is that of building relationships within the department or college and university as well as in other institutions. I have found that the people who are the most successful at getting tenure are usually the ones that come with the most social and cultural capital; that is, they have a powerful mentor and/or they have good, solid relationships with other faculty members, especially ones who are helpful in providing them with guidance on how to navigate tenure-track positions and ones they may be able to co-author articles with. Moreover, even if letters from external evaluators are written based on one's scholarship, it also helps to have a positive relationship with faculty members in other institutions who could potentially act as evaluators. This relationship can also be one where you are teaching others about your work in a more informal way rather than just through conference presentations and publications. This is undeniably a trickier process for women faculty of color, who are generally more isolated and not as well-connected in their disciplines, but it is important to attempt to engage in.

Since the tenure vote takes place within one's department or college, being seen as a good citizen and being well-liked by colleagues cannot be overrated. In the same way as with faculty outside your institution, this is an opportunity to get your departmental colleagues to learn about your work and get critical and constructive feedback from them. If for certain reasons it is hard to build those relationships within your department or college, or even if it is not, it is helpful to connect with other faculty across campus. In our university, I joined a group that was formed the same year I started the tenure process called WIRED, which stands for Women Investigating Race, Ethnicity and Difference. This proved to be an extremely helpful support group made up of women with similar challenges as I was facing personally and professionally. There could be groups similar to this in your institution, and if there are not, it may be something that you might want to think of initiating.

There are also other structural issues that one needs to look into before deciding on a position. One important aspect is the size of your unit and the number of faculty members in it; in smaller units, you may be required to do a significant number of administrative tasks. It is also a fact that colleges that have unions have better working conditions and support, and also do better at retaining female faculty members, so this is one thing to look into. Other examples of structural support that one can look for before accepting a position, in addition to groups such as WIRED, are diversity scholarships and fellowships, career or tenure workshops, a faculty equity advisor, or a vice-provost for faculty advancement (as we have).

The process of getting tenured is one that starts before starting a tenure-track position. Therefore, it is helpful to have at least one solid publication in hand before starting. There are also a number of people who are offered a position before they finish their dissertation. This is always tricky territory. If you are one of those people, it is helpful to find a way to get time to finish your dissertation, either during the summer before you start your position or possibly getting a leave in the fall of the year you are starting to do so. There are a number of things one can request in a start-up package that can be instrumental for being able to get tenure. One is any kind of time to write for publication, being supported financially in the summer to write or any release time during the academic year, or university grants to obtain release time. Another is the request funding in a start-up package that one can use in several ways. For instance, I have known faculty members who have used it to have an adjunct paid to teach a course the faculty member was supposed to teach. Some faculty members have used it to pay for a research assistant to help them with current research or to start a new research project.

Another useful task is to set forth some realistic writing goals—if you can, as a five-year plan and if not, at least for the first year or two. Writing up one's dissertation in the form of an article or a book is the first realistic and critical writing goal to establish (see Chapter 13, Getting Published and Doing Research). In addition to producing your initial publications, this writing also helps in formulating and continuing your research agenda and applying for future grants. Additionally, it is important to keep in mind the length of time it takes to send an article out to getting it published (remember that it can be rejected by a journal or require revisions, which requires a lengthy process). The timeline of writing a book proposal, sending it to possible publishers, and having it accepted is normally a multi-year process. It is also a fact that this process is becoming more challenging in the current economic climate, in which publishers are accepting fewer books for publication.

In terms of timeline and preserving and scheduling time to write, faculty who write consistently and set non-negotiable times during the week to write seem to be the most productive. For some it means writing every morning and only scheduling appointments and teaching in the afternoons; for others it means having blocks of writing time during the week where no meetings, classes, and other appointments are scheduled.

Since there are multiple demands and a number of activities to participate in, record-keeping is an important strategy to adopt for preparing your tenure file. One piece of useful advice that a senior faculty gave to me was to print out e-mails and documents, put these and other hard copies detailing teaching or service (for instance, a positive comment from a student about my teaching) in a box for the whole year, and sort these out at the end of the year for the annual review. This can then be used to document activities during each year in more detail.

Finally, it cannot be left unsaid that the most significant challenge in getting tenure, especially for women, is the extent of care-taking they may need to do outside of work. This could be because of childbearing and childrearing or having a relative to take care of. Once again, this is where knowing about and accessing off-campus and on-campus resources and support are crucial. The official leave policy for child-bearing or to take care of a seriously ill family member is usually 12 weeks. It is important to know what the official leave policy is at the larger institution and how other faculty members in your department or college have negotiated their leave. By talking to other women faculty members across my university, I have seen this being negotiated in a range of ways within the same 12-week official leave policy. There is a growing number of institutions that now have a part-time tenure position so that it takes double the amount of time to go up for tenure (I was not aware that such an option existed at my university until my fourth year). Balancing a family and a tenure-track position can be very challenging. It is imperative to have a support system personally and professionally as well as to keep a well-thought-out schedule that includes sufficient time to read and write.

SUMMARY AND FINAL ADVICE

In this chapter, I have discussed the general criteria for the process of getting tenure and putting together a tenure file, as well as identified the major challenges and strategies. Although I have made this as generalizable as possible, I have focused much of the discussion on the process, challenges, and strategies for a woman of color, like me. The major challenges and strategies I have discussed are the following:

- Recognize that the process of tenure starts even before starting the position.

- Build relationships with faculty in your discipline and negotiate for a start-up package that includes time and funding to write.
- Clarify the requirements for getting tenure and gently push the department or college to make the process explicit and articulated with documents, if it is not.
- Build relationships with faculty in your discipline outside your institution, within your university, and within your department or college to seek mentorship, feedback and collegial opportunities.
- Create a short-term and long-term schedule that is realistic and that includes non-negotiable, consistent, and sufficient time to write.

RESOURCES

The following is a list of select sources where you can find information about getting tenure.

American Association of University Professors (AAUP)
   http://www.aaup.org/

Chronicle of Higher Education
   http://www.chronicle.com/

Guide to Faculty Advancement and Promotion at UC Berkeley
   http://academic-senate.berkeley.edu/sites/default/files/committees/
   swem/swem_tenure_guide__rev_2011.pdf

National Education Association (NEA)
   http://www.nea.org

Readings

Cooper, J. E. & Stevens, D. D. (Eds.). (2002). *Tenure in the sacred grove: Issues and strategies for women and minority faculty.* Albany, NY: State University of New York Press.

Evans, E. & Grant, C. (Eds.). (2008). *Mama PhD: Women write about motherhood and academic life.* New Brunswick, NJ: Rutgers University Press.

Moody, J. (2010). *Demystifying the profession: Helping junior faculty succeed.* New Haven, CT: University of New Haven Press.

REFERENCES

Amacher, R. C. (2004). *Faulty towers: Tenure and the structure of higher education.* Oakland, CA: Independent Institute.

Snyder, T. D. & Dillow, S. A. (2011). *Digest of Education Statistics 2010* (NCES 2011-015). Washington, DC: National Center for Education Statistics. Retrieved from http://nces.ed.gov/pubs2011/2011015.pdf

CHAPTER 12

GETTING GRANTS

Ulla Connor
Indiana University–Purdue University Indianapolis

Grant proposals are documents written to solicit financial support for an ongoing or new research or teaching project. Fellowships are probably the first type of grant application that academic professionals learn. From my own experience, I remember filling out forms for a Finnish government fellowship to study English philology at the University of Helsinki. The forms were straightforward and included filling out matriculation examination scores and results from the university entrance examination. A couple of years later, I applied for a Philanthropic Educational Organization International Peace Scholarship to study for a year in the United States. This particular application was more complex; it included a personal essay and a recommendation from a major professor. Writing the personal essay was difficult. I had little practice in writing English in general, and persuasive writing in particular. I turned for help to a fellow dormitory dweller, David Zubin, a Fulbright scholar from the United States, who, with his wife Kate, tutored me in the writing of a successful personal essay to the U.S. grant source of the International Peace Fellowship. In retrospect, this experience taught me an important component of successful grant writing: the need to match your skills and wishes to the expectations of the donor.

Demystifying Career Paths after Graduate School, pages 141–150
Copyright © 2012 by Information Age Publishing
141

Since those graduate study days, I have written many successful and unsuccessful grant proposals. My grants have ranged from $500 travel grants to $500,000 research grants. In addition to writing grant proposals, since the late 1990s I have done research on the language and rhetoric of grant proposals as well as the processes of grant-seeking (Connor, 2000; Connor et al., 1995; Connor & Mauranen, 1999; Connor & Upton, 2004). Most recently, I have given seminars and workshops for international researchers about the development of successful grant proposals at my university (Connor & Harvey, 2011).

Writing to get funding is very important for academic professionals. Grant proposals are "a genre that all academics will have to come to terms with at some point of their career, usually the sooner the better" (Connor & Upton, 2004, p. 235). Greg Myers, a pioneer researcher of grant proposal writing, has described grant writing by scientists as the most basic form of scientific writing: researchers must get money in the first place if they are to publish articles. In his study, Myers (1990) looked at the drafts and final products of two biologists' research proposals and interviewed both authors about their writing processes. Myers (1990) concluded that grant proposals are from start to finish designed to persuade "without seeming to persuade" (p. 42). He found two primary elements in persuasive proposals, namely, that the writer situated himself in the academic community through his status (e.g., home institution, claims about previous accomplishments and/or funding), and the writer proposed original work but with adherence to expected conventions. In other words, to be funded, a proposal has to convince the reader about the soundness of the work as well as about the ability of the writer to accomplish what he promises.

In the remainder of this chapter, I will discuss some key elements that are required for successfully obtaining grants and fellowships and offer practical advice for second language professionals.

GRANT WRITING: WHY, WHAT, AND HOW?

Why to Seek Grant Funds

In today's competitive academic environment, where federal funding for universities (at least in the United States) is decreasing, getting grants to do one's work is ever so important. One can buy released time from teaching to do more research; one can hire graduate students to work on grants and get experience in research; and one can have travel funds to conferences to present one's research and interact with other scholars. Getting grants is hard work, just as teaching and doing research are. In the second language specialist's burgeoning career, grant proposal writing should, however, become part of the professional agenda. A motto in the next few years for professionals may change from "publish or perish" to "get grants or perish." In more and more settings, getting one's research and writing done is almost impossible without grants and scholarships.

Types of Grants

There are many kinds of grants available for academics. Research grants from private and public agencies are most desirable; they often have a rigorous peer review and, as a result, carry prestige. In addition, many carry hefty "indirects," as much as 48% of the total grant budget. Indirects are used to cover overhead costs such as space and grant infrastructure, which institutions need and appreciate. Although most of the indirects go to the institution, school, or department, a grant recipient may be able to negotiate part of the indirects toward the development of new grants. Internal grants are also available at most universities ranging from small research grants and travel grants to course development grants. These internal grants are a good starting point and work well for pilot projects, on which subsequent external grant proposals can be planned. My university provides special summer grants for junior faculty members that provide compensation for one or two months. It is also not unusual for universities to give their new faculty members a course release from teaching and/or a small research fund to encourage the start of an active professional career that goes beyond assigned teaching and service activities.

Where to Look for Available Grants

Universities have research and grant offices, which offer assistance in locating sources through computer searches using key words. These offices usually have grant writing specialists, too, who review draft proposals. In the best cases, they are familiar with successful grants submitted to a particular agency. Many individual schools at universities also may have a grant specialist, whose expertise is particularly useful in developing the budget. In addition to seeking help through the university's grant and research offices, an applicant is advised to study the websites of potential foundations and governmental offices for deadlines and guidelines. Professional organizations such as TESOL International Association announce grant opportunities as well.

Process of Obtaining Grants

The steps in the process of getting grants and fellowships are the following: identifying a funding source, writing a proposal and obtaining recommendations if necessary, obtaining signatures from the university administrators, receiving rating results and perhaps needing to revise and resubmit, and after being granted the award, writing reports of the progress and publishing the results. As is the case of publishing research articles, the process can be long, and one has to be prepared and allow time for each of the steps.

Grant Proposal Writing

In addition to the actual writing of the grant proposal text, social interactions are very important and constitute a key element of grant-proposal genre knowledge. The applied linguist and TESOL writing scholar Christine Tardy (2003) writes, based on her own research on proposal writing:

> Grant proposals function within a larger system of documents with which writers interact as they navigate through the grant-writing process. Documents such as letters of intent and grant-writing guidelines, as well as face-to-face interactions with program officers, are all interconnected genres within the grant-writing process. (p. 11)

Any private or public grant-making agency will have someone called a program officer whose responsibility is to answer grant applicants' questions. It is important that you talk to these program officers before writing a proposal, preferably face to face, at the funding agency's office or at conventions. It is also important to consider colleagues or mentors as good information sources.

Once the funding source is identified, it is necessary to study the "request for proposal" and guidelines for submission carefully. My advice: Read the guidelines, follow the guidelines; plan ahead, write, rewrite, ask others to read and comment—and be sure to submit in time. It is also important to keep in mind that the adjudication committee might consist of specialists from outside of your field. Employ journalistic writing strategies like avoiding highly specialized jargon and technical terminology to ensure that all reviewers can understand your proposal.

A successful grant writer once gave me this advice: "Like a child drawing in a coloring book, don't cross the lines, but be colorful." How to be colorful, however, is the key. As Tardy (2003) writes: "Science is not just about finding the truth, but it's also about communicating the truth. The reviewers must be convinced that your problem is important and that you can solve it" (p. 30). The next section describes how the text of the proposal should do exactly that.

The structure of grant proposal sections varies across each funding agency. Typically, a grant proposal contains the following sections:

1. Cover sheet
2. Table of contents
3. Project summary (abstract)
4. Biographical sketches
5. Project description (research plan)
    – Introduction
    – Goals (specific aims)
    – Significance
    – Innovation
    – Approach (methods)
    – Outcomes
6. Budget
7. Facilities, equipment and resources
8. Appendix

Most grant agencies give general advice for writing each section. For example, the National Institutes of Health (2010) gives suggestions such as the following for the "specific aims" section:

- Be as brief and specific as possible. For clarity, each aim should consist of only one sentence. Use a brief paragraph under each aim if detail is needed. Most successful applications have two to four specific aims.
- Don't be overly ambitious. A small, focused project is generally better received than a diffuse, multifaceted project.
- Be certain that all aims are related. Have someone read them for clarity and cohesiveness.

Many of these suggestions are useful, but some are vague and ambiguous. What is overly ambitious? What is being ambitious enough? These kinds of vague guidelines encouraged me and Finnish linguist colleagues in the 1990s, faced with European Union grant guidelines, to begin studying the language of successful proposals. The research produced rhetorical moves for grant proposals, which are described after the following brief discussion of developing budgets and bookkeeping.

Developing Budgets and Bookkeeping

The rhetorical moves make up the text part of a proposal. However, other sections are also important, especially the budget. Each funding agency has different stipulations on what elements of the project can be supported by the grant money, so be sure to clearly follow each individual funder's budget restrictions. Another tip is that funders want to know you can do what you are proposing with the money you request, so be realistic when developing the budget. Review the budgets for personnel and other expenses very carefully and with the help of your university, department, and school grant office. Administrators at your university often care more about the budget than the research content, so work early with them to hash out the budget and be sure to allow enough time for reviews and submission.

Once granted the funds, set up a systematic grant account to keep track of expenses and be prepared to write reports at the end of the grant period. If changes in the budget take place—for example, your mailing expenses are higher than expected or the honoraria budgeted for interviews are lower than you budgeted—most funding agencies require you to ask for these changes even if the total amount would stay the same. For annual and final reports, consult the guidelines provided by the agency.

RHETORICAL MOVES IN PERSUASIVE GRANT WRITING

Genre research on grant writing (Connor & Mauranen, 1999; Swales, 1990) provides useful insight into how to write effective proposals. Rhetorical moves are the functional parts in a text that can be identified in a given genre (i.e., research articles, grant proposals, presentations) for some specific rhetorical purpose. They are specific to each genre. Following are the rhetorical moves that were identified in the genre of research grant proposals and account for virtually all of the content in a grant proposal. These moves may appear throughout different sections of the grant proposal in different orders:

> *Territory or importance of the field:* establishes the situation in which the research is placed or physically located. There are two types of territory: 1) that of the "real world," or how the study is related to problems in society, and 2) that of the field of research in which the proposal itself takes place.
>
> *Reporting previous research:* consists of reporting or referring to earlier research in the field, either by the proposers themselves or by others.
>
> *Gap:* indicates that there is a gap in knowledge or a problem in the territory, whether in the "real world" (for example environmental, commercial, financial) or in the research field (for example, point-

ing out that something is not known or certain). This move serves to explain the motivation of the study.

Goals: is the statement of the aim, or general objective of the study. In other words, it explains what it is the researcher wants to get done.

Hypothesis: in some grant proposals, a hypothesis or research question move is used instead of the goals move.

Means: include the methods, procedures, plans of action, and the tasks that the proposal specified as leading to the goal.

Achievements: describe the anticipated results, findings, or outcomes of the study.

Benefits: explain the intended or projected outcomes of the study that could be considered useful to the "real world" outside the study itself, or even to the outside world.

Competence: contains statements to the effect that the research group proposing the work is well qualified, experienced, and generally capable of carrying out the tasks set out.

Compliance: makes explicit the relevance of the proposal to the funding organization objectives, usually with highly specific references to directives and/or the set goals of the program in question.

Importance: presents the proposal, its objectives, anticipated outcomes, or the territory as particularly important or topical, much needed or urgent with respect to either the "real world" or to the research itself. (Connor et al., 1995; Connor & Mauranen, 1999)

Sample Moves Analysis

The following are sample moves from the introduction section of a Lilly Foundation-funded grant proposal by the Indiana Center for Intercultural Communication, titled "Project for Health Literacy and Patient Adherence." Each move is identified in bold in the margin.

DESCRIPTION OF PROJECT

Health literacy plays an essential role in the ability of individuals to effectively manage their own health care, and yet a report by the Institute of Medicine (Nielsen-Bohlman, Panzer, & Kindig, 2004) acknowledges that the 90 million Americans with low literacy **Territory** probably also have low health literacy. The report further states that even individuals with adequate health literacy face challenges in the complex literacy demands of health care contexts.

Health literacy is defined by the Institute of Medicine as "the degree to which individuals have the capacity to obtain, process, and understand basic health information and services needed to make appropriate health decisions." Reading ability is one component in health literacy, another is numeracy; background knowledge of medical terms, concepts, and health care systems also contributes to health literacy.

Studies show that patients with lower reading ability and/or lower health literacy have worse health outcomes for a variety of chronic diseases in comparison to high-literate patients (Kalichman & Rompa, 2000; Williams et al.,1998; Schillinger et al., 2002). Health literacy is a factor in the complex of behaviors that relate to medication adherence (Dewalt & Pignone, 2005), and is reported as lower among minority groups and non-native speakers (Gazmararian et al., 2005).

Reporting previous research

Both the US Food and Drug Administration and the European Union recognize that current written medical information must be more effective. The FDA is now calling for initiatives to make medical information more comprehensible to patients and consumers (FDA Guidance, July 2006), and the European Union has called for testing of information with patient groups to ensure ease of use (Directive 2004/27/EC). Among the written information of concern to these government agencies is the pharmacy-generated Patient Information Leaflet (PIL) in the US and the mandatory Patient Package Insert (PPI) in the EU. An analysis of the EU template (Askehave & Zethsen, 2003) found the PPI in Europe to be poorly designed for comprehension by the consumer, and the European Medicines Agency has now called for comprehensible summaries to supplement the PPI. In the United States the *Annals of Internal Medicine* editorially (July 19, 2006) called for research and development to provide systematic and comprehensible written information to patients at every level of literacy, but there has been little systematic research on PILs and only rudimentary study of prescription medicine labels.

Gap

An interdisciplinary, trans-national team based at IUPUI in the Indiana Center for Intercultural Communication (ICIC), proposes to study health literacy across cultures here in the US and across national borders, investigate multiple dimensions of health literacy (legal, behavioral, linguistic) and foreground health literacy as essential for patient self-management of chronic diseases. The team recognizes that cultural beliefs and values play a role in accessing and processing information, and that immigrant groups and underserved populations face challenges to full health literacy. In the case of immigrants, the challenges involve a lack of language competence (knowledge of the language of health), a lack of cultural competence (understanding of the beliefs and values implicit in

Competence

health care in the United States), and a lack of discourse competence (how to navigate the health care system as a whole).

The goals of the three-year project are:

1. To develop and test a model that detects similarities and
   differences in the use of health literacy in relation to patient
   medication adherence across cultural boundaries and differing education levels;
2. To develop guidelines to prepare better information about
   medication for patients among differing cultural groups and
   educational levels.

Goals

SUMMARY AND FINAL ADVICE

After you successfully complete your project, you will wish to disseminate the findings. When you publish results of a study funded by a grant, do not forget to acknowledge the source of funding. If multiple authors are involved in a grant, set the ground rules about publishing at the beginning of the project, following the research ethics guidelines of your institution's research review board.

A few last pieces of advice:

- Do not get discouraged in the process. A good rule of thumb to remember is that only one in five proposals gets funded, at least in the first round. Therefore, the key is to write and write and write.
- Remember that grant proposals, unlike research articles, can be submitted to multiple sources at the same time.
- Learn from non-funded proposals. If no written feedback is given, it is perfectly acceptable to contact the agency for comments.
- Keep in mind that a non-funded proposal can be revised for another submission, either to the same funder or another one.
- Remember that with the success of getting a grant comes responsibilities. The work needs to get done, and reports need to be written about how the funds have been spent and what has been accomplished.

REFERENCES

Connor, U. (2000). Variation in rhetorical moves in grant proposals of US humanists and scientists. *Text, 20,* 1–28.

Connor, U. & Harvey, L. (2011, May). *Specific grant proposal writing: an ICIC workshop for non-native English speakers.* Workshop conducted in collaboration with the

Indiana University School of Medicine Office of Postdoctoral Affairs, Indiana University Purdue University Indianapolis.

Connor, U., Helle, T., Mauranen, A., Ringbom, H., Tirkkonen-Condit, S., & Yli-Antola, M. (1995). *Tehokkaita EUProjektiehdotuksia: Ohjeita kirjoittajille* [*Successful grant proposals: A guide for researchers in the European Union*]. Helsinki, Finland: TEKES.

Connor, U. & Mauranen, A. (1999). Linguistic analysis of grant proposals: European Union research grants. *English for Specific Purposes, 18,* 47–62.

Connor, U. & Upton, T. A. (Eds.). (2004). *Discourse in the professions: Perspectives from corpus linguistics.* Amsterdam, Netherlands: John Benjamins.

Myers, G. (1990). *Writing biology: Texts in the social construction of scientific knowledge.* Madison, WI: University of Wisconsin Press.

National Institutes of Health. (2010). *Quick guide for grant applications.* Retrieved from http://deainfo.nci.nih.gov/extra/extdocs/gntapp.pdf

Swales, J. (1990). *Genre analysis: English in academic and research settings.* New York, NY: Cambridge University Press.

Tardy, C. M. (2003). A genre system view of the funding of academic research. *Written Communication, 20*(1), 7–36.

CHAPTER 13

GETTING PUBLISHED AND DOING RESEARCH

Guofang Li
Michigan State University

After five to six (or more) years of hard work, you have finally completed your doctoral studies and landed a tenure-track position of your dreams in the foreign land you now call home, and you feel that you have learned how to do research and how to write in a second language. You have the proof of a thick dissertation! You are relieved and you are about to relax. Then you go to the first faculty orientation meeting; you hear about the complex tenure and promotion process and you are told "*publish or perish*;" your sense of success and relief quickly dissipates. You enter another state of urgency, and you realize that getting a Ph.D. was just the beginning of a long path ahead, and you need to know how to publish your research to make your work known to scholars other than your dissertation committee members in a relatively short period of time, as the next review of your performance is just one year away!

If you are lucky, you may have learned all about academic publishing through your involvement in various projects, papers, and presentations with your professors and fellow students in your doctoral program, and you are well on your way to publish your research and to secure tenure.

Demystifying Career Paths after Graduate School, pages 151–162
Copyright © 2012 by Information Age Publishing
All rights of reproduction in any form reserved.

On the other hand, if you graduated from a research-intensive program but failed to learn how to turn research into publications in competitive, peer-reviewed journals, you may need a crash course on how to publish and not perish. Or you may be a current graduate student who is trying to publish a course paper or a paper based on a practicum project, but you are not sure how to start and what to expect. This chapter is Publication 101, a crash course on academic publishing. I will outline different publication venues and types of publications as well as the process of getting published, followed by suggestions and strategies for graduate students and beginning scholars.

DESCRIPTION OF THE SYSTEM: THE VENUES, TYPES AND PROCESS OF PUBLICATION

In general, there are several types of publication including book chapters, journal articles (peer-reviewed papers and non peer-reviewed commentaries), books (edited and sole-authored), book reviews, and conference proceedings. The corresponding venues of these types of publications are book publishers, journals, and conferences. The first three (book chapters, journal articles, and books) weigh more than the last two kinds of publications during your tenure review process; therefore, you should focus more on these three types of publications. Among the first three types of publications, peer-reviewed journal articles are more valued than book chapters, because these articles often go through a rigorous blind review process that often leads to high quality publications characterized by ground-breaking research results and good writing, especially in content, style, and organization. Books are also valued in some disciplines, like the humanities, as books allow scholars to elaborate on more comprehensive ideas and findings otherwise too complex for a single article. Books are designed to be more broadly accessible for a larger audience. However, not all disciplines require books for tenure. Likewise, the decision whether to publish a book or not sometimes depends on your research topic and your research methods. Not all dissertations are suitable for publishing as a book.

Each type of publication can also be categorized by the target audiences, such as a research-oriented or practitioner-oriented one. A research piece places more emphasis on rigorous research methodology and is often published as a book for an academic market or in an academic journal. In contrast, a practitioner piece focuses more on implications for professional practice and therefore often appears in a practitioner-oriented journal or as a book targeting a professional market. In the following, I outline the publishing process for the three major types of publication and the major tasks involved.

Peer-Reviewed Journal Articles

According to Bowen (2010), there are "four broad, sometimes overlapping, categories of scholarly journal articles," including "*research* (reporting original research based on systematic data collection and analysis); *review* (critically reviewing literature or an entire study); *methodological* (discussing an innovative research method, design, or paradigm); and *theoretical* (presenting an original theory or assessing existing theories)" (p. 866).

The basic process of publishing a peer-reviewed journal article (online or in print) involves preparing a manuscript, finding a journal that best matches the content, style, and method of the manuscript, and submitting it following the journal's submission guidelines. Once a manuscript is submitted, it usually goes through a blind review process through which the journal editor assigns two to three scholars that best match the topic of your article to evaluate it. This review process usually takes three to four months. Upon receiving all the comments from reviewers, the editor then summarizes the comments and makes a decision on the status of your manuscript. There are four statuses: accept without revision (extremely rare), accept with minor revision (sometime requires another round of review), revise and resubmit (major revision), and reject (no chance for resubmission). The editor's letter and deliberation will help you revise and improve the manuscript and consider the next steps of action. If the manuscript is accepted without revision, hurray! Nothing much for you to do, but this almost never happens. If you receive "accept with minor revision," revise it right away following the reviewers' suggestions. If it is a revise and resubmit, take your time and do a serious round of revision before resubmitting it back to the journal. Sometimes, you find that considering the reviewers' suggestions would require too much compromise on your part (like a complete overhaul of your theoretical framework, which you are reluctant to do). In that case, you might decide not to pursue revision but send the manuscript to another journal. If it is rejected, you should still read the editor's letter and reviewers' comments carefully, and consider revising and submitting it to another journal or venue.

The most important tasks of publishing a journal article are to prepare a publishable manuscript and find an appropriate journal. For beginning scholars, the first manuscripts you work on should be based on your dissertation, not on new research that you try to conduct at your new post. While your dissertation is more than 100 (or 200) pages long, a refereed journal article is no more than 30 double-spaced pages. How to convert a lengthy dissertation into a publishable journal article of 30 pages is a very daunting task. One of the first things you need to think about is how to distribute the findings of your dissertation over several articles to maximize the quantity of works for publication. However, scholars often recommend no more than three or four articles should stem from a dissertation (Bowen, 2010). Bowen (2010) suggests that "the typical types of papers that can be generated from a dissertation and their corresponding chapters" (using a qualitative method) can include "(a) critical reviews of the literature; (b) methodological innovations; (c) specific findings or results; (d) implications for policy, practice, and/or research; and (e) insider experience conducting research" (p. 866).

Once you have a plan for converting your dissertation into different articles, decide on the order of articles you are going to work on. Usually, it is good to start with a research journal article that reports the most important findings of your dissertation study. Typically, a research journal article should include introduction, statement of the problem, rationale for the study, review of the literature, research methodology (including data collection and analysis), presentation and discussion of findings and results, conclusions and implications, and finally a reference list.

As you work on writing the manuscript, the other homework you need to do is to find a journal that is most applicable to your field of expertise and the particular study you are reporting. You can find information on different journals in your field through different channels—for example, by consulting your advisor and professors, searching through online listings, browsing your library collections, and checking with your professional associations. Also, look at your own reference list to see where the articles you cite were published. Typically there are top-tier and second-tier journals. Browse some past issues of each journal and pay attention to the scope and themes, the methods, and the structure of the articles that were included in the journal. This should give you a sense whether your own article fits the scope of this particular journal.

Once you decide on a journal, read the journal's submission guidelines and strictly follow them when you prepare your manuscript for submission. Each journal follows a certain style (such as APA, MLA, or the Chicago Style) and has specific requirements regarding things such as page length, tables, figures, and illustrations, as well as the submission process.

Finally, you need to write a cover letter to accompany the manuscript. The cover letter should indicate what is being submitted, a brief description of the work and its significance, and your contact information—your mailing address, email, phone, and fax numbers. Typically, the cover letter should not exceed one page.

Book Chapters

In addition to journal articles, another publication venue is book chapters. Different from a journal article, which requires you to take the initiative to decide where to send it, a book chapter is often invited by a book editor who knows about your work. Sometimes, you can also respond to an editor's call for manuscripts. Typically, a book editor will ask you to write on a certain topic related to the theme of the book. You need to submit a short abstract about the chapter you are to contribute first. If it fits the overall scope of the book, you will then be asked to submit a full manuscript. The editor usually sends you a list of authors' guidelines (including a timeline) for you to follow. The guidelines are very similar to the submission guidelines required by journals. Sometimes, the editor will ask you to structure your article in particular ways or address certain questions so that your chapter is consistent with the rest of the chapters. Therefore, the bottom line of preparing a book chapter is to be in close contact with the book editor.

Book chapters are also subjected to a review process, though it is not as rigorous as the journal article review process. Once it is submitted to the book editor, the editor may elicit reviewers to review individual chapters in addition to his or her own review. Sometimes, the book publisher also sends out the whole book manuscript out for review before publication.

I want to note that not all invited chapters are accepted for publication. I have, for various reasons, rejected invited chapters in the past. Invited chapters can be rejected due to similar reasons that journal manuscripts get rejected: seriously flawed research, poor writing (poor language quality, poor organization), poor analysis, poor argumentation, and/or poor conclusion, or lack of fit with the overall theme of the book.

Books

If you decide to convert your dissertation into a book, you will need to identify a publisher, write a book proposal, and prepare a book manuscript. The process of identifying a publisher is similar to identifying a journal. The important thing is to find a good fit between the publisher and your book. You can identify one or multiple potential publishers by consulting your advisor and professors or peers, browsing the catalogues of the publishers, and paying attention to publishers of the books that are central to your research study. You can also find out information from your professional conferences. Usually many publishers have display booths at conference exhibitions, and their acquisition editors are often available to talk to potential authors. You can just go visit their booths and make appointments with the editors about your book project.

Once you have identified a book publisher (or several potential publishers), you will need to work on your book proposal. Most publishers' websites have instructions on how to submit a proposal. In general, a book proposal should contain the following information: title of the book, author contact information, overview of the book (including description, scope, and purpose), market and audience, need for your book and its competition, format, length, timetable, and outline of book contents. The overview gives the editor a general idea of the proposed book, what it is about and why it is needed in the context of your broader field of study. For market and audience, you will need to address who your book is targeted for (e.g., undergraduate or graduate students, researchers or practitioners or both), why these groups would find your book useful, and what kinds of courses might use your book as texts. This is followed by a description of the competiveness of your book in the market: what is unique about your book in comparison to other books of similar topics already published? What contribution does your book make to the field? What are the similarities and differences between your book and other similar books out there? As well, you will need to indicate how long your book will be—for example, how many chapters, how many pages, and how many words—and your timeline for submitting a full manuscript. Finally, it is essential to attach a table of contents with abstracts for each chapter. This allows the editor to have a much deeper understanding of what your proposed book is about and why it is important to publish it.

Together with the proposal, most publishers ask you to submit one to three sample chapters. You should send your best chapters. Some editors make a decision on your proposal based on their own judgment of the merit and market analysis. Many editors will elicit experts in your field for comments on the proposal to help them make a decision on the book offer. If the reviews are positive, the editor will offer you a book contract that outlines basic terms and copyright issues. Once the book contract is signed, you are in a formal agreement with the publisher. Note that different from journal articles and book chapters, which you can only submit to one outlet, you can submit your book proposal to multiple publishers. But in my opinion, editors do not want to waste their time if they know you might go with other publishers. Since the academic world is very small, it is better to let the editor know in advance that you are submitting to other publishers or submitting it to one publisher at a time. Along with the book contract, the publisher or editor will also send their author's guide on how to prepare your final manuscript. Similar to preparing a journal manuscript, follow the guidelines.

As described above, all the three types of publication involve a similar process: finding an outlet that is a good fit with your manuscript and preparing the manuscript following specific guidelines. If your manuscript is accepted, you will need to revise, following reviewers' and editors' comments. Once the revision is accepted, your manuscript will enter into the production stage, which means it is going into print! You are almost there!

Journals and publishers usually have professional copyeditors to edit your work and will typeset your article for print. You will be asked to review the copyedited manuscript before it is printed. In general, this is the time to make minor language corrections, but not any substantial content changes. Once you proofread the copyedited version, the manuscript will be sent to the printer, hence completing the whole publication process.

SUGGESTIONS AND STRATEGIES FOR GETTING YOUR RESEARCH PUBLISHED (FAST)

Now that you have some basic knowledge about the publishing process, I share, based on my experience, some strategies and suggestions on how to get published efficiently within the five years before your tenure review takes place.

Start with Your Dissertation Data

Although it is expected that your first publications (articles and book) come out of your dissertation, many new graduates are anxious to start new research projects. My advice is to publish on your dissertation data and related topics first. Once you have a few manuscripts in the pipeline, think about starting a small-scale, easy-to-manage research project, since it takes a year or longer to conduct a study and collect new data. As I will explain in this section, it takes time to publish one article and you need to spend most of your time on writing, not on collecting new data when you are new to the job! From my own experience and from the experiences of friends and colleagues, I've come to the conclusion that if you do start a new project, it should be linked to your dissertation—otherwise you won't have time to get fully up to speed on the relevant literature, methods, and so on and to publish things in time for your tenure review.

Diversify with a Focus

Since most institutions, especially research-intensive universities, require both quality (publications in top-tier journals) and quantity (for example, some institutions require a minimum of 12 publications, which means about two or three publications per year) to grant tenure, it is important that you complete sufficient numbers of publications within five to six years. One of the first suggestions for increasing your chances of getting published and ensuring quality and quantity is to diversify the venues and types of your publications. This means you must have a few articles in the pipeline and know different journal rankings in your field. Submit the articles about your major findings or the articles you are confident about to top-tier journals and others to second-tier journals. Top-tier journals have higher rejection rates, but they provide very good feedback on your paper. Take these comments seriously. If you receive a decision other than rejection, revise following the suggestions and comments and send it back to the journal as soon as you can. Some editors (e.g., Levy & Schlomowitsch, n.d.) suggest not to let the manuscript sit more than a month before resubmission. If you receive a rejection, still consider revision and send it to another journal. Depending on the revision, if you address the issues adequately, you can resubmit it to another top-tier journal. If you feel that the chance of getting published in a top-tier journal is low and you are in a time crunch, send it to a second-tier or middle-ranking journals. The same strategy applies to the papers you submit to second-tier journals.

Though it is important to diversify, it is also important to stay focused in terms of building a portfolio of your work and making a name in a particular field of study or area of research. For example, I published many articles in different journals and edited books as well as numerous books. A consistent theme of my research is home literacy and second language learning. This theme is my "identity" to my colleagues in the field. If researchers in the field think of me, they think of me as an expert in second language learners' family literacy and family and school partnerships. You want to stay focused so that you can develop a professional identity. This is especially important for graduate students and beginning scholars. If the topics of your publications vary very widely and there is no unified theme, you may find it difficult to position yourself and claim one area as your expertise during the job search.

Pay Attention to the Timeline of Your Papers

Since you have to attend to both quality and quantity issues of your publications, you need to be mindful of the timeline of each publication. As mentioned earlier, the review process usually takes about three to four months. Say it takes you two to three months to write the paper, and then another three to four months to be reviewed. After you receive the reviews, you will spend about one to two months to revise it. Depending on the extent of revision, your paper may need to go through another round of review, which takes another three to four months, and then if your paper gets accepted, you may still have to do some minor changes. Once it is accepted (that is, in press), it will take a few months (or longer) to be printed, as the manuscript has to be copyedited, typeset, and then proofed by the authors. Since the process of publishing one paper may take up to a full year or longer, it is critical that you are mindful about the timeline of your papers that are in the pipeline. Sometimes, if you really need to have some publications out fast, you may choose to send your strong manuscript to a middle-ranking journal to speed up the process. Once you have some publications accepted or in press, you can spend more time on other pieces and aim for top tier journals.

If you have several papers under review, it might be worthwhile to start a time log to manage the process. Most journals now have online manuscript submission processes, and you can track your paper status online. The editor or the manuscript system will send an acknowledgment of receipt once you submit the papers. Along with the acknowledgement, the editor will tell you about the review process and the timeline. It is important for you to follow up with the editor about the status of your paper once the review deadline has passed and you have not heard from the editor yet. I had a couple of bad experiences as a result of not following up. On one occasion, the original editor got sick and there was a change of editorial team while she was on leave. During the transition, my manuscript was forgotten—for a long time. When I finally realized that something was wrong, almost half a year had passed. I contacted the editors (old and new) and finally received the reviews—a year later. Worse yet, the previous editor liked my piece and provided really positive comments before she left the editorship. However, the new editor did not share her views, and as a result, I did not receive a favorable decision. After this experience, I realized that I could not afford to wait for another round of review with this journal, so I decided to submit the piece to another journal and it was accepted with very minor revision.

So, as my experience above indicates, sometimes you can consider resubmitting your manuscript to another journal without revision, though this is not recommended if your paper has major problems. The benefit of resubmission without revision is that it allows you more time to work on other papers and projects. If you anticipate that you will have very little time to revise the paper within the next three to four months, it is a good idea to resubmit it to another journal.

Use Conference Presentations to Get Feedback and Finish Drafts of Papers

As faculty members, we all attend conferences. Conferences are a good place for professional social networking and for professional learning. One good way to make conferences more productive professionally is use them as a venue to get feedback from session attendees, chairs, discussants or fellow presenters. Though not all conferences require a fully completed paper, it is still beneficial to finish a draft of your paper. Use conference deadlines as incentives to finish a draft of your paper. Send it to your session chair or discussant or an interested colleague to solicit feedback. Take note of audience feedback and questions when you present and try to incorporate those that you think can improve your paper. Conversely, if you have finished a paper, sometimes it is a good idea to present it at a conference first to get feedback. Sometimes, the conference organizers or editors will solicit papers presented for the conference preceding for an edited book, which is another important outlet to publish your work!

Have Your Work Copyedited

For second language professionals writing in a second language, some language errors are unavoidable. While language quality is not the most important thing that makes a strong manuscript, it is a very important aspect. Manuscripts laden with language errors often distract reviewers and editors from understanding or attending to the content of your paper, hence reducing the chance of acceptance for publication. Several studies on manuscript review processes have found that writing quality plays an important role in reviewers' recommendations and editors' decisions on articles submitted. Coates, Sturgeon, Bohannan, and Pasini (2002) surveyed language errors in 120 medical manuscripts submitted during 1999 and 2000 and found that carelessly written articles often "either had a direct or subliminal influence on whether a paper was accepted or rejected" noting that "on equal scientific merit, a badly written article will have less chance of being accepted" (p. 279). Similarly, after an analysis of 706 manuscripts submitted to *Psychology Bulletin* from 1996 to 2001, Eisenberg, Thompson, Augir, and Stanley (2002) found that the technical quality of a paper is the second most important factor (following strength and clarity of the argument) associated with acceptance. These studies suggest that you must pay attention to language and mechanics before submitting your manuscript to increase the chance of getting published.

There are several ways to help with this—you can ask a close colleague, friend or family member who is willing to help. Make sure you find ways to reciprocate the favor (e.g., taking him or her out for dinner), as it takes hours to read and edit a paper! You can also pay a professional editor to do the editing for you. Levy & Schlomowitsch (n.d.) recommend that whoever you find, it is important that the person understand the content of your paper or have some experience in your area.

FINAL ADVICE: WRITE, WRITE AND WRITE!

Finally, in order to have a sufficient number of publications in the pipeline and to improve your writing skills, you need to keep on writing. One of the biggest challenges beginning scholars face is finding time to write amidst a myriad of teaching, research, and service responsibilities. Here are a few tips to ensure you engage in more writing.

- *Have a writing plan.* Make a short-term and long-term plan on the articles you plan to write. Give yourself a rough timeline for each article. Keep a log (together with the timeline log I suggest earlier). The log helps you track the progress of your writing and helps you stay focused. With an individual piece of writing, I often divide it into several smaller sections so that I can complete one section at a time and not feel overwhelmed.
- *Ensure big blocks of writing time.* Writing takes time and concentration. Try to block a long enough period of time for writing every week (e.g., one day or a couple of mornings or afternoons). Also, it is important for you to figure out when you write best and arrange time accordingly. For example, I write better in the morning and am not so productive in early afternoons, so I try to get most of my serious writing done in the morning but leave other, less demanding tasks to the afternoon. Cluster your appointments so that you can protect your writing time. Every time you leave your writing session, make sure you note down what to do next to help you get right back into the writing.
- *Make good use of small chunks of time.* Sometimes it is not possible to block a long period of time for writing. In this case, you need to make the best use of the small chunks of time available. I often use a to-do list, assess the time needed for each item, and then do it according to the time I have. That is, I do the items or parts of an article that require least time when I only have small chunks of time. This way, I get small things accomplished easily and make space for bigger chunks of time for serious writing.
- *Find alternative ways to keep engaged in writing.* There are many alternative ways to help you keep on writing. For example, you can join or form a writing group with other junior faculty members. This kind of support group can be helpful to move you along with writing. Another way is to have a writing retreat—go somewhere reclusive (such as camping, or lakeside resort). You can do it alone or with some writing buddies. This is a wonderful opportunity to form or strengthen friendships and get writing done!

RESOURCES

Belcher D. & Connor, U. (Eds.). (2001). *Reflections on multiliterate lives.* Clevedon, UK: Multilingual Matters.

Casanave, C. P. & Li, X. (2008). *Learning the literacy practices of graduate school: Insiders' reflections on academic enculturation.* Ann Arbor, MI: University of Michigan Press.

Casanave, C. P. & Vandrick, S. (Eds.). (2003). *Writing for scholarly publication: Behind the scenes in language education.* Mahwah, NJ: Lawrence Erlbaum Associates.

REFERENCES

Bowen, G. A. (2010). From qualitative dissertation to quality articles: Seven lessons learned. *The Qualitative Report, 15*(4), 864–879.

Coates, R., Sturgeon, B., Bohannan, J., & Pasini, E. (2002). Language and publication in "Cardiovascular Research" articles. *Cardiovascular Research, 53*(2), 279–285.

Eisenberg, N., Thompson, M. S., Augir, S., & Stanley, E. H. (2002). "Getting in" revisited: An analysis of manuscript characteristics, reviewers' ratings, and acceptance of manuscripts in *Psychological Bulletin. Psychological Bulletin, 128*(6), 997–1004.

Levy, D. & Schlomowitsch, M. (n.d.). *Special report: How to get published.* Retrieved from http://www.law.upenn.edu/cpp/alumni/jobseekers/GetPublishedSpecialReportACADEMICWORD.pdf

CHAPTER 14

INVOLVEMENT IN LEADERSHIP ROLES IN PROFESSIONAL ORGANIZATIONS

Shelley Wong
George Mason University

The first time I ran for a leadership position in an international professional association, I ran on an advocacy platform—as an outsider. The impetus for putting my name on the ballot was a sociopolitical concerns column I read in the association newsletter by Professor Robert Kaplan, one of the leaders in the field of Teaching English to Speakers of Other Languages (TESOL). Robert Kaplan wrote that he had always thought that TESOL (now known as TESOL International Association) was a professional association, not a political organization, but that he had been wrong. He argued that TESOL needed to be both a professional and a political association. What struck me about this article was the author's honesty, and his courage to say publicly that he had been wrong. He wasn't afraid of sharing his insights about why he had changed his position—and by so doing was even a stronger advocate for our profession, the students, and the communities we serve.

Demystifying Career Paths after Graduate School, pages 163–176
Copyright © 2012 by Information Age Publishing

Like Bob Kaplan, I felt strongly that TESOL needed to be an advocate for English as a Second Language (ESL) programs for immigrant communities. I had experienced first-hand teaching in a high school in which there were not enough classrooms for ESL students, and I taught some classes in a trailer, one class in the teacher's lounge, and one class in the auditorium foyer. I was so inspired by this article that I decided that TESOL was the kind of organization I wanted to be more involved with, and I decided to become a candidate for election to the board of directors.

This chapter will discuss challenges, strategies, advantages, and successes of assuming leadership roles in professional and scholarly associations such as TESOL (Teachers of English to Speakers of Other Languages), NABE (the National Association for Bilingual Education), NAME (the National Association for Multicultural Education), ISLS (the International Society for Language Studies), AAAL (the American Association of Applied Linguistics), and AERA (the American Educational Research Association). Being a leader in professional associations affords you the opportunity to become a stronger advocate for your profession as well as the students and families you serve. Through policy statements and educational research initiatives, professional associations can advise and work closely with national, provincial or state, and local departments of education as well as governmental and private agencies that develop educational and public policies.

DESCRIPTION OF THE SYSTEM, CULTURE, AND EXPECTATIONS

Participating in a Professional Organization

How can you get involved in leadership positions? How do you go from being in the audience at a conference to being part of the conference program and an active leader in the association? How do you move from being an outsider to becoming an officer or president of a professional association? You might say, "I'm just beginning! How can a graduate student or early-career professional eventually take a leadership role with established professors who have been in the field for years?" Involvement and becoming a leader in professional associations is one of the best ways for non-native English speakers (NNES) and people of color to learn about their field of study as a community of scholars. But first, you need to participate in an organization by attending its conferences.

Active participation in conferences held by those associations enables you to actually *experience* the discourse, and to learn by *doing* (Wong, 2005). Attending conferences affords new scholars the opportunity to interact with internationally known experts in the field, learn about the latest research, and participate in the latest debates in the field. Many of the key authors of the books and articles you have studied in your graduate program will be discussing and debating the latest issues in the field at the conferences. In addition, going to conferences is a way to meet others who are working on the same issues that you are working on in your area of specialization.

Oftentimes, our research interests are so narrow and specialized that we cannot find anyone at our own institution who shares our interests. You may feel isolated and lack perspective. The chances are that by attending a large convention with 10,000 participants from all over the world, you will be able to find others who can share bibliographies with you and recommend articles and books of others who have done similar work. Developing expertise and defining your research interests can be accomplished through establishing relationships with others. Often when you read a published piece of research, the work in a journal article seems so objective and definitive—so polished and authoritative. You may wonder about the story behind the article—the kinds of struggles that the authors encountered to get the piece published. Conferences are a way for you to see these scholars' works in progress, to learn about the ethical challenges and dilemmas they encountered in conducting their research, and to understand how they developed their research tools—in other words, the "how," not only the "what" of their research. Through participating in conferences, you can develop your profile as a researcher, which is a fundamental qualification for assuming leadership in a given organization. Then, what is the process of becoming a leader? In order to understand the process, we need to know the system of a professional organization.

Organizational Structure and Getting Involved

Non-profit educational and scholarly societies or organizations are typically governed by a board of directors or a governing board who are elected by the membership of the association. For a small local organization, the election process for officers could take place at a business meeting, with nominations for the slate of candidates taken from the floor. But in a large national or international association, there is usually a nominating committee to ensure that the candidates for office reflect the geographical base and diverse areas of interest of the association. Those who seek to be candidates for leadership positions on the governing or executive board are usually vetted by a nominating committee. Most non-profit academic associations in the United States have a constitution, bylaws, or standing rules that state the duties and responsibilities of the officers. Following parliamentary procedures, Robert's Rules of Order are used to conduct board meetings, and decisions that were made are recorded in the minutes of the meetings.

Duties of leaders in professional organizations can be found in by-laws or standing rules, but the best way to find out about the organizational culture is to attend membership meetings at a conference or special event, as well as to volunteer. As you assist with the work of a committee or publication, don't be afraid to ask questions and show your willingness to do what is needed to get a job done well. If you are willing to help out for the good of the organization (whether selling raffle tickets or helping with a website or newsletter), people will ask you to volunteer for other duties and to assume more responsibilities.

Consider volunteering in a conference organizing committee as a first step towards becoming an "insider"—participation in tasks such as registration, meeting speakers at the airport, and contacting publishers and sponsors will all enable you to participate and support the organization. From the ground up you will meet people and start networking by volunteering.

Another volunteer opportunity is to get involved in a Special Interest Group (SIG). Participation in a SIG is a way to meet with a smaller group of like-minded people. Some associations allow you to join more than one SIG without a charge. Others charge a fee for each SIG you join. Typically you vote in only one division or SIG. Consider attending a SIG business meeting at a conference and volunteer to submit articles to SIG newsletters. At any conference or convention, there are business meetings of the entire organization as well as business meetings of the entities or structures within the organization. While newsletter articles are not "valued" for promotion and tenure at research universities, they do count as service and they enable you to develop your voice as an advocate and a member of the profession. They also allow you to gain visibility in the SIG. Many professional associations have apprentice systems that enable you to "shadow" the leader in a different capacity (whether as chair-elect, treasurer, or representative to the assembly or council). Volunteering to be a reviewer of proposals for conference presentations is yet another way to get first-hand experience and to gain the knowledge of what makes for a successful proposal within a particular association.

While we see more and more newcomers being active in professional associations, it is never too late to get involved. Throughout your career, you will be introduced to many different gatherings—big and small—and opportunities to choose which one(s) to invest your energies in and contribute your talents to. TESOL, for example, has graduate forums for master's and Ph.D. students as well as orientations for first-time attendees. Most associations have reduced fees for membership and conference registration for graduate students, and some have incentives for early-career professionals because they want to attract a new generation of members.

How to Find the Right Organization to Join

How do you find the "right" association to attend, given limited time and money? Consider participating in at least two (optimally three) of the following levels of organization: local, state or provincial, regional, national, and international. Consider attending a large national or international conference (for example, with 10,000 attendees) and smaller conferences. The large conferences will provide an incredible variety of presentations and publishers' exhibitions with a dazzling range of publications and multimedia resources. Small conferences often give you opportunities to interact in depth with leading experts in the field.

Look up on the Internet the authors and researchers you admire and find out where they have presented recently. Ask other professors, colleagues, and advisors whose work you respect which conferences they attend. And within each conference, pay attention to which division or SIG they present in and are involved in as officers.

It is not always easy to ascertain which conferences and venues are most valued in your institution, as different colleagues have different opinions about what associations are the best. For example, because I work as a teacher educator in a college of education, the American Educational Research Association is considered to be an important conference. Because there are different fields of study and specializations within any department, it is always important to seek advice from your mentors so that you can best present your work to others. Remember that you are ultimately your own best advocate to explain to other colleagues why attending and presenting at a particular conference demonstrates your growth as a scholar and professional.

Running for Office

After you have accumulated some experience, consider running for an elected position (e.g., SIG chair, committee chair, officer of the executive board) within the organization. Although each association has its own requirements, the ballot generally includes a statement of a candidate's vision for the association, key publications, and previous committee work.

In large associations, there are different ways to be elected to leadership positions. Sometimes there is a business meeting in which there is a call for nominations for officers of the division or committee. There may be an announcement in the association newsletter from the nominating committee requesting candidates to submit a statement of interest. If nominations for a position are made during a face-to-face meeting, being nominated by someone who is a respected leader is helpful. In some associations, who nominates you is important. Don't be afraid to ask a colleague to nominate you before the meeting.

When I first ran for the board of directors of TESOL, I wrote a statement of interest for the ballot that emphasized my desire to see the association be more involved in sociopolitical concerns and advocacy. While the other candidates I ran against had a longer resume of service to the profession, my vision statement for social change that involved immigrant communities was certainly perceived to be stronger. After serving on the board of directors, I continued my service through the interest section and committees of the association. By the time I ran for president, I had had experience as a leader in many of the structural entities, including standing committees whose leadership is appointed by the president, as well as elected positions such as chair of the Teacher Education Interest Section.

Assuming Responsibilities as a Leader

Once you get elected to be the president of an organization, there are numerous tasks you must engage in. First, you are a public spokesperson for the association. This involves writing presidential messages in newsletters, recording podcasts for the webpage, and representing the association at research symposiums, affiliate conferences, and meetings with other associations. Being a spokesperson for the association may involve meeting with departments of education at the federal or state or provincial levels.

Second, as an officer you have fiduciary responsibility to protect the nonprofit, tax-exempt status of the association and its assets. This will generally include legal and financial oversight and fundraising. As the past president of TESOL, I served on the finance committee, which worked with the association staff on the budget and met with auditors, investment consultants, and attorneys.

Third, you are responsible for chairing meetings. This includes preparing agendas and budgets for the board meetings and the annual open business meetings of the membership of the association. Officers of TESOL (or the executive committee, which is smaller than the full governing board) are entrusted with implementing the decisions of the board of directors or governing board in between board meetings and communicating with the board. The meetings of the board of directors and the annual business meetings of the membership follow Robert's Rules of Order. Learning how to run meetings is another challenge of leadership. In large associations, meetings can be contentious.

Fourth, you are responsible for personnel decisions, including appointing search committees. During my tenure on the executive committee and board of directors, we were responsible for appointing search committees for the selection of journal editors and a new executive director.

Finally, you are responsible to listen to the membership and to translate their aspirations, needs, and visions into concrete programs and initiatives. Most associations engage in strategic planning processes to ensure long-term planning and successful implementation to help the organization meet its goals (Christison & Murray, 2008).

Benefits of Being Involved and Taking a Leadership Role

There are several benefits for getting involved in a professional organization. First, it provides you with a deeper understanding of the close interconnections between local issues and global processes. A slogan from the 1960s is "Think globally; act locally." You can only truly understand your local situation when you meet others who are doing similar work in other parts of the world. The networks of colleagues you develop through your membership and service in professional and scholarly organizations will provide scope and perspective to your work. For example, if you serve on a newsletter committee, you will reach out to solicit articles from members at many different institutions and from different geographical locations. If you work on a sociopolitical affairs committee, you may be learning about issues of concern within your region or internationally. Through this kind of service, you may realize that you are not alone, but through participating in a professional association you are acting with other professionals to be part of the solution addressing a systemic problem.

Second, the global connection allows you to find your professional and intellectual home. As a beginning NNES professional or a scholar of color, you may find that your workplace or home institution is actually not a place where you feel "at home." Finding a home in a professional or scholarly association allows you to seek out allies and like-minded colleagues and to view your local projects as part of larger issues within the field. It affords a site for you to hone your skills in research, presentations, and publications, while engaging in professional development and advocacy.

Third, you can disseminate the knowledge and experience you have gained through a conference to your colleagues after returning home. For example, you can report on what you learned (e.g., the latest research, debates, techniques) in the form of a newsletter article or a presentation at your own institution or a local affiliate. You will be able to apply what you have learned from other colleagues from diverse localities and contexts to initiate projects at your home institution and the local communities you serve.

Fourth, perhaps most importantly, your participation in leadership and advocacy can enhance diversity within the association. By participating in business meetings you can make suggestions about the theme or invited speakers for the next conference to make it more inclusive and to reflect more diverse perspectives. You can work toward increasing participation from communities that have traditionally been excluded from the association.

CHALLENGES AND STRATEGIES FOR SUCCESS

Public Speaking

My involvement with my professional association eventually led me to the presidency. One of the greatest challenges I faced as TESOL president was public speaking. You may be surprised to hear that a native speaker of English would be afraid of public speaking in English. It is a myth that being a native speaker makes you a good public speaker. Public speaking, like other components of leadership, is a skill that can be learned (Coombe, England & Schmidt, 2008). I remember when I was president-elect, sitting in the audience listening to President Jun Liu deliver a dynamic plenary speech. I wondered to myself, "How would I ever give a plenary in front of several thousand people in the audience?"

I was not accustomed to teaching large lecture classes, nor had I spoken to large audiences outside of the United States. My first opportunity to speak to an affiliate outside of the United States occurred when I was asked to go to Panama to stand in for a board member, John Schmidt. John became my mentor. He introduced me to Toastmasters, an international organization for public speaking. There are Toastmasters clubs in locations throughout the world. I highly recommend that you attend a session to see what opportunities it may afford you (or your students). I did not have the time to attend weekly meetings but found that three visits provided me with some valuable insights and tools for public speaking.

The major lesson I learned from John was the importance of storytelling. Storytelling enables you to connect with your audience. People can more readily remember the content of your presentation if you tell a story to "hook" your point. A story can make abstract principles come to life. He summarized the principle as follows: "Tell a story and then make a point. Or make a point and then tell a story."

Some of us will never get over our stage fright. And while some of us will never be great public speakers, we can all become more effective speakers. Improvement in public speaking is a process, just like everything else in life. And all discourse conventions—such as chairing a meeting, speaking before audiences, and communicating effectively in professional organizations—can be learned. I have learned to write a script for my plenary speeches. By writing out a script, I am less apt to ramble and can be more economical with my words. However, there will always be times when you are called on to speak extemporaneously without a script. I remember that I was told just before I went up to the stage that the person who was supposed to present an award could not be there. Fortunately, I was familiar with the work of the awardee and was able to speak from the heart about his contributions. Although my remarks were not as eloquent or polished as a written text, my sincerity came through in my impromptu remarks. In these cases, trust yourself and speak from the heart.

Your experience in conference presentations can become a foundation for your public speaking skills. Utilize your strengths in doing presentations. Work with what you know best. What is your expertise? Technology? Special Education? Are you strong in math, business, or music? Consider crossing the practitioner-researcher divide to utilize your expertise in one area to develop strengths in another. Think about all the areas in which you are an "expert."

Respecting Diverse Opinions While Holding on to Your Vision as a Leader

A common challenge in working in large associations and organizations is how to respect diverse opinions while holding on to your vision as a leader. One strategy to deal with this challenge is to develop a model for consensus that takes into account diverse perspectives. If you have a vision of leadership that is transformative and aligned with critical social analyses, there is so much work to be done. But where do you start? Although you recognize so many burning issues of social injustice that you would like to address, your term of office and your resources are limited. An issue that is important to you may not be a burning issue for everyone. Focus on one or two important projects to work on and carry them out to the end. I selected two major issues to address: peace and immigration. TESOL has held a number of peace forums through the years. In my presidential year I convened a Cultures of Peace conference, which addressed peace from diverse perspectives such as using drama, addressing bullying and efforts at peacemaking in a Palestinian interfaith elementary school in Bethlehem. The conference program featured conflict resolution in elementary, middle and high school, higher education, and adult school contexts.

A second issue that I focused on was rights for immigrant students. The TESOL President's Award was presented to the UCLA student group IDEAS (Improving Dreams, Equality, Access and Success), which advocates for passage of the DREAM (Development, Relief, and Education for Alien Minors)

Act, legislation that would allow undocumented students who were brought to the United States as children and graduated from U.S. high schools a pathway to citizenship (Wong, Shadduck-Hernández, Inzunza, Monroe, Narro, & Valenzuela, 2012). Many of these students have grown up in the United States and yet are not allowed to work or receive scholarships to go to college. Without a way to legalize their status, they are in danger of being deported and forced to work in the underground economy. Professional organizations can provide legitimacy to the claims of those who are the most marginalized. Through their publications and meetings, they can put forth research reports and policy recommendations to create spaces for advocacy in otherwise hostile environments.

Giving Voice to Marginalized Groups

People from non-European cultural perspectives, scholars of color, and others who are engaged in changing mainstream-dominant institutions in the United States often find it difficult to understand and relate to the systems and structures of the institution. This is because its institutional practices may be foreign to their cultural understanding of how systems operate and are managed. In order to make a professional association a transformative site for change, it is necessary to solicit individual concerns and needs and to involve as many members as possible in raising awareness about social justice issues.

Institutions can change only when the members have information about how to get involved, and underrepresented voices have access to information and opportunities to serve on committees, boards, and agencies. It is often said that knowledge is power. An important strategy is to share information with others about different opportunities for leadership and involvement. Don't forget to give encouragement to new leaders and to acknowledge the little victories—it could take the form of a telephone call or a note or e-mail message (Bailey, 2008). By acknowledging and calling attention to the newer voices for change, you are providing them with institutional support to become stronger leaders. They will become more involved and take ownership of the change if they can see that their own work joins that of others, which would create a snowballing effect to transform the professional organization as a whole.

Encouraging People to Become Leaders

How do you get more people involved? Leaders of professional associations are volunteers and have family and professional responsibilities daily.

We can all serve as mentors to support and encourage people. Give them opportunities. Ownership and consensus around an organizational change process is crucial to help people become aware of their abilities to change as well as uncover the realities that the organization will offer for resistance. Organizations are similar to organisms in that comprised of people they need fresh air, movement, and nourishment to thrive and be vibrant.

SUMMARY AND FINAL ADVICE

- *Learn the institutional structure and its governing rules.* Attend the business meetings of the association. Who are the "movers and shakers?" Identify the stakeholders and power makers. Within every organization there are different cultures and rules for getting on the program, getting articles published, getting a resolution through, airing issues of concern, and developing policies and initiatives.
- *Seek out mentors who can help you navigate various parts of the system.* Look for mentors who know the bylaws and standing rules of the association, and learn these rules yourself by proposing a resolution or policy statement. How are policy statements developed? How are resolutions passed? Don't be afraid to ask questions and challenge the institution constructively. Don't be afraid to think outside of the circle.
- *Don't take things personally.* This is easier said than done. Being in a leadership position at the top can be lonely and stressful. You may be attacked or outnumbered. Don't internalize the abuse. A corollary to "don't take things personally" is to not take yourself too seriously. Remember that you are only one drop in the ocean, as Gertrude Tinker Sachs, the TESOL convention chair during my presidential year, often reminded me. For every success in the struggle for justice, there are many sacrifices and defeats. Remember, the struggle for inclusion and social justice is a protracted one and it takes many contributions from many people. Be strategic. And remember that you are not alone. This is why it is especially important to find allies and to develop a "kitchen cabinet"—a few trusted, unofficial advisors who can give you a broader perspective.
- *Self-care is important: exercise, diet and sleep.* Physical health is related to mental health, spiritual health, and balance. (See Chapter 17, Balancing Professional and Personal Life). Make sure that you have time to rest and reflect. Try to achieve balance by looking for good in bad situations. And remember that while there are so many tasks crying out to be done, doing a few things well is a more powerful legacy than trying to do everything.

- *Utilize your positions of power to create new spaces for historically excluded voices and to plant seeds for change.* Look for opportunities that reflect your own special identities and the causes you support or believe in. This may take the form of a special workshop, task force meeting, or hearing on an area of social justice that has not received sufficient attention. For example, AERA held a research workshop on lesbian, gay, bisexual, transgender and queer (LGBTQ) issues in Education. AERA is a large association of thousands of members, but by convening this special workshop, a small group of people was able to identify relevant research, assess gaps, and consider opportunities and challenges in building a future research agenda. Special task forces and caucuses have been utilized by women, scholars of color, NNES professionals, and other oppressed and historically underrepresented populations in various associations to "make a difference in expanding knowledge, raising awareness, and building a more robust base of educational and social indicators, which can contribute to addressing or ameliorating beliefs or behaviors grounded in bigotry or bias" (Levine, 2010, p. 601).

RESOURCES

American Association for Applied Linguistics (AAAL)
  http://www.aaal.org

American Council on the Teaching of Foreign Languages (ACTFL)
  http://www.actfl.org

American Educational Research Association (AERA)
  http://www.aera.net/

American Psychological Association (APA)
  http://www.apa.org

Association Internatinale de Linguistique Appliquée/International Association of Applied Linguistics (AILA)
  http://www.aila.info/

Dialogue Under Occupation (DUO)
  http://dialogueunderoccupation.org/

International Association of Teachers of English as a Foreign Language (IATEFL)
  http://www.iatefl.org/

International Reading Association (IRA)
http://www.reading.org

International Society for Language Studies, Inc. (ISLS)
http://www.isls.co

Modern Language Association (MLA)
http://www.mla.org

National Association of Bilingual Education (NABE)
http://www.nabe.org

National Association for Multicultural Education (NAME)
http://www.nameorg.org

National Council of Teachers of English (NCTE)
http://www.ncte.org

TESOL International Association
http://www.tesol.org

UCLA Improving Dreams, Equality, Access and Success (IDEAS)
http://ideasla.org/index/

ACKNOWLEDGEMENTS

With appreciation to Mary Romney, Ryuko Kubota, Yilin Sun, and Maryam Saroughi.

REFERENCES

Bailey, K. (2008). Passing on the light: Encouragement as a leadership skill. In C. Coombe, M. L. McCloskey, L, Stephenson, & N. J. Anderson (Eds.), *Leadership in English language teaching and learning* (pp. 29–37). Ann Arbor, MI: University of Michigan Press.

Christison, M. A. & Murray, D. (2008). Strategic planning for English language teachers and leaders. In C. Coombe, M. L. McCloskey, L. Stephenson, & N. J. Anderson (Eds.), *Leadership in English language teaching and learning* (pp. 128–140). Ann Arbor, MI: University of Michigan Press.

Coombe, C., England, L., & Schmidt, J. (2008). Public speaking and presentation skills for ELT educators. In C. Coombe, M. L. McCloskey, L, Stephenson, & N. J. Anderson (Eds.), *Leadership in English language teaching and learning* (pp. 50–61). Ann Arbor, MI: University of Michigan Press.

Levine, F. (2010). AERA holds research workshop on LGBTQ issues in education. *Educational Researcher, 39*(8), 600–601.

Wong, K., Shadduck-Hernández, J., Inzunza, F., Monroe, J., Narro, V., & Valenzuela Jr., A. (Eds.) (2012). *Undocumented and unafraid: Tam Tran, Cinthya Felix, and the Immigrant Youth Movement.* Los Angeles, CA: UCLA Center for Labor Research and Education.

Wong, S. (2005). *Dialogic approaches to TESOL: Where the ginkgo tree grows.* New York, NY: Routledge.

CHAPTER 15

WORKING AS A
JOURNAL EDITOR

Suresh Canagarajah
Pennsylvania State University

When the chair of the search committee for *TESOL Quarterly* (*TQ*) asked me to consider applying for the position as editor, I didn't take her seriously. I knew that the position was open, but never gave thought to applying for it. Even after two decades in the language teaching profession, I still deviated idiomatically and grammatically from the privileged varieties of English. Though I knew all the sociolinguistic reasons why my Sri Lankan English was not ungrammatical or inferior, I was mindful of the fact that academic publishing was governed by what scholars call the Standard Written English (SWE). More importantly, I had always been a critic of the biases and inequalities in academic publishing. Journals seemed to give preference to Eurocentric research practices and genres of writing, and scholars from first language backgrounds dominated academic publishing.

However, the fact that the search committee considered me a possible candidate despite my controversial place in the profession suggested to me that some scholars were probably thinking outside the box. Perhaps they took my criticism seriously and wanted to see how publishing practices could be reformed. I had to ask myself if it was time to move from being a

Demystifying Career Paths after Graduate School, pages 177–189

critic to an agent of change. Could I be an advocate for the research and writing styles of professionals from diverse backgrounds, especially those who are multilingual and non-Western? Having published in the mainstream publishing circles and coming from the periphery (having started my teaching and scholarly career in Sri Lanka), I could be an effective mediator between both professional communities. Furthermore, being a multilingual, I was well positioned to work towards the acceptance of other languages and English varieties in publishing. Therefore, I put my hat into the ring, motivated by a vision of change.

I have now completed my term as the editor of *TQ* (2005–2009). This chapter is a reflection on the challenges and achievements during my editorship. I hope that the chapter will inspire other second language professionals to serve as editors in the diverse academic publishing venues we currently have in our field. I want to mainly focus on editing refereed "international" academic journals (such as *TQ, Modern Language Journal,* or *Applied Linguistics*), as they occupy an important place both in knowledge construction and institutional evaluation. There are implications for editing other types of academic journals. For example, there are regional journals (focusing on research and themes related to a specific geographical areas, such as *Language Education in Asia* or the *Journal of Asia TEFL*), national journals (related to themes of relevance to a country, such as the *Indian Journal of Applied Linguistics*), and institutional journals (which encourage their students or faculty to apprentice into publishing, such as the *Texas Papers in Foreign Language Education,* published by the University of Texas at Austin). Though these journals are refereed and make a good contribution to knowledge dissemination, they don't enjoy the impact factor and prestige enjoyed by the international journals. There are also practitioner-based journals, such as *The Reading Teacher* or *Language Arts*, which focus on teaching concerns and may not insist on empirically-based research articles; and professional journals, which encourage sharing of classrooms reports, professional concerns, and policy issues, such as the *Council Chronicle* published by the National Council of Teachers of English. It is advisable for scholars to develop a repertoire of writing styles, and write for a range of journals in their profession.

The objective of this chapter is to outline the special mission, challenges, and opportunities for second language professionals in editing academic journals. I elicit lessons from my own experience that may help my colleagues in editing endeavors. Before doing that, I have to introduce the system and culture of refereed academic publishing.

DESCRIPTION OF SYSTEM AND CULTURE

The research article is by all accounts the archetypal genre of knowledge construction. One's research gains legitimacy and validity after going through the refereeing process and breaking into print. One's findings are not treated as "knowledge" until they get published in refereed academic journals. There are other pragmatic reasons why academic publishing is a high stakes activity for scholars. Because of its role in knowledge construction, one's tenure and promotion in universities are based on one's record of publishing in academic journals. There are also material rewards attached to publishing. Based on one's publishing record, one may get grants for further research or prestigious fellowships and scholarships. For all these reasons, academic publishing is becoming very competitive. It is not only the universities in the United States or Europe that adopt the "publish or perish" philosophy anymore. Countries such as China, Iran, Singapore, and Argentina are also requiring their faculty members to publish prolifically in journals with the highest impact factor in the West to earn their tenure and promotion.

The genre of writing and research practices favored by academic journals are shaped by the philosophy of modernity and the rise of empirical science. The research that is considered valid is that which is disciplined and rigorous, with systematically obtained data, employing high-budget instruments and procedures. In keeping with the positivistic values motivating these research practices, the genre that is preferred features the IMRD (i.e., Introduction, Method, Results, Discussion) structure. The genre simulates the inductive approach typical of empirical science. The article first outlines the basic assumptions and research questions motivating the research, then describes the methods employed to test these assumptions, and provides the data obtained, before offering an interpretation of the findings.

Second language professionals sometimes have problems with these research and writing practices for both cultural and material reasons. Materially, they don't have the time or resources for sustained research of this nature. Culturally, they have different traditions of knowledge construction. Many multilingual communities value more intuitive and personal modes of knowing, and suspect the objectivity of modernist science that encourages them to keep their feelings and values behind. Forms of informal observation and socially immersed ways of knowing find representation in narratives and personal reflections that qualify as knowledge. Second language scholars may also value rhetorically engaged, value-laden, and committed forms of writing, which might be perceived as biased in mainstream academic and publishing circles. There are other material reasons why their writing may diverge from the preferred genres of the publishing industry.

As they don't always have the latest publications, they may not frame their articles in ways that are relevant to the current conversations in the West.

More importantly, there are considerable tensions generated around the preferred language in the publishing industry. SWE is not the neutral variety as it is claimed to be. As second language professionals know very well, their own idiomatic uses, locally coined vocabulary, and creative grammatical structures are often treated as errors and their texts considered unedited by journal editors and reviewers. As I have personally experienced, any amount of editing will not take away our accents as they are influenced by localized usage and norms that go back many centuries in some of our communities. We are so steeped in our traditions of English usage that we are not always aware of the extent to which our norms are locally shaped. Though it is possible to get the help of native speaker colleagues or paid editors to suppress our accents, many of us don't like to do so. The peculiarities of our English are important for our voice and identity.

These differences can lead to profound consequences for knowledge production. As the voices (and research and knowledge) of second language professionals are inadequately represented in academic publications, the knowledge that shapes linguistics, education, second language teaching, and other fields is somewhat skewed. It is based on the experiences, research, and values of privileged scholars. As this knowledge often shapes policies, pedagogies, and teaching material, the one-sided knowledge construction leads to other unfortunate consequences. The policies and pedagogies may not relate to the communicative needs and interests of diverse student populations. This imbalance in knowledge production is detrimental for all of us in the profession. Even native speaker scholars have much to learn from the experiences and competencies of second language speakers, as they have to deal with language practices in a globalized world with plural cultures and discourses. For all these reasons and more, second language professionals have to consider editing as a service that they have to perform for the profession. They have to make their voices heard, help their colleagues publish their research, and engage with the publishing industry for reform.

Those who are motivated to help their colleagues break into publishing and open up spaces to democratize the publishing industry may be heartened to realize that the current academic climate and publishing culture are showing signs of change. There is a general backlash against the reductive positivistic values of knowledge-making. Many have begun to critique the limitations in the dominant research and writing practices. Rather than being a hindrance, our identity, values, feelings, and imagination enrich our research and findings. Also, knowledge is always local. Rather than attempting to eliminate the contextuality and contingency of our research, scholars are now acknowledging them openly. Along these lines, scholars are also realizing that there are alternate forms of research that convey knowledge. Modes of narrative research, self-reflexive inquiry, autoethnography, case studies, action research, and participatory research engage frankly with one's values and experiences for knowledge-making. As these forms of research gain validity, the genres of writing are also changing. People now realize that except in the case of experimental research, especially in the natural sciences, it is unwise to insist on the IMRD structure. Qualitative research practices are leading to creative new genres that authors need to discover in relation to their studies and objectives as they write. There is also a general sensitivity to the one-sided knowledge construction in the academy, as journals, professional associations, and publishing houses explore what can be done to provide spaces for more diverse voices. Demystifying the publishing process, mentoring authors from non-dominant settings, and providing greater access to publishing are efforts being undertaken now—efforts that second language professionals should take up.

DESCRIPTION OF EXPECTATIONS

Journal editors play a significant role in the gradual shift of academic discourses and publishing practices discussed above. How does one become an editor? Usually, journals issue a call for applications when the term of the current editor expires. Typically, a search committee consisting of leading scholars in the field handles the process. An application letter should highlight one's experiences in publishing, reviewing, and editing. It is possible that some may have edited a special topic issue or a book. Such experiences should be mentioned in the application letter. When the search committee has formed a short list, it may provide some tasks for candidates to assess their abilities. For *TQ,* candidates are asked to write a reviewer response for a sample submission, and then write an editorial decision letter based on that review. They are also asked to answer a questionnaire that seeks to understand their orientation to developments in the field, to writing, and to publishing. After these tasks, the search committee interviews the candidates. The search committee typically looks for a candidate who is a sound researcher, a good writer, a broadly informed scholar, and an effective manager of responsibilities, with a vision that addresses the critical needs of the discipline.

Once the selection is made, the candidate has to negotiate the necessary resources with his or her institution and the journal. The resources provided for editing are a well-kept secret, as publishers don't want to be pressured to offer more than they want to. The type of resources provided by publishers varies. Some commercial publishers are able to offer an editor an honorarium, funds for a course buy out, and also student/secretarial assistance. In the case of *TQ*, TESOL expects one's institution to match its support. TESOL provides funds for a single course buy-out, and expects one's institution to offer another. It provides an honorarium of $4,000 for a year, and expects one's institution to provide student support. These arrangements can vary depending on one's personal context. Some institutions are not willing to offer too much. I know of a candidate selected to edit *TQ* who couldn't take up his appointment as he couldn't get his university to provide the matching resources. One has to impress upon one's university administrators the importance of housing a prestigious journal in order to persuade them to contribute adequate resources. In these financially difficult times, some editors have to use their own resources earned as faculty members (i.e., their own graduate students and release time for research) in order to handle their editorial responsibilities.

Though editorship is treated as half-time appointment in many contexts, most editors find that it takes a lot of their time from personal research and even teaching. Many universities don't waive their expectations for research and publications when one is editing a journal. Therefore, it is important to continue one's typical academic routines when one edits a journal. One needs good time management skills and a strong sense of priorities in order to balance the editing responsibilities with the other institutional expectations. (See Chapter 17 for more on time management.) Training the student and administrative assistants well to manage the editorial office can help the editor spend time on the more important issues of reviewing, decision-making, and editing, and less on record keeping.

The editorial responsibilities are diverse. In the case of commercial publishers with more resources, some of these responsibilities can be shared with others. Here is a sample of the work involved:

1. Correspondence relating to submissions. One has to acknowledge receipt of manuscripts, seek reviewers for them, send reviewer comments and decisions, and answer queries relating to the journal.
2. Keeping records of different versions of a manuscript, multiple rounds of reviews for those manuscripts, and correspondence relating to them.
3. Sending articles for review. When a manuscript is received, it has to be checked for relevance to the journal and following the guidelines. Checking if authorial identity has been masked can take a lot of time. This is because self-references may have occurred unexpectedly, and it might still be possible to guess the author's identity despite names being removed. Once the manuscript is deemed to be relevant, the editor has to choose the best reviewers for the submission. Two or three reviewers are usually needed. Though all submissions that are relevant are usually sent out for review, recently

journals have become more discriminating, as they simply don't have the reviewers for all the submissions they receive. Reviewers also may complain that their valuable time is taken up with submissions that are not of a good quality. Some editors, therefore, adopt a more rigorous screening process, rejecting submissions that don't have a good chance of getting published.

4. When the referee reports are received, the editor has to read the feedback judiciously. The editor has to read the submission more closely once more to judge if the feedback is balanced. In case a split decision is reached, an additional reading by a fresh reviewer may be required.

5. In writing the decision letter, the editor has to highlight the most important points in the referee feedback. Though it is easy to arrive at a decision of outright rejection when both referees recommend it, in most cases the feedback is split. In such cases, the editor has to judge the significance of the contribution for the field in offering a chance to revise and resubmit. Typically, journals have the following categories of decisions: reject, revise and resubmit, accept with revisions, and accept. During my editorship, no article was accepted in the first round of reviews. In decision letters seeking revision, the editor has to give clear guidance on what changes are expected.

6. Once the submission is accepted, the editor still has to read the article closely to negotiate more specific changes with the author. These may involve issues of style, clarity, citations, organization, context, and copyright permissions. After these issues have been satisfactorily addressed, the editorial office sends the manuscript to the publishing office. In most cases, there are in-house copyeditors who check the manuscript more closely for the style conventions, clarity, and mechanics.

7. When the article goes to print, the editor oversees the proofreading. First, the individual articles have to be proofread with the involvement of the authors. Once the authors are satisfied with the final changes, the whole issue of the journal has to be proofread. After publication, the publishing or business office takes over the distribution and marketing of the journal.

8. Though the above is a perspective on what is involved in the day-to-day life of a journal editor, there are broader responsibilities as well. These include the following: appointing the members of the editorial board, negotiating policy with the publishers, relating to the concerns of readers and authors, and engaging proactively with the disciplinary changes. I will deal with these issues in my narrative on how I negotiated them as editor of *TQ* in the sections to follow.

CHALLENGES AND ACHIEVEMENTS

When I became the editor of *TQ*, I was interviewed by TESOL for my mission statement. Among other things, I provided the following as the objectives I wanted to accomplish during my editorship:

- I intend to help *TQ* keep up with changes in scholarly research practices. In many disciplines, research has become more participatory, reflexive, critical, and local. The research approaches in TESOL still largely follow the controlled, impersonal, and positivistic mode of traditional modernist inquiry. *TQ* has to present a wider range of research approaches.
- I intend to help the journal negotiate more boldly the diverse modes of representing research findings. In many journals, introspective or narrative writing sits side by side with the more impersonal articles reflecting the traditional introduction, methodology, results, discussion (IMRD) structure. I would like *TQ* to be more open to atypical forms of scholarly rhetoric.
- I also want to facilitate a more inclusive international conversation on mutual disciplinary interests. Linguists and teachers in places such as India, Singapore, South Africa, and the Middle East are developing interesting new orientations that fall outside the current paradigms in the profession. Their work gets published locally, if it gets published at all. I intend to be more proactive in accommodating the work of nontraditional researchers. I want to explore ways to mentor new authors, encourage referees to provide more constructive commentary to help these authors in the revision process, and increase *TQ*'s readership outside elite research and academic institutions.[1]

This is an idealistic statement. I knew that academic publishing conventions won't let me achieve many of these matters easily. In refereed publishing, the editor doesn't make decisions about the publishability of an article unilaterally. The assessment of the referees plays an important role in decision-making. Furthermore, articles cannot be solicited for publication by editors in such journals. Articles are submitted by authors. There is little room for the editor to push through genres and themes he or she likes, as articles go through an impersonal double-blind review (i.e., where the authors and referees don't know each other's identities) before publishing decisions are made.

There are other constraints an editor faces. New genres and research practices cannot be published too fast, as readers of the journal may not be acquainted with those to appreciate them. There may even be a backlash against the editor as the diversification of voices may create the accusation that standards are being lowered. If such an impression persists, the readership of the journal might decline, the impact factor go down, and prestige suffer. This is a disservice to the profession and to the authors who get published in the journal. If the knowledge represented in the journal is to shape the discipline in significant ways, the journal should not let the quality of the research represented and articles published decline. I wanted to be mindful of *TQ*'s traditions and practices as I initiated changes gradually.

There are also institutional constraints. An editor has to work within the expectations of the publisher or professional organization sponsoring the journal. The publisher has policies about the number of pages permitted for each issue. Though editors would like to expand the range of articles published (more sections for personal narratives and scholarly exchanges, for example), the publisher may not provide the space to do so. While editors usually have the freedom to publish the material they want, policies relating to price, pages, and distribution don't come under the editor's purview. Policies can also place ideological constraints that can limit editors in subtle ways. Often the publishing managers and/or professional organizations have already drawn the policy for the journal based on their objectives and mission. Though these are rarely blatantly discriminating, they can have subtle leanings in one direction or the other. *TQ*'s policy, for example, is published in the journal as follows: "*TESOL Quarterly's* mission is to foster inquiry into the teaching and learning of English to speakers of other languages by providing a forum for TESOL professionals to share their research findings and explore the ideas and relationships within second language teaching and learning." Since this focus on English and teaching practice is connected to the goals of the professional organization, they are hard to renegotiate. For example, though *TQ* can improve its impact factor by publishing more research articles in each issue, it cannot abandon the sections devoted to teaching issues or the Forum for professional reflections. Its commitment to pedagogical concerns cannot be compromised for the sake of research. For the same reason, all authors should make the pedagogical implications of their studies clear. Many good studies devoted to purely descriptive findings about linguistic structure, textual patterns or language acquisition cannot be published in *TQ* if their pedagogical implications are not made clear.

Within such constraints, one of the first and easiest changes I could undertake was to diversify the editorial board. Editors have the privilege of inviting scholars as board members. I tilted the balance of the board toward more representation to multilingual scholars from non-Western communities. Diversifying the editorial board is important for many reasons. The fact that board members evaluate manuscripts means that they will be able to understand the unconventional research or writing practices received from their own or related countries. They will be able to engage proactively with policy-making, helping initiate changes that are more relevant to diverse countries. They may also help provide access to the journal in their own countries, helping widen the readership among their students and colleagues. Participating in the inside workings of the journal, they may also develop the knowledge to mentor their students and colleagues more effectively for publishing. A broadened editorial board also ensures that atypical research and writing practices are identified for publication in the journal.

Since the members of the editorial board help make publishing decisions, the editor can do much to shape their reviewing practices. For example, *TQ* started carrying the following statement in its invitation to reviewers: "Although it is often appropriate to discuss the way the paper is written, we urge you to be mindful that many of our authors come from communities where World Englishes are spoken and may display different norms." Such a statement will alert reviewers to the diverse varieties they will see in the submissions and avoid disparaging remarks that damage the self-worth and motivation to publish for novice authors. The editor may have to intervene directly at times to educate reviewers or modify their comments for authors. Ironically, I found that some American reviewers treated the language and style of British authors as either unedited (because of their spelling system) or lacking rigor (because of their conversational writing style). I had to intervene and inform reviewers that these authors used a different spelling system and writing style that could be mistaken for being nonacademic.

Editors can also influence the quality of the feedback provided. Reviewer response is usually of two different kinds: judgmental or mentoring. The former would be very brief and direct, and convey the assessment of the referee on the publishability of the article. The latter offers more elaborate and constructive feedback on how the author may revise the submission for publication in this or any other journal. For novice authors, the latter kind of feedback is more useful. It takes a lot of effort on the part of reviewers to read manuscripts closely and offer detailed comments for improvement. I limited the reading load of board members and also recruited good scholars from outside the board to facilitate the writing of detailed mentoring reviews.

A more radical change I worked towards was to establish a mentoring program for nontraditional authors. This developed from a subcommittee set up to increase the voices of nonnative authors in the journal. I went on to use the services of members in this board for more extended mentoring help for nontraditional authors (defined more broadly to include also native speaker authors who may be off-networked in publishing). Since this assistance cannot be provided for everyone, as submissions to *TQ* are too numerous, I used my editorial discretion to recommend the submissions that were close enough to publishing with a bit more mentoring assistance. The revised articles were sent to a fresh round of double-blind review before a publishing decision was made, in order to avoid preferential treatment for these authors and prevent conflicts of interests.

Editors can make their own communication clear and helpful. Decision letters are not always easy to interpret. Often editors are caught between the twin needs of being collegial and judgmental that they end up with incoherent messages. This lack of clarity is compounded by the lack of experience novice authors have in interpreting decision letters. Many of us have abandoned manuscripts that could have been revised and resubmitted successfully, because we failed to understand the value editors and reviewers did see in an initially rejected manuscript. To make matters worse, some editors have to resort to using templates for decisions as there are simply too many submissions to write individual letters. During my editorship, I aimed towards personalized responses, helping authors understand the reviewers' assessment and offering suggestions on how to proceed with the submission. Even in cases where the submission had to be rejected outright without being sent out for review (as they were not relevant to our journal or didn't follow our guidelines), I tried to give those authors helpful information (such as enclosing a copy of *TQ*'s guidelines) as it was clear that these authors (mostly from outside the United States) had never read the journal. In some cases, I also offered suggestions about which journals might be considered by authors whose work didn't fit *TQ*. Editors can also make themselves open to consultation by authors. Often potential authors like to send their abstracts to get an opinion on the suitability of their work to the journal. They can save time by being redirected to more promising venues. Similarly, authors who have had their paper reviewed like to consult the editor on ways to navigate conflicting feedback. Though editorial policy on offering such advice varies, there is nothing to prevent editors from making themselves open to consultation without compromising their objectivity and impartiality.

The editor does have some leeway to shepherd unconventional genres and research approaches into publication. In cases where reviewers may waver about an unconventional submission, editors have the power to make the final decision and lean towards publication. Rarely does a submission receive a unanimous assessment by reviewers on whether they should be accepted or rejected. Besides, in leading journals such as *TQ*, no submission is accepted on the first round of reviews. Every submission goes through significant revisions before publication. In such a context, the editor can identify the types of research and genres that are gaining importance in the field and nudge them towards publication. Another area for direct intervention is through decisions on special topic issues. In this case, the editor has the prerogative to identify topics that need more prominence in the field, and invite guest editors to shape these issues. I sponsored special issues on topics such as race, migration, and narrative research, which deserved more attention in our field.

Editors can also intervene in policy in limited ways to make meaningful changes. In *TQ*, I lobbied hard for open access to the journal. It was clear that in order to get more non-native voices the journal had to be made available to a more diverse readership, especially to practitioners and scholars outside the United States who cannot afford the journal. Many journals are now freely available on the Internet. However, some publishers fear that such a facility may limit the revenue they earn through sales. During my editorship, TESOL agreed to an arrangement with *Journal Storage* (JSTOR) to post *TQ* with a five-year moving wall (i.e., issues are posted only after the fifth year of their publication, allowing people to subscribe to the journal or buy articles from *Ingenta* if they wanted them before that point).

In retrospect, though many see improvements in the diversity of voices and research practices represented in the journal, *TQ*'s rigor and selectivity haven't suffered. In fact the acceptance rate went down from 8.5% to 5% during my editorship. This suggests that I was fairly successful in maintaining the balance between the old and the new, initiating gradual changes that didn't violate the journal's traditions and status.

SUMMARY AND FINAL ADVICE

What can those second language professionals who are interested in academic editing do to prepare themselves for this service?

- *Break into the publishing world first.* It is not possible to understand how publishing works without publishing yourself. There is no handbook that can fully explain all the strategies, practices, and conventions in publishing. It is by doing it that one can learn the variations in diverse academic disciplines and journals. There is also much to learn about the complexities of negotiating the different parties involved in the publishing process.
- *Volunteer to serve as a reviewer.* Journals are always short of reviewers. As submissions are increasing for all journals, with academic institutions insisting on publications from their faculty, editors are looking for more reviewers. However, editors normally invite reviewers from among those who have already published in their or related journals.
- *Serve on editorial boards.* Scholars sometimes decline to serve as reviewers or board members as they feel they take time away from other work. However, such service earns credit from many institutions. In addition, the involvement provides professional connections that are

important for one's own career. Many scholars also find that this service helps them keep abreast of developments in the field, as they get to read the most recent research from active scholars. These forms of service also give insights into the inner workings of the publishing industry, which can help when one steps into the editorial position. It is okay to write to an editor and say that you are interested in serving as a referee or board member in that journal.

- *Read widely.* It is important to read academic publications in one's own discipline and related fields to understand the developments in research practices and writing genres. In order to develop the confidence to make sound editorial decisions and identify needed changes in the field, one has to gain a broad view of academic communication and knowledge production.
- *And what about those linguistic insecurities second language professionals often display?* Actually, that is the last thing one should worry about. Publishing is a negotiated activity. Articles are shaped products. Referees, copy editors, and editors shape the article in negotiation with authors. Though I have heard of editors who leave language issues completely to professional copyeditors employed by the publisher, I have made observations on style and language first and negotiated further changes as the process continued. My openness to diverse varieties of English meant that I had to give a sympathetic ear to authors who insisted on special language usage and lobby for them against copy editors.
- *More importantly, then, strengthen your negotiation strategies!* You have to negotiate the interests of professional organizations, publishers, editorial board members, referees, copyeditors, readers, and authors as you try to chart new paths for your field while being mindful of traditions. There are no simple tips that can be provided to develop one's negotiation strategies. Dispositions that can help are: be balanced in your approach, take into account the concerns of different stakeholders, be patient and reflective before you act, and be prepared for give-and-take.

I hope more second language professionals will consider editing a mission to represent the voices and knowledge of scholars from diverse settings and pluralize the disciplinary discourses.

NOTE

1. See http://www.tesol.org/s_tesol/sec_document.asp?CID=209&DID=3150.

CHAPTER 16

ASSUMING ADMINISTRATIVE DUTIES

María E. Torres-Guzmán
Teachers College, Columbia University

Within three months of my arrival as a junior faculty member, my senior colleague and mentor announced her pending position as president at another institution. Just like that, I became the head of the Bilingual/Bicultural Education Program. I walked into her shoes and began spinning. I felt like a kite, going where the wind blew. Mastery control from the ground was not there. I held on to the strings at first, barely managing. Eventually, the kite flew with an apparent ease that showed my confidence. I have been program head for most of my 25 years at Teachers College, Columbia University.

To squeeze in twenty-odd years of stories about administrative duties would be impossible in these next few pages. Instead, I will address two questions: 1) What kinds of faculty governance and/or administrative positions exist in a university? and 2) What would assist a faculty member making the transition to administration? The purpose of this chapter is to share with the reader some strategies that might be helpful in moving from a faculty to an administrative post.

Demystifying Career Paths after Graduate School, pages 191–203
Copyright © 2012 by Information Age Publishing

FACULTY GOVERNANCE VERSUS ADMINISTRATION

The literature makes a distinction between faculty governance and administration (Palm, 2006). The administrative work associated with academic programs, departmental units, research projects, and college-wide committees are considered faculty governance. They are what count as service to the institution. What is actually considered administration is when faculty members take on positions at the college and/or university level, in the role of associates, deans, vice-presidents, provosts, and presidents.

Recently, a colleague shared with me her experience in a hybrid position. She has a faculty line but is doing administration full time. She is not yet "one of them" or "on the dark side" (Glick, 2006; Palm, 2006; Willis, 2010). Her contract offers her the schedule of a faculty member but she spends most of her days in meetings on college-wide and policy-oriented matters. While she still identifies herself as a faculty member, her vision has changed; she went "from looking at things from the ground where individual trees grow, to the forest, 3000 feet from above" (A. L. Goodwin, personal communication, 2011).

DESCRIPTION OF THE SYSTEM, CULTURE, AND EXPECTATIONS

Service Activities Through Committees

The possibility of faculty governance and administrative positions is limitless. Much depends on what kind of institution you are in and on the hierarchies of the institution—from program, to department, to college, and to university levels. Most of the work considered as faculty governance is work you are expected to participate in as a citizen of the institution. There are many benefits derived from your participation in the institution. For you, the benefit will be the opportunity to try your hand at providing leadership beyond your own discipline.

As a faculty member you will be expected to participate in program committees, such as student recruitment and admissions, financial aid, public relations, diversity and community affairs, and many more. Most of these committees are the operational foundations of university life and will be part of your responsibilities beyond your teaching and research agendas.

In addition, you will be asked to serve as a member of the department, college, or university on different standing and ad hoc committees. Many standing committees are organized as joint administrative and faculty committees. Membership in these standing committees is either by administrative appointment, volunteering, or based on faculty elections. Depending on how you enter the membership roster, you will be representative of either administration or faculty. It is important to understand this difference, as it will position you and your contributions to the committee.

Some examples of standing committees in my institution, a tier one research-based graduate school, are: Affirmative Action, Institutional Review Board, Campus Safety, Dean's Grants for Faculty, and Dean's Grants for Students. Some of the elected committees are the Faculty Executive Committee and its subcommittees. Our institution is very invested in faculty governance, but the level of investment is likely to vary across different types of institutions. While it is expected, for example, that we participate in the governance of the college, there is a space for discernment and choice of committees. The workload and the level of involvement, in my experience, depend on the leadership of the committee and your own deliverance.

Another category of committee—the ad hoc committee—is constituted for a specific purpose. An example would be faculty search committees. These committees are very important as who you select will determine with whom you will be sharing your academic life and the direction of the intellectual life of a unit. Ad hoc committees disband when the purpose has been accomplished.

Positioning yourself in the role of service to the university is important for you as a faculty member as it determines, in the eyes of others, your leadership qualities, and demonstrates your collaborative work capacities.

Grant Administration Experience

At the program level, there are two possible entry points to the world where budgets, university business procedures, government regulations, and reconsideration of time schedules reign. The two pathways are grants and program coordination.

As the lenses into the world behind the academic stage widen, you are likely to experience a steep learning curve in different areas (Foster, 2006; Strathe & Wilson, 2006). What you attend to and the strategies you might benefit from will differ, however. As a researcher with an externally funded research or training project, you will have to attend to making sure the goals and reporting requirements are met while you interact with the human resources department with regard to hiring and personnel practices internal to your institution. You will have to follow the money trail, making sure your spending is within budget, and attend to many details of a legal nature imposed by the funding agency and your home institution. Nonetheless, you will also have the ability to structure an additional source of income for yourself within the institutional norms, and you can often negotiate a course release. Research and training grants allow you to advance your agenda within the institution. You will have to become aware of the parameters that will guide you, and these become visible as early as the proposal stage when you construct budgets for the grants. While it is still your own work, you will now be responsible for all those who work with you to complete the grant.

Program Coordination

As the coordinator or administrator of a program, the parameters of your vision are expanded. You are now responsible for making sure that faculty and staff members are doing their share in the service of the students. You will be asked to speak to the issues of course scheduling, faculty assignments, student recruitment and admissions, capital campaigns, and the like. There is great variation among institutions.

The most delicate of issues for the program administrator is that of leadership, as you have very little authority over your colleagues but need to ensure their participation in a variety of activities. You have to develop skills that are a mix between a salesperson and counselor—you have to sell your ideas and set up the support structures for joint activity with the faculty. How well you do this will determine whether you end up with a unit of disparate individuals co-existing or a cohesive and collaborative community of practice in which each individual faculty member has a role.

In the coordinator or program head position, there are generally token monetary compensations and, rarely, course releases. This remuneration, however, can be negotiated. I had neither until recently. When I changed to a department that was decentralized with respect to budgets, I received a nominal monetary remuneration but no course release. Much has to do with the traditions of each unit, which may differ even within the same institution, as well as individual circumstances. Make sure you investigate what has gone on previously within your unit and within the institution, and set some parameters that will allow you to be comfortable taking on the job.

Department Chair

Beyond the program, there is the position called chair of a department. Becoming department chair usually signals to the world outside that you have demonstrated administrative and intellectual leadership capability at some level. As you move upward in the hierarchy of the institution, the lenses of your vision and mission will widen. At the program level, you need to focus on the individual trees around you, but as you go up, the individual trees begin to blur as the forest takes shape and comes into view.

Department chair falls within the faculty governance realm, but at this level there are two parallel roles developing: a representative of colleagues in different units within the department and a messenger of administrative mandates. At the chair level, the wide-angle lens is concentrated on a conglomerate of programs. The issues of equity and unique needs of each program emerge and the chair must attend to variations among programs and to developing an interdisciplinary mindset, where connections between units are made. In addition, the chair handles issues of personnel, contract renewal, tenure and promotion, distribution of resources, conflicts among units and personnel, permissions to recruit new faculty, student demands, and alumni relations.

At the level of chair, monetary remuneration, course releases, additional administrative support, and discretionary funds are all possible. The specifics will depend on the tradition within the department and institution, and your ability to negotiate the conditions of your job.

Administrative Positions

Beyond faculty governance, administrative positions are plentiful at the university level. For a faculty member, the push into the "dark side" often results in academic positions such as associate dean, dean, assistant provost, associate to the provost, provost, vice president, associate to the president, and president.

As you move up the organizational chart, the focus requires a stronger and sharper wide-angle lens. The tasks begin to differ and become more specialized. You may, for example, be the Vice President for Academic Affairs or for Community and Diversity. Investigate what the previous individual in the position did and what achievements he or she made. This will give you some orientation to the position. Sometimes the administrative position is new, which means you have a unique opportunity to imagine and inspire others to join you in doing something never done before within the institution. You will need to develop a philosophy of action that will depend on the length of time of your appointment (Palm, 2006), on the things you care for, and on the demands made on your position from above (Griffith, 2006). Not only does an administrator have to have a vision and mission, they also must know how to work with other people's strengths to ensure the vision becomes a reality (Swain, 2006).

Some administrators, who see themselves transitioning back into a faculty status, chose to continue to teach or do research (Griffith, 2006; Plater, 2006; Strathe & Wilson, 2006; Willis, 2010). Others, however, decide to be dedicated to full-time service.

Being an administrator does have its perks: it yields personal authority, it establishes a new contractual work world in relation to schedule and remuneration, it potentially offers an operating budget with discretionary funds, and it changes the individual's relationship with colleagues. To take an administrative position or not is a decision each individual has to make. Before accepting a position, however, make sure you are familiar with the position's mandates and the domains of responsibility. Once you have decided to go forward, investigate potential areas of negotiations and push for a contract with which you can live.

The dilemmas of identity and balance loom large in the transition from faculty member to administrator. You have to shift mentally from loyalty to the clan to being cosmopolitan; your public image and relationships with faculty will go from feeling and being seen as a haltering kite to one that glides with ease. Plater (2006) proposes that you can recognize the moment of balance "when you know you will do what you believe and act according to principles that you not only recognize and understand but can articulate to others and translate into words and action" (p. 23). A message from the literature on the transition from faculty member to administrator is the call for a dynamic identity construction process that is in constant search of balance.

CHALLENGES AND STRATEGIES

There are a few challenges that all faculty transitioning into administration will have across the board. In this section, I will address the following three challenges mentioned in the literature and present my own perspective from the position of program head: 1) how to create a vision and mission that reflects the self and inspires others to join in collective action; 2) how to establish leadership in a structure of parallel hierarchies through communications; and 3) how to establish identity-in-action. The discussion of these areas will also be grounded in a perspective of attending to balance and identity.

Establishing a Vision and Evolving with It

When the kite was flying in the wind, I did not have a philosophy of action I could call my own. There was very little room for me to decide whether I wanted to take on the administrative position or not since I was the only tenure-track faculty member remaining in the program. There were some principles we had operated on, but I had to establish my own identity as the coordinator.

The literature on the transition from faculty to administration is replete with advice on developing a vision that distinguishes you from others who have had the post previously. It requires articulating a philosophy of action that incites the imagination of others while leaving space for them to contribute, and is flexible enough to change with the times. Thus, a key strategy is to *develop a vision that distinguishes you* and will inspire your colleagues to join you.

Creating a vision or a mission requires not only your personal reflections about direction but also conversation with others. Find or create occasions for such conversations. I used the program faculty meetings to encourage the necessary dialogue. The conversation, however, did not occur only at these meetings. It emerged from continuous dialogues with students and colleagues in various settings. Within a half year or so, I realized that writing memos, reports, and other everyday documents provided ample opportunities for clarifying aspects of the vision.

For example, the faculty of the program had two strong beliefs that united us. The first was that the program had to have a critical perspective because of whom it purported to serve: namely, those who were marginalized because of language. Thus, the issues of language equity and social justice had to be at the center of our work. The second belief was that reflective practices about how these issues took shape in instruction would permeate our work. These two stances were very much tied to our minority status. As the teacher candidates explored discourses about their practices in bilingual public school classrooms, it was important for us to examine the ways in which they enacted their bilingual teacher identities and thought about language policies and pedagogies.

As a result, we strengthened our connections with successful bilingual education programs that supported our students trying out new strategies in the classrooms. By doing this, we were privileging quality, dual-language instruction for minoritized populations. Eventually, some of our teacher candidates became teachers in the schools we worked with. We also engaged in professional development activities for the teachers and established a school-university partnership, where faculty, teachers, and teacher candidates entered into dialogues about language equity and social justice in bilingual instruction within public schools.

The initial gist of the philosophy of the program still remains. However, we have had to adjust our program to the changing teacher candidate population at the college. No longer do we have droves of first-generation immigrants from the Spanish-speaking world knocking at our doors. Now, our students reflect the new immigrant groups from diverse linguistic backgrounds and second-generation Latino teachers who speak Spanish as a heritage language.

Working with this new population was a bit disconcerting, but it also propelled us to (re)analyze how the world reads us, whom our admission criteria favored, and what the discourse of the international students, heritage language learners, and second language learners was. Of particular importance was how the prospective teacher candidates spoke about the need for language equity and social justice. A flurry of activity, including conversations with the students, led us to (re)articulate the vision in relation to the times and to adjust our admissions criteria.

Our program's identity has evolved with the times while maintaining its core beliefs. We moved from a parochial view of bilingual education towards multilingualism. While broadening our vision, it also became an occasion to (re)instate, in a clearer way, our commitment to privileged linguistically minoritized students. Balance between broadening and privileging was important to our identity as a program and to the impact it might have on program's growth.

Communication and Consensus Building

The programmatic decisions an administrator is responsible for are often political. Thus, you should think strategically as you listen to information and the discourses that constitute multiple perspectives on the issue at hand. This will serve to help you construct your arguments, build alliances and consensus, and move the greatest amount of support in a collaborative fashion as you make decisions and position yourself in relation to your values.

I came into an academic program that had a little more than a decade of existence, but had just received the approval to prepare teacher candidates for state-approved certification in bilingual education. It had been set up as a service program to the other academic units of the institution; only two students were majors, while 100 were minors. At that time, this program existed in the politically hostile climate against bilingual education in the state of New York. The limited enrollment of bilingual/bicultural education majors was obviously influenced by a larger amount of coursework unfairly required for them compared to other programs, which perhaps reflected the climate. The program had to be changed.

My first strategy was to *listen and gather information*. In order to understand the process for change, I listened to how others perceived why things occurred the way they had. I went to the registrar who managed the state requirements, I went to other programs in the city to see how they structured their programs, I attended state meetings about the new regulations of programs, and the like. I asked, read, and talked to every sector possible.

Next, I *constructed a counter-argument*—that our students bore the burden of paying very expensive tuition for a large number of credits. It was an equity issue. Furthermore, I felt the intellectual rationale for making a change was the need for integrating knowledge on teaching with that of multilingualism. However, in a public meeting with the State Department, I asked whether they would be amenable to a proposal based on the principle of integrated knowledge. They assured me that if it passed through the bodies of the institution, it would be accepted by the state.

I began disseminating a document on a 36-credit program, and as we moved through the different bodies at the college level, we found that there was a group of faculty members that constructed our proposal as "threatening." They felt that our proposal was hostile and unfair because their state teacher certification program for one certification required 40 credits. They felt that their students who were interested in bilingualism would flock to us. Their concerns were clear.

Alliances, conversation, and consensus building were key. After some negotiation, we agreed to a 40-credit master's degree where the students enrolled would work towards receiving both the elementary and bilingual certification. The agreement was, for the most part, a friendly one.

In the literature on the transitioning of faculty into administration, the issue of communication is big, as it was in the story above. One must involve all stakeholders in gaining information, in gaining consensus, and in moving forward. Each initiative will determine who the stakeholders will be: students, their parents, alumni, faculty members, clerical staff, other offices, businesses, government, trustees, and so forth (Strathe & Wilson, 2006).

Accompanying the conversation about communication in the literature is the admonition of balance. There is an exponential amount of communication needed in administrative positions in comparison to that of faculty. One example in the literature is on the balance that a dean needs to establish, as both the inside world of the university and the outer world of donors demand time (Harris, 2006). Sometimes an internal issue weighs heavily, while the outer world of donations and ceremonies may take over the next week. However, the specific areas of communication depend on the specific administrative position one undertakes.

Managing Rhythms and Time

The rhythm of administration can be overwhelming—the flow of questions is constant, everyone wants your attention, and everything was due yesterday. I often felt out of control and resented that my day evaporated as I figured out how to get wi-fi cables and ventilation into our office suite, discussed what ought to occupy the space of the display boards, sat mediating the relationship between two warring assistants who could not speak to each other without yelling, followed paper trails to find out why a check due months prior had not gotten to its destination, trained new assistants, made sure that our teaching personnel were on the same page with new state or college mandates, resolved a problem with a student's grade given by a former instructor who could not be found, and lunched and schmoozed with wealthy individuals to get fellowships for students. How would I come to anticipate the flow and convergence of schedules? How would I come to understand competing interests and manage them? How would I integrate these with teaching, writing and the exigencies of advising?

I had to reframe a few strategies that I thought I already knew. These strategies were *prioritizing, anticipating, delegating and asking for help from others*, and *integrating academic, teaching, and community work.*

Prioritizing meant that I had to distinguish that which was critical and demanded immediate action, that which was almost automatic and only needed a daily push, and that which could be placed on the agenda for a future scheduled time. Understanding the role of prioritizing is important for the eventual achievement of a sense of identity and balance as an administrator.

For example, attending to the press's push for an immediate response to the comments on bilingual education by the federal government's Secretary of Education is critical. In contrast, to present to the federal government's Senate Education Committee, which is an equally important request, requires only an immediate response of availability and willingness since these hearings are scheduled far in advance. Participating in the policy life of the nation is important and needs your attention when the opportunities present themselves. In the juxtaposed examples above, participation required either an immediate substantive statement or a well-thought-out and scheduled one. Here is where your values and individuality come into your prioritizing. In my case, when I did not have the time to speak to a news reporter, I would decline commenting, but I would do everything in my power to not miss an opportunity to present to the Senate. Other people enjoy the news coverage and would probably prioritize the immediate responses that are likely to create public opinion. There is no right or wrong; it is a matter of who you want to be.

The sharpened skill of prioritizing helped me filter all the information coming at me at once, to plan various events at the same time, and to sleep at night. It helped me to understand that as the head of a family, I had to balance work and family. It helped me understand that not everything can be investigated in depth but that the decisions that you make are the best you can make at the moment; this might include making mistakes. Understanding what your values are can provide you with the parameters for making decisions and establishing priorities.

Anticipating loomed big as another very useful strategy. One of the first things I asked the administrators of the college for was a schedule—the academic schedule, the administrative schedule, the faculty meeting schedules and the like. Upon receiving the year's schedule, usually at the end of the spring semester, I set up my upcoming year's schedule before going away for the summer. It is the first thing I attended to upon returning the following academic year. It has become a tool for anticipating work and pacing myself in relation to the internal routine activities I have to attend to during the semester and the academic year.

Delegating and asking for help from others is also important. I worried about my scholarship and had to make room for it in my schedule. This was a long-term project, as I did not only take on the administration of the program, but also the administration of two U.S. Department of Education training grants that called for a significant amount of accountability. One of the grants was a government-funded fellowship program, which did not have any funding for the principal investigator; the second was more flexible and initially had a stipend for administrative duties, which I eventually turned into a course release. With time, I structured the administrative work of the grant to be taken up by a project coordinator, although I would continue to administer it in the role of director and principal investigator. The day-to-day budgets, reporting, and the like were taken off my shoulders. I delegated. All of these adjustments took three to four years, because I had to learn what the parameters were of the institutions, of the grants, and of the program, but they were significant for me to find the time to write.

Lastly, and concurrently, I purposely *integrated my academic, teaching, and community work*. The latter had very little importance in academia but was very important to me. New York had a very large Latino population and I wanted to keep my finger on the pulse of it. This connection was vital for me. I applied for and received a dean's untenured faculty grant that assisted me in identifying a community and a research topic focused on an educational issue important to the Latino community. The desire to be in the community to understand what the local issues in education were also led me to different committees and commissions at the local and state levels.

Administration is primarily learned by trial and error (Strathe & Wilson, 2006). I learned that prioritizing and making smart decisions about use of time as well as anticipating and planning long-term enabled me to accomplish my goals (Griffith, 2006; Swain, 2006; Willis, 2010). I also learned that integrating my varied interests and competing demands was critical. Furthermore, learning how to trust others and delegate to them was essential in order for me to live a fuller life.

SUMMARY AND FINAL ADVICE

There are many ways in which you can participate in service at the university level within faculty governance and administration. Based on my own experience and on the literature on faculty-to-administration transition, I have touched on three main topics: creating a vision and mission, establishing leadership through communication, and understanding the rhythm of tasks. I also discussed a variety of strategies, such as listening and gathering information, establishing alliances, building consensus, prioritizing, anticipating, delegating, and integrating. All of them are grounded in issues of balance and identity. Here are my final suggestions:

- *Learn how to plan your day with sufficient room for emergencies.* At most, an administrator has only three hours of possible planned work in a day. The other five hours go to everyday office events and emergencies. Adjust your expectations of what you can do during a work day, as it will lessen your level of frustration. To acquire balance, shift your perspective.
- *Establish your unique identity as an administrator by prioritizing.* Prioritizing is an act of identity. Give priority to tasks that speak to your values. If you do not like what you see upon examining your everyday existence as an administrator, shift by focusing on responding to what is important to you.
- *When your priority comes into conflict with program's priority, reflect and reframe yourself.* Spend some time to reframe yourself by reflecting on what is important at the given moment and to your own professional subjectivity. Decisions are contextual. Think deeply about how conflicts came to be and where you position yourself to find the best decision for the ultimate recipients of education.

REFERENCES

Foster, B. L. (2006). From faculty to administrator: Education. *New Directions for Higher Education, 134,* 49–57.

Glick, M. D. (2006). Becoming "one of them" or "moving to the dark side." *New Directions for Higher Education, 134,* 87–96.

Griffith, J. C. (2006). Transition from faculty to administrator and transition back to the faculty. *New Directions for Higher Education, 134,* 67–77.

Harris, S. E. (2006). Transitions: Dilemmas of leadership. *New Directions for Higher Education, 134,* 79–86.

Palm, R. (2006). Perspectives from the dark side: The career transition from faculty to administrator. *New Directions for Higher Education, 134,* 59–65.

Plater, E. M. (2006). The rise and fall of administrative careers. *New Directions for Higher Education, 134,* 15–24.

Strathe, M. I. & Wilson, V. W. (2006). Academic leadership: The pathway to and from. *New Directions for Higher Education, 134,* 3–13.

Swain, M. A. (2006). Reflections on academic administration. *New Directions for Higher Education, 134*, 25–36.

Willis, C. L. (2010). To the dark side and back: The administrative odyssey of an academic sociologist with lessons learned. *The American Sociologist, 41*, 190–209.

CHAPTER 17

BALANCING PROFESSIONAL AND PERSONAL LIFE

Suhanthie Motha
University of Washington

> *You're on an airplane*
> *In a car. You're in a car*
> *On the bus. You're on the bus*
> *Going home as you daydream*
> *At your desk. On your desk*
> *You have a postcard of Alaska.*
> *You are never where you are,*
> *And when you are, you're leaving,*
> *Late already for something else,*
> *A meeting, a class, shopping*
> *And isn't shopping fun, you think,*
> *Like being on a sightseeing tour.*
> *But you're late and you must get home*
> *Or you're home and must get going,*
> *Late either way, exasperated,*
> *Tapping your foot to get us all*
> *Out the door. Goodbye, you wave*
> *To yourself, standing there.*
>
> —*I Saw You Tomorrow,*
> Alberto Ríos[1]

Demystifying Career Paths after Graduate School, pages 205–217
Copyright © 2012 by Information Age Publishing
All rights of reproduction in any form reserved.

Alberto Ríos' poem "I Saw You Tomorrow" drives home the vulnerabilities of a life lived without a mindfulness of the need for balance, presence, attentiveness to the moment, and even occasional stillness—the type of existence that faculty members in higher education institutions frequently find themselves living. Let me open this chapter with the candid admission that I have no special talent for balancing the professional and the personal. Because I am appreciative of the editors' intention to compile an encouraging and constructive collection narrating victory and success, I will blithely gloss over the numerous ways in which I fail to achieve balance, and I will refrain from sharing my countless, humorous-in-retrospect tales of woe. I will instead tell one brief story. When I received the invitation to contribute this chapter, I shared with my writing group my sense of being unqualified to write the chapter, my lack of ability to achieve balance being felt rather keenly at that particular moment in time. One friend replied: "Actually, Su, you are doing it. You finished a Ph.D. and got a tenure-track position at a Research I institution while giving birth to and raising two young children. Your contract has been renewed, and you are making your way towards tenure. You *are* doing it." This struck me as a revelation, and therein lies Lesson One. Much of our ability to balance lies in the framing, in how we choose to measure each of our steps. If the definition of success is a moving target, always lying ahead on the horizon, it will always remain unattainable *and* unattained. Rather, recognizing and honoring the steps behind us, those already taken, allows them to be a part of our success.

Finding balance in higher education poses special challenges for faculty of color and linguistic minority faculty. Academia has come to be constructed as a solitary and competitive enterprise, one that rewards independence and self-reliance. It is a system that can be hospitable to those who, by virtue of their identities at birth, have doors opened and signposts already planted for them along their way. Many faculty of color and linguistic minority faculty come to academia without these signposts—the socialization we receive is usually not intended to prepare us for a life within academia. We often perform a particular constellation of responsibilities and carry distinctive loads. Students are more likely to seek out faculty who look and sound like them, and we consequently often mentor students who are disenfranchised from academia, whose families are unfamiliar with the conventions of U.S. higher education (Antonio, Astin, & Cress, 2000). We are more likely to encounter hostility in our classrooms (Vargas, 2002). Our employment options may be limited by immigration and visa constraints (see Chapter 2, Seeking a Faculty Position). We frequently encounter a dearth of allies or like-minded colleagues in our home institutions (see Chapter 14, Involvement in Leadership Roles in Professional Organizations). If English is not our first language, our nervousness and insecurity may be exacerbated by concerns about interlocutors' perception of our fluency or pronunciation (see Chapter 4, Teaching-Focused University). We may encounter more material and cultural barriers to academic writing and publishing than our colleagues who are neither linguistic nor racial minorities (see Chapter 15, Working as a Journal Editor). We may be undergoing socialization into unfamiliar hiring and professional practices or workplace expectations (see Chapter 7, Moving from North America to Overseas).

Balancing the personal with the professional requires us to recognize and critique the myth of the ideal worker (Williams, 2000), the image of an ambitious worker devoted to his (for the "ideal worker" is typically male) institution and profession and who is able to have a family life only if a "marginalized worker," for instance a (usually female) partner, performs the family work. Robyn Wiegman (2000) wrote of her reaction to a toast made by her dean of faculties to the "marriage to the institution" of recently tenured faculty, including Wiegman herself. Wiegman was taken aback by the inappropriateness of the metaphor, writing: "I believe that we need to approach the labor we do in the academy as quite simply that—labor," and she disputes the metaphor of family as an "organizing principle of academic life" (p. 71). Historically, teaching in many parts of the world was construed as a vocation of sorts. Teachers' personal lives were regulated by school boards, and teachers were no longer employable once they married (Lather, 1987). The historical professional terrain of academia can create unreasonable expectations of devotion and single-mindedness that should be approached critically by faculty who are interested in developing a balanced relationship between their personal and professional lives.

In this chapter, I outline a range of strategies that I have found to be helpful on the quest for balance.

BE THOUGHTFUL ABOUT YOUR FRAMING OF THE RELATIONSHIP BETWEEN THE PERSONAL AND THE PROFESSIONAL

Think about how you want to frame the personal and the professional and what you want the space between the two to look like. The two are, of course, not truly separate, and the delineation is artificial. Do you want a demarcation? A blending? A little of both, depending on the circumstance? Sandie Kouritzin (personal communication, March 16th, 2000) has suggested blurring the lines between the two, for instance having a work desk in a playroom. Juliann Emmons Allison (2007) writes of meeting with students while her toddler son played with blocks, trucks, and dollhouses in her office. Before I had children, I was inspired as I observed a junior faculty member I knew moving calmly from room to room at conferences with her preschooler in tow, assiduously taking notes while her son sat serenely by her side, seeming to listen with great interest to talks about Vygotskian theory and recent trends in teacher education. On some levels this notion of blending works for me—for instance, much of my socializing is with colleagues. My children accompany me to campus on weekends when I need to photocopy or collect books from the university library. On other levels, however, it has become crucial that I separate starkly and find ways to focus on work while I am at work, on writing while I am writing, on students while I am teaching or meeting with them, on my daughters while I am playing with them, on my partner over the dinner table. It requires a degree of heedfulness to resist mapping out my lesson plans in my head while absently discussing the variegated shades of the snails we pass as I'm walking my children to school. I have to make a conscious effort not to mentally map out resources for my daughter's school project with one corner of my mind while my mouth is discussing the structure of a student's final paper with him.

KNOW YOUR INSTITUTION'S FORMAL SUPPORTS

Ask your benefits office about policies surrounding work-life balance, paid and unpaid family leave, dependent care leave, modification of duties, and transitional support programs. Even if you never use any of these programs, the awareness that they exist as a possibility can be helpful in reminding you of available options. You should know what formal institutional supports exist for you within your institution. The University of Washington, for instance, has a Diversity Research Institute, an Associate Vice Provost for Faculty Advancement who is charged with retention of minority faculty, and an Office of Minority Affairs and Diversity. These are all offices to which minority faculty can go, usually with an assurance of confidentiality, for advice or support in managing the various parts of their positions and in increasing the feasibility of a balanced approach to academic careers. Every college or department should have a functional, effective diversity committee. It should be composed largely of senior faculty invested in the future of the department, since junior faculty members are frequently not in a political position to advocate for themselves and their commitments. Unless you happen to be working at an institution at which most faculty members are minorities (however that term is defined at your institution), the diversity committee should not overwhelmingly comprise minority faculty members. Members of diversity committees are another potential source of support in negotiating a viable work-life balance. If your department does not have a diversity committee, a senior faculty ally should be enlisted to initiate department-wide discussions about forming one.

COLLABORATIVE COMMUNITIES

Throughout my academic career, I have relied on collaborative communities for support in all areas, particularly in achieving balance between the personal and the professional. Before I started my tenure track, my writing group, the Quotable Quills, was invaluable. Among the seven of us, we have 11 children. During our last year together before we scattered across the globe, five of us were either pregnant or breastfeeding, and our monthly Saturdays tucked away in a conference room provided a space in which we could be scholars, write, and nourish each other intellectually in a way that eluded us during the chaos of our everyday lives. My longer-term and more far-flung writing group, the Sister Scholars, includes more senior scholars whom I have observed, over the past decade, caring for aging parents, adult children with special needs, and adult siblings with disabilities; who have gone through tenure processes and promotions, coped with parents' deaths, adjusted to new family configurations, transitioned to new institutions, handled health challenges, managed relationships with partners, published copiously, and parented. My collective at the University of Washington, WIRED (Women Investigating Race, Ethnicity, and Difference), also includes a dozen parents of young children who share advice about and indeed model effective balance between the personal and the professional, who organize to support each other through difficult periods, and who check in with each other around a monthly professional goal and a "Take Care of Me" task.

Developing coalitions allows strategizing for sharing out in a systematic way the responsibilities that faculty of color often shoulder. For instance, if minority faculty at your institution find themselves overburdened by an effort to include minority faculty on most major committees, you can strategize amongst yourselves to ensure representation while protecting those in your community who might have tenure files or book revisions due at a particular time. Care of minority students and mentorship of junior minority faculty members can be shared, as can manuscript reviews of books or articles that are important to your lines of research.

BE CONSCIOUS AS YOU MAKE
TIME MANAGEMENT DECISIONS

One of my hardest learned lessons is that as we pass through life, decisions about how to spend time on an hour-by-hour basis must be made consciously. Without deliberateness and intention, it becomes easy to unwittingly spend a large percentage of your time on work you do not value and to neglect people, commitments, and work that you treasure. Rather than reflecting your best judgment and interests, decisions made in the moment are most likely to be responsive to an artificially constructed sense of urgency, academic bullying, an inability to think quickly of ways to refuse, a sense of powerlessness or defenselessness, or a desire to please. Faculty of color and linguistic minority faculty are more likely to feel powerless (Smith, Altbach, & Lomotey, 2002), to feel compelled to please, and to be victims of academic bullying (Twale & De Luca, 2008).

One concept that has been invaluable to me, the Sunday Meeting, was conceived by Kerry Ann Rockquemore (2010) and is described in her *Inside Higher Ed* online column. The Sunday Meeting is unreasonably time-consuming the first time, but it is much faster thereon in, and shortcuts become easier to devise. My interpretation of the process looks something like this: Set aside time on a Sunday to make a comprehensive list, ordered by categories, of the activities you want to carry out during the following week. The list tends to remain substantially unchanged from week to week, so less time is needed each consecutive Sunday. On it, list teaching (reading, preparing for classes, grading, coordinating with teaching assistants, office hours or conferences with students), research and writing, service (program, departmental, university-wide, national or international), administrative duties (faculty meetings, program responsibilities, admissions), supervisory work (meeting with doctoral students, reading and responding to dissertations), personal (exercise, yoga, attending to spirituality or faith, regular physician appointments, phoning your best friend or your mother, volunteer work), family (including caring for elderly parents, shopping for groceries, bathing and feeding children, helping them with homework, taking them to cello lessons, reading bedtime stories, taking your dog to the vet), and recreation (brunch with family friends, a hike or bike ride, dates). The next step is to put all of these activities on your calendar in order of priority. Of course your schedule won't accommodate all of the items you deem important. In fact, chances are that it won't contain all of the items you consider indispensable. You need at this point to decide what to do with the items that remain—delegate them, abandon them, identify ways to alter deadlines, lower your standards for their completion.

For me, the magic of the Sunday meeting comes with the consciousness that as you plan your schedule you are prioritizing and making decisions about what you value most, not only this week but in a larger sense. When you decide that your overdue mammogram cannot fit into the week's schedule, you are making a deliberate choice to cross it off the list, rather than simply allowing it to be overlooked. You are making the decision that agreeing to serve on that extra doctoral committee or attending the meeting to talk about a new program is more important than your mammogram. Once you have made your choices and scheduled out your week, observe the boundaries you set. If you allowed yourself two hours to plan that applied linguistics class on translanguaging, be willing to allow good enough to be good enough and to turn to the next item when your time is up. If e-mail is controlling you, set aside a block of time once a day to go through it, even for a month, while you refine the skills to move through your e-mail more efficiently.

At this point, a natural reaction might be to justify uncomfortable decisions you make as temporary: "This is just a busy period, I'll have that mammogram just as soon as my schedule allows it." When you catch yourself in "just for now" mode, be conscious that life will not become more manageable unless you take conscious steps to make it more manageable.

SURROUND YOURSELF WITH "BALANCE MENTORS"

"Balance mentors" are people whose ability to balance the personal and the professional you admire, people who are able to succeed in academia, whatever this might mean from your individual perspective, without compromising other aspects of their lives. Perhaps your balance mentors find ways to give priority to the work that you consider important, even if it is work that is not rewarded institutionally, such as minority student mentorship, community engagement, public scholarship, creative pedagogical practice, and advocacy work. Perhaps your balance mentors respond admirably to personal responsibilities similar to yours, such as a relative with special needs, aging parents, or small children. Perhaps they have the types of spiritual commitments you want to emulate—an ability to nurture creativity, meditation, faith, or organized religion. Perhaps they make commitments to communities you are invested in, such as indigenous or immigrant populations, public schools, or homeless shelters, or commit time to advocacy work you care about.

A balance mentor doesn't have to be institutionally senior to you. In fact, some of my best balance mentors are students (truth be told, some of my best intellectual mentors are also students). Be consciously analytical of the strategies used by your balance mentors in navigating their own personal challenges. Turn to them for advice. Last winter, I mentioned to Rachel Chapman, a balance mentor and friend in the anthropology department at the University of Washington, that I had 33 letters of recommendation that needed to be mailed that week, during the peak administrative time of my academic calendar and a period of a heavy teaching load. I wanted to write each of these letters well. Rachel shared with me a time-saving and helpful strategy. As soon as a student asks for a letter of recommendation, Rachel sends her a form letter that requests: a list of courses taken with Rachel, the grade for each class, a line summarizing the final paper for each class and an explanation of why the work is important, a CV, and two weeks' advance notice for submitting the letter. I developed my own version of Rachel's form and find that it jogs my memory, helps me to start composing the letter, and saves me a great deal of time hunting through old files and papers. If possible, ensure that you have a variety of balance mentors, perhaps from outside your department, perhaps from outside your institution, perhaps from within your department but removed from your area.

MINDFULNESS-BASED STRESS REDUCTION

A turning point for me was a class in mindfulness-based stress reduction, which I took at the urging of Manka Varghese, my colleague at the University of Washington and a wonderful balance mentor. It helped me to revisit and even reframe my thinking about life, balance, and the work that I do. It equipped me with a few basic strategies for responding gracefully to difficult situations, for managing stress and anxiety in daily life, for increased reflection on the genesis of my fears and discomfort. For instance, I learned a handful of breathing exercises that can be pulled out at those moments of discouragement. I learned to probe more deeply my reasons for overcommitting myself and to contemplate the roles of self-doubt, avoidance, ego, anxiety, and catastrophizing "what if" stories in my making of decisions that lead to an absence of serenity in life. Information about mindfulness programs and resources worldwide can be found at www.umassmed.edu/cfm.

BE ORGANIZED

Write everything down. I had an uncanny memory for most of my life, even during the pressures of doctoral work as a foggy-brained new mother. Working in higher education has tested the limits of my memory's volume. It took a few dropped balls to convince me to stop overestimating my memory. I carry one notebook into which I write all of my notes, reminders, and lists. My phone has a command that allows me, with two button-pushes, to record brief reminder messages that I then play back at the end of the day ("Change Howard's grade. Buy milk. Book auditorium for workshop. Make pediatric dentist appointment."). In the past, I thrived on spontaneity. Now, our lives are shockingly pre-arranged and predictable. We do laundry every Friday night. On Saturday mornings, our children select all of their clothes for the week and place every item into a sweater organizer so that no decisions need to be made on weekday mornings. We plan out our menus for the week before heading to the farmer's market and grocery store in order to reduce the need for unplanned midweek trips to the grocery store. We cook one or two simple dishes on Sunday that can be pulled out and plopped on the stove during the week. For now, the predictability is soothing.

LEARN TO SAY NO

In their book *The Black Academic's Guide to Winning Tenure Without Losing Your Soul,* Rockquemore and Laszloffy (2008) list 10 ways of saying no, including: "That sounds like a really great opportunity, but I just cannot take on any additional commitments at this time," "I am in the middle of _____, _____, and _____ and, if I hope to get tenure, I am unable to take on any additional service," and "I would rather say no to your request than do a halfhearted job on the committee" (p. 119). I have found that it can be helpful to expend more words and greater enthusiasm on the "I wish I could do this, it sounds so wonderful" part of a refusal than on the "but I can't right now" part of it—the actual refusal. Refusing requests for doctoral supervision is particularly difficult for faculty members who want to ensure that students of color and linguistic minority students receive the extra support that they might need in order to succeed within the academy. However, overwhelmed faculty members drowning under heavy supervisory loads are not able to provide the quality of support that their students deserve. A wise senior faculty member suggested the response: "I need make sure that some of my students graduate before I take on new students." It is frequently difficult to gauge when saying no is acceptable, and many faculty members agree to various tasks because they fear that refusing might make them appear apathetic or negligent. Asking a faculty member in another department or unit, particularly a more seasoned faculty member, about the appropriateness of saying no is one way to help make decisions. Another potential source of advice is administrative or advising staff, who may be less likely to pass judgment when you ask about the advisability of saying no.

As you make decisions about when to say no, consider the nature of the labor you are being asked to perform. Faculty of color are more frequently asked to perform caretaking or domestic labor. For instance, they are more likely to be assigned methods classes and student teaching supervision than theoretical and research classes (Lin et al., 2004). Are you being asked by faculty senior to provide refreshments for meetings, to host dinners or other gatherings, to set up for and tidy up for meetings more often than your colleagues who are not minority faculty members? If so, these may be tasks to excuse yourself from.

Think about why you say yes. This train of thought can be uncomfortable but is worth pursuing. Consider requests that you have recently agreed to against your best judgment. Why didn't you refuse? Were you afraid of retribution? Are you concerned about damage to your tenure track or possibilities of promotion? Is your fear based in a real risk? Are you afraid of someone disliking you or thinking less of you? How likely is that judgment? If it is indeed likely, how fair is it? Does refusing leave you feeling guilty? Would you rather feel guilty for saying no or overwhelmed and angry because you said yes? Do you enjoy the feeling of being needed? Are you reluctant to refuse because you are flattered by the request? Are you unable to say no because you define yourself too fully by your professional identity? As you respond to these questions, analyze any patterns that you see emerging and consider how these might inform you as you decide whether to say yes or no in the future.

BREAK LIFE DOWN INTO INCREMENTS WITH DIFFERENT STANDARDS FOR THE VARIOUS CHUNKS

Academic calendars are notoriously uneven. The University of Washington runs on a quarter system, which means that my life is divided into 11- or 12-week chunks. My heaviest load is during the winter, so I consciously drop my standards for everything I can, such as social activities and volunteering in my children's classrooms, during the winter quarter with the understanding that I will try to make up for it all during the spring. I try to plan ahead for those times, plan financially for extra babysitting, plan for extra deadlines, and perhaps beg my parents for a visit to help with childcare.

CONSIDER ZANY SCHEDULES, EVEN TEMPORARILY

The stillness and solitude of the hours before dawn make these my most productive time of day. At my busiest times of the year, I rise at 2:30 a.m. every day (maintaining day-to-day consistency makes the sleep deprivation more tolerable). Because this means that I am most ragged at the end of the day, during the hours which I usually spend with family, this arrangement it is not feasible as a permanent solution, but it gets me through my busiest periods. Consider the possibility of strange schedules for a short period, and be committed to the transitory nature of these periods, even enlisting friends or partners to sternly ensure that you return to a more human schedule on a set date.

LOWER YOUR STANDARDS

In *Bird By Bird*, Anne Lamott (1994) writes: "Perfectionism is the voice of the oppressor, the enemy of the people. It will keep you cramped and insane your whole life…" (p. 28). You can't do everything perfectly, and try-ing to do so will simply leave you unhappy and unfulfilled. Accept that you will have to cut corners, then make conscious decisions about what corners you are willing to cut.

ANALYZE YOUR CONTEXT, THEN ANALYZE YOURSELF

Think critically about the culture of work embedded in your various con-texts—your institution or department or unit. If your context encourages an unbalanced lifestyle, step back and reflect upon what steps you need to take to resist socialization into an approach that is off-kilter. Is it possible for you to achieve the balance you want within your context? If not, consider the possibility that a different environment might be better for you. Is a sense of urgency and stress always present? Are you surrounded by negativ-ity and complaining? Are you able to resist joining in, or is the mentality oppressive and impossibly contagious?

If your health, friendships, relationship with a partner, and closeness to your children or other relatives have deteriorated in recent years because of your commitment to higher education, think about the specific choices you have made that have led to this deterioration. How could your decision-making have been different? What steps can you take right now to make change? The following questions are adapted from Shanafelt's (2005) se-ries of questions to help re-evaluate and reshuffle priorities:

1. What is my greatest priority in life? Have I been living my life in a way that demonstrates this?
2. Where am I most irreplaceable? At home? On campus? Elsewhere?
3. Do I have adequate balance between my personal and professional lives?
4. Am I asking more of my partner, children, or other family members than I should?
5. What kind of a legacy do I want to leave?
6. What person or activity have I been neglecting?
7. If I could relive the past year, what would I spend more time doing? What would I spend less time doing? What changes do I need to make to help this happen this year?
8. Why did I choose my profession? What do I like most about my job?
9. What would I like my life to be like in 10 years?
10. What do I fear?

FIND YOUR INSPIRATION

Even if you are not able to turn to them frequently, be aware of the activities or past-times that help to sustain you, especially those that are unrelated to your professional field: running, watercolor painting, hiking, playing or listening to music, yoga, meditation, poetry, knitting, escape through fiction, gabbing with your best friend. I have, taped to my office walls, copies of poems such as Mary Oliver's "Mindful," May Sarton's "Now I Become Myself," Ruth Forman's "If You Lose Your Pen," and Nikki Giovanni's "Revolutionary Dreams." These provide quick existential reminders.

If you have significant personal responsibilities that tear you away from your work with regularity, your life forces a certain degree of balance. If you do not, it could become easy to spend long periods of time in front of your computer, forgetting to live the rest of your life. I suggest scheduling in recreation ahead of time, perhaps with a buddy who will ensure that you show up. Keeping a sense of humor is also vital.

BE PATIENT WITH YOURSELF

"Every thousand-mile journey starts with a single step," wrote Lao-tzu. Remember that you won't learn to balance overnight but rather will develop strategies that you refine over a period of many years and perhaps many decades. Be forgiving of yourself. If this semester you were present for your sick brother and submitted a journal article but didn't maintain a regular exercise routine nor make it to your annual physical, make your health a priority for next semester. Schedule that appointment today. Over the past dozen years, I have recalled with amazing regularity the words of my mentor since graduate school, Shelley Wong: "Start from where you are and then step forward." As you take that step forward, do *not* turn around and wave good-bye to yourself.

NOTE

1. Credit: Alberto Ríos, "I Saw You Tomorrow" from *The Dangerous Shirt.* Copyright © 2009 by Alberto Ríos. Reprinted with the permission of The Permissions Company, Inc. on behalf of Copper Canyon Press, www.coppercanyonpress.org.

REFERENCES

Allison, J. E. (2007). Composing a life in twenty-first century academe: Reflections on a mother's challenge. *NWSA Journal, 19*(3), 23–46.

Antonio, A. L., Astin, H. A., & Cress, C. M. (2000). Community service in higher education: A look at the nation's faculty. *Journal of Higher Education, 23*(4), 373–398.

Lamott, A. (1994). *Bird by bird.* New York, NY: Random House, Inc.

Lather, P. (1987). The absent presence: Patriarchy, capitalism, and the nature of teacher work. *Teacher Education Quarterly, 14*(2), 25–38.

Lin, A., Grant, R., Kubota, R., Motha, S., Tinker Sachs, G., Vandrick, S., & Wong, S. (2004). Women faculty of color in TESOL: Theorizing our lived experiences. *TESOL Quarterly, 38*(3), 487–504.

Rockquemore, K. A. (2010, September 20). The Sunday meeting [Blog post]. Retrieved from http://www.insidehighered.com/advice/surviving/fall2

Rockquemore, K. A. & Laszloffy, T. (2008). *The black academic's guide to winning tenure—Without losing your soul.* Boulder, CO: Lynne Reiner.

Shanafelt, T. (2005). Finding meaning, balance, and personal satisfaction in the practice of oncology. *The Journal of Supportive Oncology, 2*(3), 157–165.

Smith, W. A., Altbach, P. G., & Lomotey, K. (2002). *The racial crisis in American higher education.* Albany, NY: State University of New York Press.

Twale, D. & De Luca, B. (2008). *Faculty incivility: The rise of the academic bully culture and what to do about it.* San Francisco, CA: Jossey-Bass.

Vargas, L. (2002). *Women faculty of color in the classroom.* New York, NY: Peter Lang.

Williams, J. (2000). *Unbending gender: Why work and family conflict and what to do about it.* New York, NY: Oxford University Press.

Wiegman, R. (2000). Married to the institution. In S. G. Lim & M. Herrera-Sobek (Eds.), *Power, race, and gender in academe: Strangers in the tower* (pp. 71–82). New York, NY: The Modern Language Association.

AUTHOR BIOGRAPHIES

Yuko Goto Butler is Associate Professor of Educational Linguistics at the Graduate School of Education at the University of Pennsylvania. She is also the director of Teaching English to Speakers of Other Languages (TESOL) program at Penn. She is originally from Japan and received her Ph.D. in Educational Psychology from Stanford University. Her primary research interests include the influence of various psychological and social factors on young learners' second and foreign language learning both in the United States and East Asia. She is also interested in how best to assess young learners' communicative and interactive competence both in their first and second/foreign languages.

Suresh Canagarajah is the Edwin Erle Sparks Professor in English and Applied Linguistics at Penn State University. He had his education and started his teaching career in Jaffna, Sri Lanka. He teaches second language writing, world Englishes, ethnography, and postcolonial studies. His publication *Translingual Practice: Global Englishes and Cosmopolitan Relations* is forthcoming from Routledge.

Ulla M. Connor, Ph.D. is the Barbara E. and Karl R. Zimmer chair in Intercultural Communication, Professor of English, and director of the Indiana Center for Intercultural Communication at Indiana University-Purdue University Indianapolis. Dr. Connor received her B.A. and M.A. in English philology from the University of Helsinki, an M.A. in English literature from the University of Florida, an M.A. in comparative literature, and a Ph.D. in English linguistics from the University of Wisconsin. Dr. Connor has held academic positions in applied linguistics and TESOL at a number of U.S.

Demystifying Career Paths after Graduate School, pages 219–223
Copyright © 2012 by Information Age Publishing
All rights of reproduction in any form reserved.

universities including Georgetown University, Purdue University, and most recently Indiana University-Purdue University Indianapolis.

Tracey Costley has a Ph.D. in Philosophy of Education from King's College London, and she works at the English Language Centre at King's College London. Her doctoral research focused on English as Additional Language learners in mainstream educational settings in London. Her current research interests include exploring the interface between education policy and curriculum practice in relation to ethnolinguistic minority students in mainstream schooling contexts, as well as academic genres and student identity in writing at university.

Xuesong (Andy) Gao is Associate Professor in the faculty of Education, the University of Hong Kong. Previously he worked in the department of English, Hong Kong Institute of Education. His current research and teaching interests are in the areas of learner autonomy, sociolinguistics, vocabulary studies, language learning narratives and language teacher education. He has published about 40 internationally refereed journal articles and book chapters. He serves on the editorial and advisory board for *TESOL Quarterly* and reviews manuscripts for a dozen international journals.

Soonhyang Kim is Assistant Professor of TESOL and Bilingual Education program at Pace University, Westchest Country/New York City. She has been active in supporting issues relating to non-native-English-speaking professionals, including serving as a co-guest editor of *Journal of Excellence on College*, which focuses on NNES instructors in higher education, and publishing in a *Modern Language Journal* about the development of NNES graduate students' academic and professional trajectories through long-term, ongoing, multiple interventions during graduate study.

Ryuko Kubota is Professor at the University of British Columbia, Canada. Previously, she taught in Japan and the United States. Her research is focused on sociopolitical issues in second/foreign language education. She is an editor of *Race, Culture, and Identities in Second Language Education: Exploring Critically Engaged Practice* (Routledge, 2009). She has published chapters in edited books and articles in such journals as *Canadian Modern Language Review, Critical Inquiry in Language Studies, International Journal of Bilingualism and Bilingual Education, Journal of Second Language Writing, Linguistics and Education, Modern Language Journal, TESOL Quarterly, Written Communication,* and *World Englishes.*

Constant Leung is Professor of Educational Linguistics in the department of Education and Professional Studies at King's College London. He also serves as deputy head of department. His research interests include additional/second language curriculum, language assessment, language education in ethnically and linguistically diverse societies, language policy, and teacher professional development. He is associate editor for *Language Assessment Quarterly* and editor of research issues for *TESOL Quarterly*.

Guofang Li is Associate Professor in the department of Teacher Education at Michigan State University. Li specializes in ESL/ELL/EFL education, family and community literacy, and Asian American education. Li is the recipient of the 2010 Early Career Award of AERA, the 2008 Early Career Award of Division G (Social Context of Education), AERA, the 2006 Ed Fry Book Award of the National Reading Conference, and the 2001 Best Article Award from *McGill Journal of Education*. Li's major publications include three sole-authored books, *Culturally Contested Literacies: America's "Rainbow Underclass" and Urban Schools* (Routlege, 2008), *Culturally Contested Pedagogy: Battles of Literacy and Schooling between Mainstream Teachers and Asian Immigrant Parents* (SUNY Press, 2006), and *"East is East, West is West"? Home Literacy, Culture, and Schooling* (Peter Lang, 2002), as well as several edited volumes including: *Best Practices in ELL Instruction* (Guilford, 2010), *Multicultural Families, Home Literacies, and Mainstream Schooling* (IAP, 2009), and *Model Minority Myths Revisited: An Interdisciplinary Approach to Demystifying Asian American Education Experiences* (IAP, 2008).

Suhanthie Motha is Assistant Professor at the University of Washington in Seattle, Washington. Her research explores the intersection of race, empire, and identity in the context of English language teaching. Her work has appeared in journals including *TESOL Quarterly, Modern Language Journal, Critical Inquiry in Language Studies, Language Teaching, Peace and Change Journal, TESL Canada Journal*, and *Educational Practice and Theory*, in addition to several edited volumes. She currently serves on the editorial advisory board of *TESOL Quarterly*.

Originally from France and Switzerland, **Lucie Moussu** earned a master's degree in TESOL from Brigham Young University and a Ph.D. in ESL and Higher Education Administration from Purdue University. She also taught French and ESL in Utah, then Composition and Written Communication at Purdue. At Ryerson University, in Toronto, she worked for three years as assistant professor in Applied Linguistics and Writing Center director. She is now director of the University of Alberta's Centre for Writers and a faculty member in the Writing Studies Program and the Department of English and Film Studies. Her research interests include the administration of writing centers, the strengths of native and non-native English-speaking ESL/EFL teachers, and second language writing. She has published in *Language Teaching, TESOL Quarterly, Essential Teacher*, and *TESL Reporter*.

Ekaterina (Katya) Nemtchinova is Associate Professor of TESOL and Russian at Seattle Pacific University, where she teaches Russian as well as methodology and linguistics courses in the MATESOL program. Her research interests include teacher education, particularly the issues of non-native English speaking professionals in TESOL, and technology in language learning. From 2007 to 2009 she served as the chair-elect, chair, and immediate past chair of the Non-native English Speakers in TESOL Caucus/Interest Section. Her Russian language textbook *Listen Up!* was published by the University Press of the South in 2011.

Ling Shi is Professor in the department of Language and Literacy Education at the University of British Columbia. She holds a Ph.D. from the Ontario Institute for Studies in Education, University of Toronto. Prior to coming to Canada, she taught in a university in mainland China. Her research specializes in second language writing, English for academic purposes, and teaching English as a second/foreign language.

Yilin Sun has a Ph.D. from the Ontario Institute for Studies in Education at the University of Toronto, Canada. She is a Fulbright Senior Scholar (2011–2012) at National Taiwan Normal University and Professor at Seattle Community Colleges (1994–present). She has over 25 years of experience in the ELT field as a teacher trainer, researcher, and program lead, and served on the board of directors of TESOL International Association (2008–2011). She is the author of several book chapters and research papers in refereed professional journals in the field of ELT, including *TESOL Quarterly* and *TESOL Journal*. She is a frequent presenter at national and international educational conferences, and her research interests include classroom-based action research, L2 reading and vocabulary development, teacher education, World Englishes, and non-native English speaking teachers in TESOL.

María E. Torres-Guzmán is Professor of Bilingual Education at Teachers College, Columbia University. She holds a Ph.D. from Stanford University. With Bertha Pérez, she co-authored *Learning in Two Worlds: An Integrated Spanish/English Biliteracy Approach*; with Ofelia Garcia and Tove Skutnabb-Kangas, she co-edited *Imagining Multilingual Schools: Languages in Education and Glocalization*; with Roger Barnard, she co-authored *Creating Classroom Communities*; and with Joel Gomez, she co-authored *Global Perspectives on Multilingualism: Unity in Diversity*. Her latest book is *Freedom at Work: Language, Professional and Intellectual Development* (Paradigm Publishers, 2010). In addition, she has published numerous journal articles and book chapters.

Manka M. Varghese is Associate Professor of Language, Literacy and Education in the College of Education at the University of Washington, Seattle. Originally from India and raised in Italy, Dr. Varghese received her Ph.D. in

Educational Linguistics from the University of Pennsylvania. Her primary research and teaching interests include how to improve teacher education for teachers of language minority students and understanding these teachers' professional lives. She has also recently been interested in understanding the experiences of language minority students accessing higher education in the United States.

Shelley Wong is Associate Professor in Multilingual and Multicultural Education at George Mason University in Fairfax, Virginia. Shelley began her teaching career in Hong Kong, where she went as a Chinese American to study Cantonese. Over the years she has taught English as a Second Language in adult school, high school, community college, university intensive English programs, and teacher education programs in California, Ohio, New York, and the Washington, D.C. metropolitan area. She was President of TESOL 2008–2009. Her research interests are dialogic inquiry, critical discourse analysis, and sociocultural approaches to literacy and academic achievement for language minority students.

Ke Xu teaches ESL and computer-assisted language learning (CALL) at Borough of Manhattan Community College, City University of New York. As a researcher and textbook writer, he is author and co-author of six books and over 30 articles, and editor of three book series in the areas of EFL testing, EFL/ESL methodology and pedagogy, teacher education, intercultural communication, and CALL. He also worked one year in Melbourne, Australia, as an International Teaching Fellow and curriculum consultant for the Ministry of Education of Victoria. He was a member of the Jiangsu Provincial Council of Education and Jiangsu EFL Testing Board, as well as director of School EFL Programs in Jiangsu Province, China.

CPSIA information can be obtained at www.ICGtesting.com
Printed in the USA
BVOW011603310113

312096BV00003BA/40/P